MOUNTAINEERING BASICS

Lynne Foster

AVANT BOOKS

SIERRA CLUB

i

Summary: A handbook of elementary mountaineering techniques for use in basic mountaineering courses and as reading for those who would like to improve their mountaineering knowledge and skills.

Published 1983 by the San Diego Chapter of the Sierra Club and Avant Books.

Book trade orders: c/o Avant Books, 3719 Sixth Avenue, San Diego, CA 92103.
Individuals/groups order from: San Diego Chapter of the Sierra Club, 1549 El Prado, San Diego, CA 92101.

Front matter and Chapters 1, 2, 5, 6, 7, 8, 14, and Appendix E © 1982 by Lynne Foster

Chapters 3, 4, 9, 10, 11, 12, 13, and Appendices A, B, C, D, and F © 1982 by the San Diego Chapter of the Sierra Club

Photographs © 1982 by Lynne Foster

Cover design: Djordjevic, Roxburgh & Gosney

Illustrations by Mark Kingsley Brown and Matthew Simpson

Mountaineering Basics was prepared for publication at The Word Shop, 3719 Sixth Avenue, San Diego, California 92103. Production staff: Karen Flynn, Matthew Simpson, Michael Kelly, Ed Roxburgh.

First edition

Library of Congress Catalog Number 82-061637
ISBN 0-932238-24-6

Manufactured in the United States of America

Second Printing

The Sierra Club, founded in 1892 by John Muir, has devoted itself to the study and protection of the nation's scenic and ecological resources — mountains, wetlands, woodlands, wild shores and rivers. All club publications are part of the nonprofit effort the club carries on as a public trust. There are some 50 chapters coast to coast, and in Hawaii, Alaska, and Canada. Participation is invited in the club's program to enjoy and preserve wilderness everywhere. Address: 530 Bush Street, San Francisco, California 92108.

This book is dedicated
to the memory of
Henry I. Mandolf
by the San Diego Chapter
of the Sierra Club.

Acknowledgements

When debts are many, the task of enumerating them all is daunting. I will, however, plunge right in at the ghostly beginning without further ado. I say "ghostly" because those without whom I could not have started, let alone completed, this new handbook were those who produced the original *Basic Mountaineering* book. Much of this new book is based on their experience and knowledge, and whatever value these pages may have is due in great part to their efforts in the past. Their names are too numerous to mention here, but they are set down in the opening pages of the original book.

My present helpers, to whom I owe an equal debt, have also been many. First on my list is Betty Fellows, our Chapter Treasurer, who has been my faithful go-between in the inevitable battle of the budget. Her ability to stretch our Chapter's funds to accommodate this much-needed new book has been nothing short of miraculous. Then there are the reviewers, who read though and gave advice and information on the whole manuscript or selected chapters. Chuck Berry and Ted Young brought the "Rock Climbing," "Winter Travel," and "Snow and Ice Climbing" chapters up to date, in addition to making extensive comments on several other chapters. Betty Fellows and Wes Reynolds contributed many helpful comments on the book as a whole. John Hanna single-handedly wrote Chapter 4, "Hiking Navigation." Bill Alley began the revision of the "Outfitting" chapter and Jim Harrison did the preliminary chapter and subject rearrangement. Roger Schlatter will find that many of his equipment check list suggestions have been incorporated. Linda Michaels, our very efficient San Diego office person, helped me in many ways. Bob Hartman, our present Chapter Chairperson, has given his patient and unfailing support during the nearly two long years *Mountaineering Basics* been in preparation. And to anyone else who has helped with the book, but who has been overlooked here, my very great thanks.

Some of the publications which were particularly helpful in preparing this new handbook include: the last edition of *Basic Mountaineering* (of course) and the last two editions of the Basic Mountaineering Course Notes (both published by the San Diego Chapter of the Sierra Club); *Mountaineering: Freedom of the Hills* (published by the Seattle Mountaineers, edited by Harvey Manning); *Walking Softly in the Wilderness: The Sierra Club Guide to Backpacking* (published by Sierra Club Books, written by John Hart); *The Complete Walker* (published by Alfred A. Knopf, Inc., written by Colin Fletcher); *American Red Cross First Aid* (published by the American Red Cross); and *Medicine for Mountaineering* (published by The Mountaineers, second edition, edited by James Wilkerson.) LF

A History of This Book

The history of the San Diego Chapter's original *Basic Mountaineering* book, first published in 1961, is a long one. Surprisingly, this history begins not in San Diego but in Seattle, Washington, where since 1935 the world-famous Seattle Mountaineers have been giving a course designed to effectively train people in safe mountaineering methods. The foundation for the Chapter's original mountaineering book was begun in the early 1950s, when two members of the Chapter's Rock Climbing Section took the Mountaineers' course. One of these members also became involved in the Mountaineers' Climbing and Lecture committees. Inspired by their members' experiences with the Mountaineers' courses, the San Diego Chapter's Rock Climbing Section (and their co-sponsor, the San Diego Parks and Recreation Department) organized and presented their first mountaineering course in 1957.

In 1960 the Seattle Mountaineers finished compiling and developing the mountaineering course information they had already gathered into a master outline of lecture material. They then published what is still, after many editions, one of the most complete books on the subject — *Mountaineering: Freedom of the Hills*. Between 1957 and 1960 the San Diego Chapter, building on their own experience and taking the Mountaineers as their guide, had been putting together their own basic mountaineering course outline. From this base, the original *Basic Mountaineering* book grew — and was first published in 1961. It was the first mountaineering handbook to be published by any Sierra Club chapter and is fondly called, to this day, the "Red Book." The second edition appeared in 1965, and a third in 1970. While being revised for the 1970 edition, the useful text of the book was expanded from 118 pages to 135 pages.

The Red Book has been reprinted a total of seven times: an enviable testament to its acceptance and popularity among wilderness seekers. The original *Basic Mountaineering* book and its two revisions were the result of the untiring work of the late Henry I. Mandolf, a long-time member of the San Diego Chapter. Mr Mandolf's love for and knowledge of the mountains and his devotion to wilderness preservation made him an inspiration to all who knew him. This book is gratefully dedicated to him by the San Diego Chapter.

However, even the best and most useful handbooks often eventually need not just a revision, but a complete reworking. And so it was that the Old Red Book was honorably retired and you now hold in your hands a *new* Red Book. Yes, still red, but not just revised. The book has been totally rewritten, expanded to 256 pages, reorganized, and redesigned. In addition, the new book has brand-new illustrations and a slightly different title: *Mountaineering Basics.**

The new Red Book, like the old, is meant to be a *summary* of basic mountaineering information — to be used not only by people who want to improve their wilderness skills, but also as a teaching aid for mountaineering courses. It is not intended to be an encyclopedia of mountaineering.

It is important to note, also, that the spirit of this new book, *Mountaineering Basics*, is in harmony with that of the original Red Book. Henry Mandolf could not have put it better when he said: "The greatest reward will be to have contributed to the safety and enjoyment of those many people who are beginning to find their way into the mountains and the desert. The country is there and the people are looking for what it can give them. May they discover it and long enjoy and protect its forests, water, wildlife, and wilderness."

---

* Some of you will doubtless ask why the title was changed. The reason is a simple one. Many book lists are arranged alphabetically by title. Thus, putting the word "mountaineering" first may enable more people to discover the book.

MOUNTAINEERING BASICS

Table of Contents

Part III – Climbing and Other Challenges

Chapter 11 – Rock Climbing

Chapter 12 – Winter Travel

Chapter 13 – Snow and Ice Climbing

Chapter 14 – Desert Travel

Appendices

Illustrations

FOREWORD

More and more people are turning to the outdoors — and particularly to wilderness — for recreation. When people go on foot into the mountains or desert, in winter or summer, to enjoy the wildflowers, clean air, rivers and lakes, quiet, solitude, and challenge, they need to know how to travel safely, responsibly, and pleasurably. *Mountaineering Basics* is meant to fill this need, to be a summary of information useful to people who regularly spend some of their time in the wilderness and to be used as a teaching aid for elementary mountaineering courses.

The basic skills of what people usually call "mountaineering" — with some commonsense modifications — are applicable to traveling on foot not only in the mountains, but in the desert, in the foothills, and in winter as well as in summer. Mountaineering basics include skills such as obtaining the proper equipment, planning a trip, packing a pack, physical conditioning, planning meals and cooking on the trail, using map and compass, first aid, winter camping, rock climbing, and using but not injuring the wilderness. We hope the book will be useful not only to those of you who are beginning to find your way into our deserts and mountains, but to those who wish to improve their mountaineering knowledge and skills. May you all long enjoy and protect the wilderness of our vulnerable and precious planet.

Part I: MAKING READY

Ancient Bristlecone Pine Area, Inyo National Forest

The wildest health and pleasure grounds accessible and available to those seeking escape from care and dust and early death are the parks and reservations of the West.

— John Muir

Chapter 1
Getting into the Spirit

1.1 Why a Wilderness Experience?

Let's start with a definition of "wilderness." Throughout this book the term "wilderness" is used in a much broader sense than a government agency uses it when referring to an area that has received official designation as wilderness. We use the word "wilderness" to mean any uninhabited, uncultivated, or unspoiled area—whether mountain, foothill, desert, or seashore. Some wildernesses are outstandingly beautiful, some are unique, and some are both; most are accessible to outdoor recreationists. This being so, it is not surprising that as population increases and the pollution and congestion of urban life grows, people are increasingly seeking out our wildernesses. In these unspoiled areas people find opportunities for a variety of high quality outdoor experiences free from urban pressures: picnicking, day hiking, camping, backpacking, fishing, cross-country skiing, rock climbing, kayaking, canoeing.

Although wilderness belongs to everyone, and is accessible to most, in general it offers its finest recreational experiences to people who don't mind walking, who find their pleasure more intensely satisfying when it is laced with some effort. In the wilderness you can find more than beauty and simplicity—you can find challenges, problems, and sometimes even emergencies: the challenge of completing a strenuous hike; the problem of how best to keep your food safe from camp robbers; or perhaps an emergency involving a down jacket left at the last rest stop! These experiences are pleasurable or memorable in very personal ways—perhaps because in the wilderness we experience the fruits of individual self-reliance and group cooperation in more direct ways than we do in urban life, where the results of our individual efforts are so often diluted by trivia as to be almost undetectable.

3

Wilderness travel has much to offer — and, unlike most recreational athletics, it has much to offer people who feel they are non-athletic or who do not enjoy competition. Such people often find, quite by accident, that one of their favorite forms of recreation involves some kind of wilderness experience. Which is not to say that there are no competitive "wilderness games"; anyone who has ever watched a very intense group of peak baggers in action can easily assure you of that.

The wilderness is, of course, more than just a reservoir of recreational opportunities or a place to exercise our aesthetic or athletic sensibilities — though these are indeed important uses of wilderness, provided they are pursued in a "low impact" mode (of which, much more later). The word "reservoir," though, can help us understand something about why the wilderness is much more than a place to play. The wilderness is indeed a reservoir: a reservoir of biological diversity from whence our species came and upon which we and those who will come after us directly depend for our health and well-being. It is in the still-vast wildernesses of ocean, river, forest, sky, desert, and mountains — reservoirs of clean air, water, earth, and rock — that the toxic waste products of our cities, factories, power plants, and motor vehicles are detoxified and eventually returned to us once again in life-giving forms. It is in these wildernesses that live the myriad interdependent plants, animals, insects, and microbes whose genetic diversity, flexibility, and stability make it possible for them, and us, to adapt to a wide range of environmental conditions. But this range has its limits, as is well-illustrated by the growing number of extinct or endangered species.

But why should we worry if a few species become extinct? Haven't species been becoming extinct ever since there were any species? Naturally, the answer to both parts of this question is "Yes." We have to worry because not only are we pushing species over the brink into the bottomless pit of extinction at a more breakneck speed than at any time in life's evolutionary history, we are at the same time busily creating environmental conditions which will assure that few new species will ever take their places. In addition, we must consider carefully how this continuing fall in "diversity stock" is affecting our planet's "ecological economy."

An often-used and effective way, though admittedly a partial one, of visualizing the complex relations between organisms and their environment is to imagine our species as the leaves on a tree, and the rest of the tree (including roots) as everything else in the world. Now, what happens to the leaves when you start lopping off branches, roots, bark, etc., more or less indiscriminately? Natural succession and clearcutting are quite different processes. Utility commisions, timber companies, dam builders, and missile site seekers to the contrary, our planet's most precious assets are its untouched alpine highlands, virgin forests, free-flowing rivers, high peaks, deep gorges, flower-filled meadows, lovely

4

lakes, desert dunes, seashores, wildlife, and plants—its reservoirs of life-giving and life-enhancing necessities. Keep this in mind whenever you go into the wilderness, and each visit will sharpen your awareness that in both a pragmatic and a transcendent sense, "everything is connected to everything else." Once you experience this awareness you'll find it hard, if not impossible, to be unconcerned about protecting and increasing our planet's remaining wildernesses. All of which is probably one of the best answers to "why a wilderness experience?" Remember those leaves we were talking about, and don't wait until you start to wither to start enjoying and protecting our wildernesses.

1.2 Wilderness Ethics

The purpose of this book is to help you enjoy wilderness travel safely, pleasurably, and, above all, responsibly. In order to do this, you need to acquire some skills and techniques—most of which are used for enhancing your enjoyment of wilderness travel, but a few of which are occasionally needed for survival purposes. (Despite the fact that our wildernesses are shrinking away and we find it harder than we once did to get lost or stranded, it is still entirely possible to get into serious trouble on a weekend backpack or even a day hike.)

Responsible wilderness travel in our time is a bit more complicated than it used to be, primarily because the number of wilderness users is increasing and the amount of wilderness is decreasing. Increasing use, decreasing area, and leftover "pioneer" habits add up to the "impact problem." And because wilderness means not just the country, but also our experience of it—particularly the experience of solitude and naturalness—the impact is at least twofold: damage to land and injury to experience.

Our shrinking wilderness can no longer absorb high-impact, pioneer-type outdoor habits. The days of the frontier are over. In our crowded world, preservation, not pioneering, makes it possible for all who visit the wilderness to delight in it. It is time to make an ethic of low impact wilderness use, of sparing the land; each of us must be thoughtful of the other, and of the generations to come after us—there is no excuse for adding new scars to the land. Responsible use, briefly, means choosing your route, your gear, your destination, and your behavior on the trail and in camp with the welfare of the wilderness in mind. To spare the land, camp and travel by the rules of "low impact."* Seek out less-known, less-used areas; don't play pioneer, but take the landscape as you find it (the perfect camp is found, not made); don't camp on meadows or at timber line; carry out all trash and garbage; use stoves for cooking and build fires only when absolutely necessary; accept the restrictions

* The how-to of low-impact suggestions will be discussed in some detail in later chapters.

necessary for protecting the land (keep in mind that the door to wilderness cannot be endlessly, limitlessly open); intrude on others as little as possible (no radios or pets—be inaudible and invisible); use proper sanitation practices; travel only in small groups (8-10 maximum, preferably 6 or under); don't cut switchbacks, stay on the trail. In other words, "take nothing but pictures, leave nothing but footprints" (and keep even those inconspicuous).

Speaking of ethics, also remember this fact: each of us has the chance to speak out for wilderness, to help in protecting it by influencing the political decision-making system. Write letters to your congresspeople, state legislators, and local officials expressing your concern for wilderness. Keep informed on issues involving wilderness. (Often the best way to gain this information is through your local conservation organizations such as the Sierra Club, Friends of the Earth, Audubon Society, Wilderness Society, League of Conservation Voters, and so on.) Help by attending meetings of environmental groups and going to public hearings where the political issues are discussed. To cite only a few examples, such efforts have established new national and state parks, expanded the national wilderness system, and created the Environmental Protection Agency. *You can make a difference!*

Chapter 2
Physical Conditioning and Preliminary Planning

2.1 Getting in Shape

One of the appeals of wilderness travel is its simplicity. You are there, the country is there, and you're ready to see and experience. Even if someone else is leading the way, though, you have to put one foot in front of the other. Often those feet must go uphill—sometimes only up a gentle slope, but more often up a steep one. Are you ready for that? If you've only been walking from your car to your desk and back again lately (unless you leave your car some distance away), you're probably not. So what can you do to prepare for an enjoyable, safe, sometimes strenuous wilderness experience? Well, the best exercise for hiking is hiking, and though few of us are fortunate enough to live where we can walk out our door and go hiking any time we feel like it, no matter where you live there's a place to begin conditioning yourself for wilderness travel. Some people prefer to jog or run a few miles on the local school track or in a nearby park, on dirt or grass (which give a little, and so are easier on the body than cement and asphalt); others prefer long, brisk walks (4 miles an hour or so). But no matter what kind of conditioning program you choose, the important thing is to stick to it and pursue it regularly, several times a week.

When conditioning yourself for wilderness travel, you want not only to acquire strength and endurance, but the ability to make substantial elevation gains without tiring yourself excessively. Whatever your present physical condition, you should begin improving it progressively—walk before you jog, and jog before you run (and do stretching exercises before any of the above). Exercise training for mountaineering is based on progression and equilibrium. Progression results in improvement regardless of your starting level. Equilibrium is the balance your body maintains during sustained exercise—when you are in good condition you can climb all day in relative comfort.

Ideally, to train most effectively you should have access to a running track (or the equivalent) for endurance, steep stairs for developing climbing muscles, and a bicycle for leg exercise. In jogging or running your aim should be two to three miles. By the time you can run three miles, your body is in equilibrium and any longer distances will depend primarily on your motivation. If, so to speak, you're starting from the bottom of the fitness barrel, the fitness experts recommend that you begin with an activity you can easily manage—for example, walking briskly for one mile almost every day for a week or two. Next, you walk two miles, then three. If your aim is to jog or run, you could then begin running a quarter mile, walking a quarter mile, and so on, until you find that you can run about three miles without walking at all. A twelve-minute mile is walking. An eight-to twelve-minute mile is jogging. Under an eight-minute mile is running. For ease in mountain climbing, try to step up your time until you are running eight-minute miles. For speed, run 100 yards all out, walk 100 yards, etc.

Not everyone is interested in the highest fitness level, though. If you can walk a brisk three miles without feeling tired, you're ready to enjoy almost any day hike or light backpack at low elevations. For more strenuous, longer, higher elevation, heavier backpack trips, you'll need to condition by walking a couple of miles further each time, up to five to seven miles, and doing it more often. If you can do this or run three eight-minute miles back-to-back you're probably ready for almost any kind of wilderness travel you have skills for (except Everest, K-2, et al.). This extra conditioning is necessary when you hike to higher elevations (above 5,000 feet) because the higher you go, the less oxygen there is available in the air. This puts a burden on both heart and lungs. Progressive conditioning prepares your body for altitude and will enable you to hike in comfort after a short period of adaptation (overnight for up to 8-9,000 feet, more for higher altitudes). Running out of energy is no fun.

Elevation gain training is unique to mountaineering. You can train by climbing short or long flights of stairs, fuel breaks in the foothills, or steep city hills. When climbing stairs (or anything else), first climb part way, then all the way, then every other step, then faster, until you reach your limit. If you have the time, do it five or ten times. There is one basic rule: do it regularly and progressively. When it becomes easy, place a greater demand on yourself. If you train progressively your body will begin to equilibrate easily.

There are three basic signs that your conditioning program is effective:

1. Stable resting heart rate of 60 beats per minute or less; a rapid return of heart rate to baseline after exercise.

2. Stable morning weight.

3. Stable and reproducible 12-minute test.*

An increase in heart rate and/or weight and a decrease in the distance covered in 12 minutes indicate a loss of conditioning. Weight loss, constant fatigue, and frequent illness might indicate excessive exercise. Don't be afraid to push yourself a little, but use common sense when doing so.

Aerobic exercise, the kind we have been discussing, when practiced regularly and for sufficient lengths of time, stimulates heart and lung activity and results in fitness and endurance—a phenomenon sometimes called the "training effect." If you want to train for heavy-duty, high altitude mountaineering (and you have no physical condition that would prevent you from doing so safely), it is recommended that you accumulate 50 to 70 points per week.* For example: cycling 10 miles in 33 minutes gives 13.5 points; jogging 3½ miles in 22 minutes gives 23½ points; and running two miles in 15 minutes gives 11 points.

According to the fitness experts you can achieve aerobic fitness* by maintaining your appropriate "target" heart rate for 20 minutes, four times a week (excluding warmup and cooldown periods). The target heart rate varies with age, level of fitness, and sex; it can easily be calculated from the following chart:

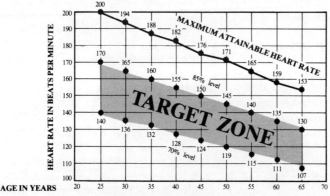

As we grow older, the highest heart rate we can reach during all-out effort falls. These are "average" values for age.

1. **Target Heart Rate Zone**

* For complete information on the 12-minute test, the "point" system, and aerobic fitness in general, see Dr. Kenneth Cooper's *The New Aerobics* (available in paperback).

9

It is possible for even a young, fit person to strain his/her heart with in-appropriately strenuous exercise. The target rate, if measured regularly and kept within the recommended limits, can not only allow you to monitor the progress of your exercise program, but can help advise you whether you need to work harder or ease off. For your heart's sake, use it.

2.2 Obtaining Wilderness Permits

A successful trip depends on careful planning. In planning a trip, one of the first steps is to check out the regulations for the area you will be traveling in. This also goes for areas which are not actually designated wilderness areas, such as Forest Service lands, Bureau of Land Management lands, National Monuments, State parks, and so on. During the past few years, the National and State Park Services and the National Forests have established additional regulations for using public wilderness areas. These regulations sometimes apply to non-wilderness areas such as undeveloped campgrounds in National Forests. Thus, you often need permits and reservations for car camping as well as for trail or cross-country travel. Although you may dislike these restrictions, the rules have evolved as outdoor use has increased; they are set up to avoid overcrowding, minimize environmental impact, and to give all wilderness travelers a quality experience. You can help assure this quality by abiding by the regulations.

To enter any of the Wilderness or Primitive Areas in the National Forests of California, even for a day hike, you must have a permit issued by the park or forest ranger in charge. The permits are free to anyone agreeing to follow simple rules intended to protect the visitor as well as the wilderness resource; they can be obtained in person, by mail (see Appendix F for mailing addresses in California), or sometimes by telephone, from your point of entry. With few exceptions, a permit for one wilderness will be good if you hike into another one—even from a National Forest into a State or National Park. Obtain the permit from the area where your trip is to start. The permit is good for one trip and for a specified period of time. Only one permit is required for a group travel-ing together. Most wildernesses have limits on the number of groups and on the size of the group that can enter at each trailhead. Sometimes there are limits on the number of people who can enter per day. You can avoid a possible filled area by having an alternate plan (the agency can usually tell you which trails are less used in a given area) and/or entering on weekdays instead of weekends. Some permits restrict you to camping on-ly in certain areas for a given length of time. If an area is overused or a high fire hazard exists, wood fires, stoves, or even camping may be pro-hibited. Many areas, such as the Mount Whitney Trail and parts of the John Muir Trail, are on a reservation system during the summer. Obtain your reservation by writing or calling for it well in advance of your trip.

2.3 Leading a Trip

A successful trip depends a great deal on good leadership. For large group trips (8 to 10 people) a leader and assistant leader are usually selected by the group, with the assistant leader frequently taking the essential responsibility of bringing up the rear, so that no one gets left behind inadvertently. The leader may be anyone in the group, though for more difficult trips it should be someone with a sound basic knowledge of mountaineering. If you are organizing a trip and/or planning to lead one, you and all group members should discuss the equipment, route, food, choice of other group members, dates, timing, possible weather, alternative plans, and obtaining wilderness permits and/or reservations.

Trip planning should include determining where the closest telephone will be and/or possible routes of evacuation in case of emergency. It is preferable that at least one group member has made the trip previously. Decisions should be made democratically and cooperatively, except in cases where it is obvious that one group member is more skilled or knowledgeable in certain situations than all the others. Generally the greater the difficulty of the trip, the greater need there is for a leader.

An effective leader will use the principle of minimum authority — she or he will be unobtrusive, tactful, empathetic, and concerned about the group members' capabilities and feelings. Good leaders consult with the group when a situation presents itself where some doubt exists as to the proper course of action. This results in an enjoyable, voluntary, and democratic relationship between leader and group members.

Even if you have a formal leader, all members of the group should still consider themselves responsible not only for their own safety, but for the safety of the other group members. In a small group there may be no definite leader, but in emergencies a more experienced group member often steps forward to guide the group in making the necessary decisions. If your group is large and your objective difficult to attain, the leader may not gain the primary goal (perhaps a difficult peak), but will be satisfied that some of the group was able to achieve the goal and that his/her leadership made this possible.

On any trip each person has a responsibility to get along well with the rest of the group so that everyone can enjoy the trip, a responsibility to other groups to act in such a way that your presence is welcomed, and a responsibility to future travelers to protect and spare the land so that they too can enjoy the wilderness as much as you have.

2.4 Traveling with Children

Hiking or camping with young children takes even more careful planning than for all-adult trips, but the rewards (e.g., growth in the skills of cooperation and self-reliance) make any work for the adults well worth the trouble. When planning such a trip, you will of course choose an objective suitable to the children's ages; Mt. Whitney would not be a good choice for toddlers ,not to mention adults whose most strenuous activity in the preceding months has been walking from desk to water cooler. Because *Mountaineering Basics* is primarily an introductory summary of necessary wilderness skills, it's not possible to fully discuss how to get the most out of your hike, car camp, or backpack with the kids, but here are a few helpful hints:

Selecting a Trip

Trip destinations should be suitable to the experience, training, and interests of both parents and children. Destinations should also be suitable to the equipment on hand and to the children's ages.

Food

If you'll be eating differently on the trail than at home, try out the new food items at home first (keep refrigeration or lack thereof in mind). Plan a diet with adequate protein and more carbohydrates than usual. Carbohydrates give quick energy — it's amazing how fast crankiness and inability to go up a hill will disappear after an infusion of nuts and dried fruit.

Health

Children are more susceptible to outdoor miseries than adults, but recover faster than adults. Make sure all have had their tetanus shots. Enlarge your first aid kit to include children's medicines. On the trail, be very careful that water is safe to drink — when in doubt, boil or treat it (see Section 7.2).

Safety

Children past the toddler stage should each have a whistle and the Ten Essentials with them at all times (and have been drilled in how to use them). Wandering toddlers can be staked down with harness and short rope if necessary. Make sure children understand common dangers such as deep water, snakes, animals, poison oak, yellowjackets, and getting lost.

Recreation

Hiking goals should interest the older kids. Cover babies' play areas with a tarp (although bugs are high-protein fare, regular indulgence is not advised). Bring along a few favorite books, toys, and art materials. Try to camp with or near other groups with children.

Miscellaneous

Start your child's life in the wilderness with *short* trail trips, as long, boring, and/or painful early trips often leave children with an almost indelible desire never to walk up another hill. If reservations are required, be sure you have them. Interminable wanderings, followed by setting up camp hungrily in a strange, dark, usually non-level place, are nobody's idea of a good time — even if you can find the tent stakes. Avoid weekends and holidays if possible, unless you know of little-used campgrounds and trails. When hiking, have frequent rest/snack/play stops for kids. Talk with other camping families to get more helpful hints.

Chapter 3
Outfitting

3.1 The Ten Essentials

Experienced wilderness travelers agree that there are certain items of equipment you should never be without beyond the end of the road. In an emergency these essentials cannot be improvised and they could save your life. These items are the nucleus of your total equipment package and are mandatory for any outing regardless of apparent conditions and circumstance. The "Ten Essentials" should be carried by each person. This is just common sense, considering the many possible emergencies that can occur. Of course there are other items that each person will consider essential (the most common "11th essential" is toilet paper). In time and with experience we all develop our own personal "essentials" list. Here, however, are the standard "Ten Essentials":

To find your way	1. Map of the area
	2. Compass
	3. Flashlight
For your protection	4. Sunglasses
	5. Extra food and water
	6. Extra clothing
For emergencies	7. Waterproofed matches
	8. Candle or fuel tablets
	9. Pocket knife
	10. First aid kit

1. The **MAP** is a guide to your wilderness experience. Without it and without the knowledge of how to use it, though, your experiences may prove to be something less than enjoyable. Many available maps show trails and landmarks in wilderness areas, but the most useful one is a

U.S. Geological Survey Topographical map (sometimes referred to as a "topo").

2. Without your **COMPASS** you can't be totally sure about your direction. The map is accurate, but do you have it oriented correctly? Map and compass together provide the necessary tools for finding your way.

   There are many compasses on the market; the one you choose will depend on how serious you are about mountaineering. All compasses will do the basic job in skilled hands, but one which is liquid-damped and has a straight edge for map orientation seems most convenient for general use.

3. A **FLASHLIGHT** is basically an emergency tool and should be maintained with that in mind. Choose a flashlight with a switch that is not easy to turn on accidentally. Carry extra batteries and bulb, so that you have at least eight hours of emergency light at all times. Batteries lose their strength quickly in low temperatures, so when it is cold keep the flashlight in a pocket close to your body.

4. **SUNGLASSES** are an absolute must. The human eye is delicate and can be harmed by sun glare or excessive light such as occurs on snow and ice, and in the desert. Preferably, the sunglasses should be designed to prevent side glare, to absorb ultraviolet rays, and should have some ventilation to prevent fogging. Such glasses are, however, more expensive than the usual drugstore variety. It is a good idea to carry an extra pair on a long trip, because they are easily lost or broken.

   When on glaciers, on snow, or in the desert, wear sunglasses even when it is cloudy. Amber lenses permit better distinction of details in flat light, as on snow or sand; green or gray lenses are fine for general use. If a lens should break and you do not have a spare, cover the frame with tape and cut a slot or cross in it.

5. Carry **EXTRA FOOD** in a special container and place it away from your regular food supply. Carry food that keeps well and perhaps is not particularly appetizing (it will tend to stay untouched until that emergency situation arises). High-energy fruit bars, high-protein candy bars, and nut bars are suitable. **EXTRA WATER** means carrying about half again as much water as you think you'll need on your outing.

6. **EXTRA CLOTHING** should include something warm, something windproof, and something waterproof. Each of these items is usually designed for its specific function — seldom do you find clothing that satisfactorily incorporates two, let alone all three, of these functions. Warm clothing (wool) is usually not windproof or waterproof; wind parkas are not warm clothing and should not be waterproof (though if you spray them with Scotchguard you can make them water-repellent); rain gear is waterproof and therefore does not breathe, so it cannot be worn comfortably while hiking. Each item has its place and should be carried at all times; you can never tell when the weather might change.

7. **WATERPROOFED MATCHES** should also be carried away from your normal daily supply so they will be available when you really need them. Waterproof containers are good, but if the matches fall out in the rain or if the container leaks the matches become quite useless. The best bet is to buy or waterproof your own matches (with melted paraffin) and then store them in a waterproof container.

8. **CANDLE, FUEL TABLETS, OR OTHER LONG-BURNING FIRE STARTERS** are necessary when trying to start a fire with damp kindling.

9. A **POCKET KNIFE** is a necessary, all-around tool. It is especially good for splintering damp wood to make kindling. A simple pocket knife is adequate, but many people prefer the more elaborate versions which provide can openers, scissors, corkscrews, saws, tweezers, screwdrivers, awls, toothpicks, can openers, etc.

10. The **FIRST AID KIT** can be called the most important essential. There are prepackaged kits on the market which (even though expensive) provide a good start for the beginning wilderness traveler. However, after spending some time in the wilderness and learning mountaineering first aid requirements and skills, most people find that only a homemade kit will provide all items needed when venturing beyond the end of the road. (For first aid kit contents, see Section 9.2.)

3.2 Clothing

John Muir may have hiked through the Sierra with a heavy overcoat and a notebook as his only items of equipment, but not so the backpacker of today. Today's gear is more specialized and much more expensive. Were Mr. Muir given a cash register tape on what today's outdoor person carries on her/his back, he might decide to stay at home because of the expense involved. A jacket, a sleeping bag, boots, a pack, a wool shirt, and all the rest can easily amount to several hundred dollars.

Perhaps the best indication of the market backpackers have created is the number of manufacturers now in the field. This competition may help advance the state of the art ("build a better backpack and the world will . . ."), but it also makes it difficult for the newcomer to choose which items to buy.

This chapter is not intended to tell you *what* to buy — that's largely a matter of individual needs, what you already have, what you can borrow, and what you can afford. Instead, we'd like to call to your attention some of the features you should look for when making your selections. Mistakes are costly; it may be years before you can afford to replace the wrong sleeping bag. In any case, the following general advice perhaps will be helpful in selecting your equipment:

— Do not rush into buying all equipment at once. Many types of equipment can be rented (packs, sleeping bags, tents). After renting you may have a better idea about the kinds of equipment you prefer.

— Observe what others are using and ask why. More experienced mountaineers have definite opinions as to why they prefer one form of equipment to another. Their opinions will aid you in evaluating sales claims.

— Set up a priority list of essential equipment. Some items will probably have to be second-hand, in order to keep the original cost within your budget.

— Consider buying equipment such as boots, socks, special items such as rock climbing gear, etc. from stores specializing in mountaineering equipment. Their stock is varied and their advice often helpful. On request many will provide illustrated catalogues and give reliable mail order service.

— Evaluate to what extent you may be able to use home-made equipment.

Mountaineering equipment falls naturally into two broad categories: *basic equipment,* such as the Ten Essentials (already discussed in Section 3.1), clothing, footwear, sleeping bags, packs, tents and other shelters; and *special equipment,* which includes items needed in rock climbing, ice and snow climbing, and snow camping. "Basic equipment" will be discussed in this chapter; "special equipment" will be covered in Part III, "Climbing and Other Challenges."

Shirts, Pants, Shorts

Wear several light layers rather than one heavy layer, especially in the winter, so you can make use of the insulating air layers in between and adjust your body heat to your activity level by taking off and putting on layers. One hike with a thick shirt and down jacket will convert you to the "layering method". An example of the layer system would be undershirt (with or without sleeves), cotton-polyester long-sleeved shirt, wool shirt or sweater (cardigan), windjacket (or parka), and cotton-polyester shorts or long pants (wool in winter). Of course the appropriate items will depend on the weather and the season.

All-cotton items take a long time to dry when they get wet, so unless the weather is very hot and dry and you prefer the slow-cool evaporation of cotton clothing, cotton-poly clothing is the best choice for items not meant to be especially warm (underclothing, light shirts, shorts, long summer pants, etc.). A plus is that cotton-poly clothes are lighter than all-cotton.

All-synthetic clothing is usually not as breathable as cotton-poly (or cotton) and so is too warm for hot weather and tends to be clammy in cold. For cold weather, wool clothing (again, in layers) is the best choice. Wool retains its insulating qualities even when wet and it dries quickly; it's also, on a weight-for-weight basis, warmer than cotton or synthetics (unless there's a new synthetic out that we haven't heard of). Some people prefer shorts for hiking, even in cool weather, but even then you should always carry a pair of long pants.

Jackets

Because there are so many derivatives of the original mountain parka, it's difficult to decide which to buy. A windbreaker with a hood is a must. These are usually made of very light, tightly woven, nylon fabric. A windbreaker has the virtue of weighing very little and of stuffing into a very small space (it's great for putting on at a rest stop—if you remember to put it in an accessible place).

Down or synthetic filled jackets are used by almost all wilderness travelers (except perhaps in high summer or at low elevations). If you're camping at over 5,000 feet, the temperature can drop below freezing after sundown, though it may be in the nineties during the day. A jacket should have regular and handwarmer pockets, should snap and zip (two-way), have a removable hood, be adjustable at the wrists, and have a drawstring at the waist or bottom edge. If you'll be using your jacket in rainy country, remember that synthetic fills, though slightly bulkier, keep most of their insulation qualities when wet and also dry quickly. Except in winter, many people use a down or synthetic filled vest instead of a parka. This has several advantages: a vest is lighter, takes up less room, is cheaper, and, in conjunction with a wool shirt and windbreaker, keeps you as warm as you'll need to be on most late spring, summer, or early fall trips (except for very high altitude ones).

Many people also carry some sort of rain gear—a waterproof poncho with hood (which can be draped over you and a pack, if properly designed), a cagoule (knee-length rain parka with hood), or rain jacket and pants. Most of this rain gear is made of coated nylon taffeta or ripstop. However, there are some new laminated fabrics on the market (e.g., Gore-Tex) which, though expensive, are said to be more comfortable as rain gear because they "breathe"—that is, let air in and moisture out so that you don't get as wet on the inside of your raingear as you do on the outside.

Hats

Wear a hat, by all means (color of your choice), but get one that will keep the sun off in the heat of the day and keep down the loss of body heat at night. If this sounds like you'll be carrying two hats, you're right—but it's worth it for the comfort. Hats with large brims that go all the way around usually don't fit between your head and your pack, unless it's a day pack. A wool watch cap is great for cool weather or evenings, but death on hot, sunny days. Many people find a soft, light-colored (to reflect some heat) cotton or felt cap with a front-facing or narrow brim just the thing for daytime, but no good when tossing and turning in the sleeping bag. Both hats weigh, together, less than those flashy Stetson types you often see — and they fit into much smaller spaces, usually don't blow off, and are much more comfortable.

3.3 Footwear

Selecting the proper boots for your feet and for the use you intend to make of them is very important. Hiking on trails or cross-country with or without a pack can sometimes put a great strain on your feet — though just how much strain depends on your feet, the terrain, the distance traveled, and last, but certainly not least, on your footwear. The time to think about buying a good pair of hiking boots or shoes is *not* when you are feeling those blisters on your heel getting larger and larger with every step you take, but several weeks before you start on that day hike or backpack. The right footwear can make the difference between your having the impulse to finish the hike on your hands and knees and having your feet and legs feel just pleasantly tired. But let's not wallow in the details of gruesome and painful possibilities, let's talk about how to avoid those blisters and bruises by selecting the right boots or shoes for your feet and hiking habits. A pair of boots is the single most important piece of hiking equipment you will buy. In order to make that selection wisely, you need to know something about types of boots, which kind of boot is appropriate for which kind of activity, how boots should fit your feet, and how to care for boots.

Types of Boots

Lightweight Trail Boots or Shoes: Trail shoes are meant for gentle forest trails where the footing is relatively easy, the load (if any) is light, and strong support is not required. Trail shoes vary considerably — from "campus boots" and "waffle stompers" to very respectable light-weight boots. Trail shoes are quite popular because they are light, require little breaking in, and fit the fashion of the day. Some running or sports "training" shoes are good for light trail use, too. One of the advantages of these lighter shoes (in contrast to the heavier boots) is that because they are light, they don't eat up the trail as badly as the deep lug soles of the heavier boots. There's really no point in buying a heavy, or even medium, pair of lug-soled boots if you're going to primarily be doing on-trail day hikes. Lightweight shoes and boots range in price from about $30 to $50.

Medium-Weight Hiking Boots: These boots are designed to support and protect the foot under a variety of outdoor conditions. They are built for use on rather rugged, rocky trails by hikers carrying 25- to 45-pound packs. Constructed in a totally different manner than light trail shoes or boots, they are tougher, heavier, and stiffer. They require a breaking-in period and usually cost from $50 to $90. This kind of boot comes closest to being an all-purpose boot; a pair weighs 3½ to 4½ pounds, with the optimum weight being four pounds or less.

Heavyweight and Winter Boots (Mountaineering Boots): These boots are special-purpose boots and are normally too heavy for summer use (some climbers, however, prefer them for year-round wear). For extended winter trips, a double boot is sometimes useful for extra warmth. These boots are large, stiff, heavy, and hard to break in; they are designed for serious, rigorous use on ice, rock, and snow, where insulation, protection, and performance are vital to both success and survival. These boots usually weigh 4½ to 6½ pounds and cost up to $200.

Kletterschuhe (Rock Climbing Shoes): These shoes usually have no heels and are only half the weight of mountaineering boots. The uppers are usually suede leather without lining. The lug shoes are less than half the thickness of mountain boots. Some use a hard rubber or steel insert for better edging on small holds. These shoes should be double-stiched and fit snugly. To preserve the important qualities of a good Kletterschuhe it should not be used on the trail.

Boot Construction

Although many boots look much alike, there are subtle differences — especially in the way the upper is attached to the sole. The five main construction methods are: cemented, inside stitched (Littleway), Norwegian welt, Goodyear welt, and injection molded.

Cemented: This is the most inexpensive type of construction and is found only in the trail shoe/boot category. Cemented boots can be recognized by the absence of stitching and the lack of a midsole (the midsole is the layer of leather or rubber between the upper and the outer sole). Cemented construction gives the boot considerable flexibility, but not good protection or support. Some of these boots/shoes cannot be resoled.

Inside Stitched (Littleway): These boots have the upper turned under and sandwiched between a stout inner sole and midsole. The "sandwich" is fastened with a double row of lock stitching concealed within the boot. The stitching is protected from abrasion, moisture, and drying. Because the soles can be closely trimmed, these boots can double for rock climbing. Both midsole and outer sole are easily replaced. The shortcomings of this method of construction are that soles tend to be stiff and uppers do not always conform to the shape of the foot. Inside stitching is found on many trail shoes, nearly all rock climbing shoes, and some hiking boots.

Norwegian Welt: This is the oldest and most common type of boot construction. Boots with this construction have several rows of stitching along the perimeter of the boot where the upper meets the sole. One row of stitching angles inward, connecting the insole with the upper, and the other secures the upper to the midsole. This is the strongest welt used in manufacturing hiking and climbing boots.

Goodyear Welt: The Goodyear welt, like the Norwegian, is stitched from the outside. The upper is stitched directly to a raised rib on the insole and to a narrow piece of leather (the welt) which goes completely around the outside of the boot where sole meets upper. The welt is then stitched to the midsole. Many U.S. manufacturers use this type of construction. Welted construction is the most desirable way of making quality boots.

Injection Molding: Injection molding is a relatively new process. In attaching the upper to the sole, molten neoprene, applied under pressure, takes the place of stitching and cement. There are two main types: lug sole molded directly to the upper, and separate midsole, usually of rubber, sandwiched between the molded section and the outer sole. The latter boots, unlike the ones without a midsole, are easily resolable and are usually mountaineering boots. Injection molding offers economy and light weight and has some advantages over stitching—i.e., no wear and rotting of thread, no penetration of water through needle holes, and (when designed as such) sole stiffness appropriate for technical rock climbing.

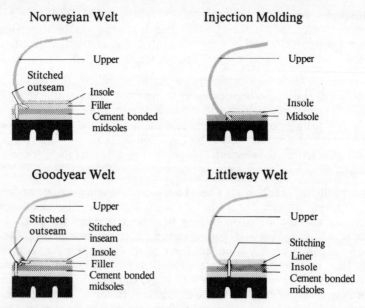

Norwegian Welt

Upper
Stitched outseam
Insole
Filler
Cement bonded midsoles

Injection Molding

Upper
Insole
Midsole

Goodyear Welt

Upper
Stitched outseam
Stitched inseam
Insole
Filler
Cement bonded midsoles

Littleway Welt

Upper
Stitching
Liner
Insole
Cement bonded midsoles

2. **Boot Welts**

Leather

Boot leathers vary in quality. The tanned cowhide most often used for uppers can be classed as either a "split" or "top" grain. When the hide comes off the animal it is too thick for boot uppers and consequently must be split into sheets of varying thickness. The outside or top layer is called "top grain"; it is ideal for boot uppers because of its tough, flexible oiliness and natural resistance to water and moisture. All other layers are called "splits." Though inexpensive, split leather is inferior because it tends to stretch and is difficult to adequately waterproof. A "rough out" leather may be reversed grain (smooth side in, rough side out) or it may be a sueded split.

Lining

Boots should be lined with leather and padded in the instep and heel areas. A heel counter will help keep the foot from moving and prevent blisters. Try to find boots with a box or stiffened toe and a nylon, fiberglass, or steel shank (full length of foot) which is semi-stiff or stiff.

Scree Collar

The top of the boot should have a scree (pebble) guard. A hinged, one-piece tongue will keep out dirt and water.

Height

Except for special purposes, boots should not be too high or be restrictive around the calf. Very high boots give no more support to the ankle; they also allow too little ankle flex on steep trails and may lead to an irritated Achilles tendon. In general, 5½ inches is an appropriate height (men's size 9).

Boot Laces

The braided, flat, nylon type of boot lace stays knotted better than the round variety. The boot lace texture should not be too rough or you'll find yourself developing raw, sore fingers.

Soles

One of the very best boot soles available is the Vibram sole. Its weight and rigidity are well balanced and it is very resistant to wear because of its high carbon content. The Vibram Roccia is fine for light backpacking (25- to 35-pound pack) and on-trail use; the Vibram Montagna (deeper tread) is better for heavy backpacking, off-trail use, and mountaineering.

Fitting

When buying your boots, take the time to fit them properly—if they don't fit, they can turn what should be a pleasant hike into a grueling ordeal (and grind your feet into hamburger). Here's a boot-fitting procedure you might try: put on a thin pair of undersocks (e.g., Wick-Dry orlon blend or Quiana nylon) and a medium- to heavy-weight pair of wool or wool blend socks. With the shoe unlaced, check to see if you have a thumb-width of space in front of the toes. Push your foot until the toes touch the front of the boot—you should be able to just get a forefinger in back of your heel. If you can get two fingers in, the boot is too large. Now lace up the boot—barely tight at the toes, tight at the instep and top of the foot. Bend forward, flexing the shoe fully—your heel should not lift more than 1/8 inch from the boot sole.

Your boot must be long enough so that when it is laced snugly the toes will neither fall asleep nor hit the front of the boot while hiking downhill. To test this, lace the boots and scuff your foot forward to simulate the motion of walking downhill. (Do this on a 45-degree slope if you can). The heavier the pack you plan to carry, the harder you should scuff.

When you first lace up a new pair of boots there should be about ½ to 1 inch between the rows of laces (to allow for stretching as the boots are broken in). Your toes should be able to wiggle, but the ball of the foot and the heel should be held firmly.

Breaking In

Good boots will mold to your feet—poor or too-heavy boots (or incorrect breaking in) will mold your feet to the boot (not very good for the feet) and possibly damage the boot.

When beginning to break in your boots, wear two pairs of socks (as noted in "Fitting") and lace the boots properly (so your heel and ball of your foot don't move more than ⅛ inch). Take several short one- to three-mile hikes, always checking for "hot spots" or actual blisters. Walking up and down steep hills will help break in all parts of the boots. Most boots will be feeling pretty good after 10 to 30 miles of hiking.

If your boots don't seem to be breaking in after about 20 miles, you can try the following techniques (with great care!) to help them along. To reduce stiffness and to aid the molding of the boot to the foot, use a rubber hammer or similar instrument to lightly tap the box toe or heel counter areas. To help mold a very stiff boot to your foot, pour warm (130- to 140-degree) water into each boot, let stand for 10 seconds, pour out quickly, then wear the boots until dry. You may need to change socks during the drying process. This technique simulates an accelerated hiking trip in warm weather and helps to mold the leather faster. It could weaken the boot if the water is too hot or if you don't dry the boot completely. Finally, for stiff, blister-producing areas around the heel, the boot can be pressed on a wood form to round out blister-forming areas. Use a one-inch diameter pole with a smooth, rounded end and press against the stiff spot on the inside of the boot, using only hand pressure.

Socks

Socks serve several vital needs: they cushion the feet against the shock of each step, they reduce blisters caused by foot-to-boot friction, they insulate the feet from extremes of heat and cold, and they absorb perspiration. Usually a light liner nylon or orlon sock worn under a heavier wool sock is a good combination. Wearing two socks provides sock-to-sock friction, reducing the chance of blisters. The heavier outer wool sock should be nylon-reinforced at toe and heel (otherwise, these areas will wear out before the rest of the sock). Wash the wool socks in a mild detergent (use cold water) and air-dry them so they will not shrink, will retain their shape, and will not lose their natural oils. Experienced hikers know that their choice of socks can make the difference between misery and comfort.

Boot Care

Cleaning: After removing most of the dirt with a brush or dry cloth, use saddle soap and a little water to clean the dirt out of the pores of the leather; wipe with a clean, dry towel and brush (if boots are rough-out).

Waterproofing: Silicones such as Sno-Seal can be used with chrome-tanned leathers. Silicone compounds "inflate" the leather fibers and restore the natural water barrier while maintaining the leather's breathability.

Oil-tanned leathers should be treated with oils and greases such as Snow Shoe. Neats-foot oil, mink oil, or Leath-R-Seal can also be used on oil-tanned leathers. Leath-R-Seal is a wax and shellac combination and is a good seam sealer (be sure you are using it on properly tanned leather). Plain wax can also be used on either type of leather. Use liquid silicone compounds on sueded leather.

Drying Wet Boots: Wet boots should be dried slowly and completely at close to room temperature. Do not put boots in the oven, over a heater, or close to a fire.

Repair: A good-fitting, quality pair of boots is worth repairing. Here the key is not to wear out the lug sole *and* the midsole. The lug sole can usually be replaced, as can some midsoles. If the scree guard collar disintegrates, it also can easily be replaced. Even the box toe can be repaired by sewing a new leather cap over it. See your friendly, local hiking boot repair shop for these operations.

Foot Care

Not only your boots but your feet need to be kept in good shape if you are to avoid blisters and other foot miseries. When wearing your boots, keep your toenails short. Socks should be changed at least twice a day and, if wet, immediately. You can stop by a brook or spring to cool your feet, rest them, and change socks. The socks can be tied on the outside of the pack to dry. When you rinse your feet, do it quickly so that the skin doesn't get soft (softened skin makes blistering easier).

The best cure for blisters is prevention. Wearing a liner sock underneath a heavier sock reduces friction between boot and foot. Feeling for "hot spots" on your feet or ankles is the only way to catch a blister before it occurs. If you feel a certain area is warm, chafed, and slightly red, take the time to put on some "Moleskin" (available at any drug store—and, hopefully, in your first aid kit). Cut an oval or round piece that will more than cover the area that's "hot"; notch it to make it lay flat, with no wrinkles; apply to clean, dry skin and leave on until the end of the hike (or day). If you hike regularly, your feet will eventually toughen up and you'll no longer need the Moleskin. After a few hikes, you'll also learn where your tender spots are and can apply the Moleskin before beginning to hike.

Blisters should never be regarded lightly. They can lead to serious infection. Keep your feet as clean as possible at all times. If a blister does develop, you may have to drain it in order to relieve the pressure and pain. To do this, sterilize a needle or the point of a knife in a flame. After applying antiseptic to the blistered area, carefully puncture it on the edge, not on the top, and squeeze all the fluid out. Immediately apply more antiseptic and cover with a small bandage of sterile gauze or a bandaid. If no more hiking is planned, this should be enough, but if you are going to keep hiking, place a piece of Moleskin over the whole thing, bandage and all, to prevent further irritation. This, however, is only one of many ways to treat blisters. You may have already discovered another method which works well for you.

3.4 Sleeping Bags

On a wilderness trip a good night's sleep often depends on an appropriate sleeping bag. Also needed are a pad providing thermal insulation and some cushioning, a ground cloth, and (if it's very cold) a few extra clothes (wool cap, long underwear, wool socks).

The average new backpacker tends to buy more sleeping bag than he/she needs. Remember that a sleeping bag is part of a system which includes a good pad, tent or other shelter, and your clothing. A sub-zero rated bag may spend most of the year in a closet because it is too hot to sleep comfortably in most of the time. Buying a three-season bag and renting a sub-zero bag when you need one is a reasonable approach. Before buying any sleeping bag, try several (borrow from a friend or rent) to determine just how much sleeping bag you need. From the standpoint of comfort and good rest, your sleeping bag is one of the most important (and expensive) pieces of equipment you will buy; and one on which you should not compromise.

The materials used in a sleeping bag are primarily for insulation. The bag does not generate heat, but only conserves what the body produces. A bag which is too warm can cause you almost as much discomfort as one which is not warm enough, a fact which should be kept firmly in mind when making your selection.

Fillers or Insulating Materials

Most sleeping bags are filled with down (goose or duck) or a synthetic — e.g., Hollofill, Celanese Fortrel, Polarguard (long continuous filaments) or Dupont Dacron Fiberfill II (masses of short fibers). Goose down has a typical loft of 550 cubic inches/ounce, duck down of 400 to 450, and Polarguard, 375. "Loft" is the height to which a sleeping bag puffs up when properly shaken out and laid freestanding on the floor; it is a rough indicator of insulation, of how warm the bag will keep you. A rough loft/temperature rating guide goes something like this: 5 to 6 inches = +15 to 25 degrees F; 6 to 7 inches = +5 to 15 degrees F; 8 to 9½ inches = -10 to -40 degrees F.

The total bag weight for down fill (regular size) with seven- to eight-inch loft should be no more than four pounds. For a synthetic fill bag of similar quality and temperature range, the maximum should be no more than five pounds.

Of course, there are many other factors involved in keeping warm — the bag itself is just one part of the picture. Other insulation factors are: preventing ground conduction loss by using a ground sheet and pad; and preventing convection loss in wind by using a tent, bivvy sack, or tarp (which also prevent dew from settling and soaking the bag). Also, people differ greatly in their rates of metabolism, and the same person's metabolism will vary depending on physical condition, tiredness at the moment, etc. The type and quantity of food consumed before going to bed is very important in determining how warm you will sleep. Eating some protein and complex carbohydrates before turning in will help you sleep much warmer because of increased blood sugar available for heat production.

Bag Shapes and Construction

The four most common sleeping bag shapes are the mummy, the semi-mummy, the barrel, and the rectangle. The first two weigh less, are less bulky, and conserve body heat more efficiently; thus, they are the most popular with wilderness travelers.

The best way to explain the various methods of constructing sleeping bags is by illustration. In down bags, the baffles are pockets holding the filler material; in polyester bags, they hold the batting in place. The basic baffle patterns used are: box wall (square), slant wall (parallelogram), V-tube (overlapping Vs), double quilt (laminated); and, last and least, sewn-through (these seams have cold spots).

Most bags with down as filler use the slanted baffle design; most synthetic-filled bags use the offset double quilting or triple layer (double quilt plus sandwich layer) design.

The inner and outer shells of a sleeping bag may be cut either differentially or with a space-filler cut. The latter cut is a design in which inner and outer fabric shells are the same size. A bag that is differentially cut has an inner shell that is smaller than the outer shell. This cut keeps the thickness of the insulation uniform, preventing cold spots caused by the body pressing the inner and outer shells together (the thermos bottle principle). Differential cut is not as important in the larger semi-mummy bag as it is in mummy bags.

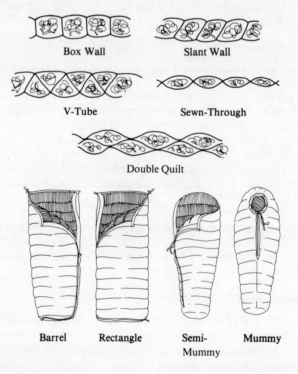

Box Wall   Slant Wall

V-Tube   Sewn-Through

Double Quilt

Barrel   Rectangle   Semi-   Mummy
                         Mummy

**3. Sleeping Bag Construction and
Sleeping Bag Shapes**

Well-designed sleeping bags have an oversized draft tube or flap in back of the zipper to prevent cold air coming through the zipper. These draft tubes should be 10 to 13 inches in circumference or three to four inches in diameter, offset by three inches, and not sewn through. The flap should extend down beyond the end of the zipper about one to three inches. Some flaps have a stiffener added to prevent the zipper from catching or snagging it.

Fabrics

Fabrics used in most bags are either ripstop or nylon taffeta. For the outer and inner shells this is usually 1.5 to 2.2-ounce material; if down is the filler the fabric should be "downproof" (a tight enough weave that down cannot slip through—212 threads/inch). Most bags have 1.9 ounce shells. The material should be fade- and abrasion-resistant, stain- and water-repellent, and smooth.

Zippers should be YKK #5 or #7; 10-toothed nylon, Delrin, or plastic coil; 70 inches long; and two-way to allow ventilation control.

Synthetic vs. Down Fill

Whether you are looking at clothing or a sleeping bag, the basic consideration is "How dry can I keep my gear?" If you expect to hike when sudden rain is a distinct possibility, Polarguard or the like would be a better choice in a bag. If you expect to use your sleeping bag inside a tent where condensation is not a problem, down would be a good choice. For the rough use kids give a piece of equipment, the easy washability of synthetic-filled items may be the deciding factor.

In deciding whether to buy a down or synthetic bag, you might keep in mind that down (all kinds) soaks up water and loses nearly all its loft when wet. A waterlogged down bag is nearly useless for any purpose other than that of mopping up the campsite. One experience with wringing wet down often results in the purchase of a synthetic-filled bag. A synthetic bag loses only a little of its loft and almost none of its insulating qualities when wet. You can squeeze it out and dry it in the sun (with a little breeze) in one-half to one hour. Down bags sometimes take *days* to dry!

Cleaning

Both down and synthetic bags need cleaning to maintain loft and breathability, and to remove salt and dirt. If you send your down bag to a professional cleaner who has experience in cleaning down products, make sure they use only "Stoddard Fluid" (a petroleum distillate) and not "Perk" (perchloroethylene). The best method of cleaning down bags is to handwash them. To do this, use an extremely mild soap, so it will not remove the natural oils in down. If you use soap such as Ivory Snow or Ivory Flakes, be sure you do so only if the water is soft, otherwise you'll never be able to remove the hardwater scum from your sleeping bag. Woolite, Nu-Down, or Fluffy (the last two are especially made for cleaning down) are good for use in hard water. Use no cleaners contining chlorine.

If you are going to wash your bag yourself, fill the bathtub half full of lukewarm water and first gently soak the bag for a little while. Then work the suds in by pushing down on the bag with open hands, gently kneading. Do not twist or wring. Dirt will appear as the suds are worked through. Sponge off especially dirty spots. Do not try to lift a wet bag out of the water—the baffles may rip out! Instead, after gently pressing out the water, gather the bag up in your arms, supporting all its weight with your hands from underneath. Press out all the water you can. Then roll the bag into a laundry basket and put it in a front or top loading machine. Use the "gentle" or "delicate" spin cycle to remove excess water only. The best method of drying the bag is in a large commercial tumble dryer that can be set for low or not heat. Before putting the bag into the dryer, inspect the drum for sharp edges and spots of oil or grease which could stain your bag. Put the bag in with a pair of clean sneakers (laces out); their weight will help break up the down clumps. Run the machine at the lowest heat possible as long as necessary. Wash down jackets in the same way.

Synthetic-filled bags should *not* be dry cleaned, (the fill is degraded by dry cleaning solvents), but should be handwashed like down-filled bags. Polarguard bags are an exception. These bags have a stronger construction which allows them to be machine washed on gentle cycle. Also, washing usually improves the loft of synthetic bags.

Pads and Ground Covers

Whether you use a tent or not, you will need a groundsheet to put under the tent or under you and your pad. The groundsheet should be light, waterproof, and sturdy; some find that an inexpensive tube tent works fine. You'll need a pad under you to insulate your body from the cold, cold ground and, if you're thin, to cushion your bones a bit. The lightest pad and the one which will insulate you the best is a closed-cell pad; the most common brand is "Ensolite." Thickness varies from ¼ inch to ½ inch. The thickness and length you buy will depend on your personal needs and how cold you expect the weather to be. The thicker, open-cell pads cushion you more, but are bulkier, heavier, and soak up water. Air mattresses are relatively heavy and do not insulate you well—not to mention the problem of punctures (ever tried repairing one in the dark?). There is, however, a new, many-celled air mattress that a lot of hikers swear by. This new mattress inflates itself, is light, and insulates better than regular air mattresses because the cells are small so air can't circulate and carry heat away as easily as in conventional air mattresses.

When choosing a pad or air mattress, keep the following in mind: temperature and weather where you'll usually be traveling; weight, bulk, and abrasion resistance of the item (open-cell foam pads need a waterproof cover); and length and thickness needed for comfort.

3.5 Packs

We could write a whole book about packs, but will refrain from doing so out of consideration for our cost and your sanity. Instead, we'll confine ourselves to a few brief descriptions of types of packs, their general uses, and a few suggestions on what to look for when you buy one.

Types

Day packs: Just what they sound like. Used for non-overnight hikes, or even just for going to the library or store on foot or bike. Some people with fairly large day packs manage to strap a sleeping bag on the outside and make it do for a weekender. Look for wide and/or padded straps, light waist belt (unless you're never going to put more than five pounds in it), waterproof material, non-metal zipper, and some means of fastening miscellaneous items on the outside.

Internal Frame Packs and Soft Packs: Internal frame packs usually have a sturdy, triangular frame of steel or high-impact plastic over which the bag is attached. A soft pack has approximately the same design, but without internal frame. Both have a low center of gravity because the load is held close to the small of your back, thus giving you better balance than with an external frame pack. These packs are usually used for off-trail hiking, cross-country skiing, rock climbing, scrambling, etc. They come in varying sizes, from those appropriate for overnights to those carrying enough for major expeditions. Look for: adjustable frames; wide, padded shoulder straps and waist belt (the belt should also have a quick-release fastening with no sharp edges); some means to cinch up the bag if it is not full (otherwise gear will shift around, throwing you off balance); some means of fastening skis, climbing equipment, and so on, on the outside; and waterproof materials (check seams carefully).

External Frame Packs: These packs are used for both on-trail and off-trail (cross-country) travel. Most pack frames are welded; some are screw-fitted. The least reliable are those with sloppy welds, so give the pack a careful inspection at the store. Beware of sharp tube bends; bending fatigues metal. The added tubing designed into the pack to make it stand upright may be functional or just more weight. A wide belt strap allows most of the weight to be placed on hips and legs, the strongest parts of the body. Shoulders and arms are then free, making breathing easier than with packs whose whole weight hangs on the shoulders. These packs are comfortable on trails, but due to their high position they are

4. Types of Packs

Day Pack

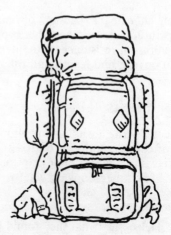

Internal Frame Pack

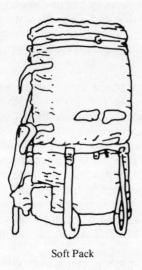

Soft Pack

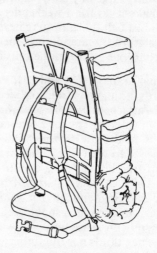

External Frame Pack

less suitable for skiing or travel off-trail through brush or large rocks. Look for waterproof pack bag and a sturdy frame that is well welded, not soldered. Bolted frames are OK if properly keyed. Be sure to try on any pack for good fit; the comfort of this style of pack is particularly dependent on good fit to your body dimensions. There should be at least four lengths for you to choose from. Shape of bag and number and shape of pockets are up to you. As with all pieces of major equipment, if possible you should either borrow or rent several kinds before deciding on what kind to buy.

3.6 Tents and Other Shelters

Again, several volumes could be written on this subject, but will not be. Suffice it to say that good, light, well-made tents are expensive, so rent a few tents, share your friends' tents, look in catalogues, visit mountaineering stores, and talk to quite a few tent owners before you make the big purchase.

Tents

When researching your tent purchase, look for the following: waterproof, bathtub floor; untreated (non-waterproof) upper walls and roof (to allow moisture to escape — otherwise it may rain indoors when it isn't even raining outside); waterproof fly to keep out the rain; mesh-covered cross-ventilation openings (with provisions for closing tightly if necessary); a door which can be unzipped at the top for ventilation and which begins at or above the junction of the bathtub floor and upper walls; ease of setting up (can you set it up in the cold and windy dark, with gloves on, on the side of a hill?); replaceable parts; light weight (not more than three pounds/person); small stitching (eight to ten stitches/inch); ample reinforcing in high-wear areas; tent poles seated on grommets attached to tab on tent bottom (or poles may sink inconveniently into the ground or through the tent floor if there is an inside frame); flat, felled seams.

Quality backpacking tents come in many shapes and sizes, but most hikers buy what is referred to as a "three-season" tent; that is, a tent generally good for all seasons except winter. If you need a winter tent, be sure to consider wind stability, weight (most are made of heavier materials, and the average weight/person is four to five pounds), cookhole (a zippered opening in the floor), two entrances (the usual and a snow tunnel, sort of like an expandable sleeve that you can crawl through), snow tunnel vents at each end (so snow doesn't blow in), a door that can be opened at the top (in winter, ventilation is more of a problem than in summer, especially if you are cooking indoors), snowflaps (extra material around the base of the tent on which you can pile snow or rocks to make the tent more stable in wind), catenary cut if tent is an A-frame (this is a built-in sag of the roof line which takes up the usual slack in the tent sides so that when the guylines are tight the tent walls flap very little in the wind), and a frostliner.

You can buy a two-person tent for $25 to $300, but the amount you pay often has little relation to your satisfaction (or lack of it) with the tent. A tent should be lightweight, yet sturdy. It should be roomy enough so you won't get cabin fever when you're trapped inside it during a two-day rainstorm. Roomy is in the eye of the beholder, though — there are backpackers who can exist for weeks quite happily in the new "bivvy sacks." These are glorified versions of the old cagoule trick, in which you first put on all the clothes you had with you, then pulled tight the hood, sleeve, and bottom drawstrings (with your knees under your chin) — and hoped you'd stay dry and warm all night! The new bivvy sacks are actually miniscule one-person tents; though you can't sit up in some of them, they do give you some breathing space, some netting for ventilation, protection from the wet, and are very light in weight (one to two pounds).

Winter Tent

Standard Tent with Fly

Tarps Pitched as Shelters

Poncho Pitched as Shelter

Tube Tent

Bivvy Sack

5. **Types of Shelters**

Other Shelters

A good tarp, handily pitched, can be quite satisfactory, except in heavy rain, wind, or in winter. The best quality tarps are often made of coated nylon and sport quite a few heavy-duty grommets; they are usually sized 7 x 9 feet, 9 x 11 feet, and 10 x 12 feet. Weights vary from two to three pounds and prices from $25 to $60. If you already have a tent, but don't think you'll need it for a particular trip, try taking along the rain fly for emergency shelter — it works very well.

Tube tents are fine for occasional weekend outings and emergencies, but don't plan on using one on a long trek. Tubes are usually made of two- to three-mil plastic, are about nine feet long and three to five feet in diameter, and weigh one to three pounds. You can buy one for $4 to $10. Tubes are easy to pitch, in that you just run a cord through one and fasten it tightly between two anchors. You'd best leave the ends open, though, or you'll find yourself without enough air to breathe comfortably.

If you're really desperate for shelter, you can even use your poncho — if it's a pretty tough one of coated nylon, complete with grommets and an extension that is meant to fit over your pack when you're wearing it.

3.7 Homemade Equipment

Many mountaineers enjoy making some of their own equipment. The introduction of strong, synthetic, colored fabrics has increased this trend so that now many mountaineering equipment stores and catalogues carry large yardage assortments and quite a few accessories for the do-it-yourselfer. There are even books on the subject which give helpful design and sewing instructions. And, of course, there are numerous kits for making just about any fabric article from an "outdoor office" to a tent. You can make gaiters, mittens, rain gear, parkas, sleeping bags, ditty bags, pack bags, ponchos, and so on. Besides the fun of making your own camping gear, there is also the fact that doing so is *much* cheaper than buying same ready-made! We have only enough space here to tell you a bit about the possibilities and to give you a couple of simple ideas to get you started (see Appendix C for patterns and instructions for gaiters and mittens).

Fabrics

Nylon fabrics are the most versatile of the synthetics used for mountaineering garments and equipment. They are available both in plain and ripstop weaves and come in different weights and colors. In ripstop materials, tears and rips can only go a short distance. Most stores carry ripstop in various weights. Nylon fabrics are water-repellent, not waterproof — unless they have been coated with another synthetic (polyurethane). The uncoated nylons are usable for parkas, tents (except floors and flies), windbreakers, and sleeping bags.

Cotton and polyester fabrics (sometimes called 60-40 cloth — 60% cotton and 40% polyester) are good for parkas, windbreakers, and other items which need to be water-repellent, but not waterproof. This cloth can be made water-repellent by spraying with Scotchguard or something similar.

Mountaineering catalogues usually list which materials are suitable for certain purposes. Some listings are very accurate and up-to-date. A recent innovation in outer shell fabrics is Gore-Tex, a material providing a barrier which is said to be both waterproof and breathable.

Sewing

The pattern for any item you want to make should be laid out accurately on the material ahead of time, for these lightweight fabrics are expensive. Cutting should be done with pinking shears or a "hot knife" along lines you have laid out on the fabric according to the pattern.

Nylon and cotton-polyester fabrics may be sewn with a home sewing machine. For nylon fabrics especially, correct tension must be maintained so that the lock of the thread is in the center of the lay of the fabric. Be sure to use the synthetic thread recommended by the manufacturer of the material. Size 16 thread is recommended for load-carrying seams; size 24 thread can be used for garments and sleeping bags. For synthetic fabrics the needle must be sharp and of the right size. If the needle is too large, it punches holes which are hard to make waterproof; if too small, the thread frays. A number 16 needle for size 30 thread and a number 18 needle for sizes 16 and 24 threads are suggested.

When stitching synthetic fabrics, either a slight zig-zag or a straight line of eight to 12 stitches/inch is satisfactory. All load-carrying joints must have at least two seams so that the thread acts in shear. Seams and hems should be arranged so that no opening faces upward on the outside of a garment or tent.

If you have remnants left after making some item, you can make an assortment of "stuff" or "ditty" bags with drawstrings. These are very handy for keeping your pack well-organized during a trip.

Part II:
AWAY FROM THE
ROADS

John Muir Wilderness, near Mammoth Lakes

It is far safer to wander in the woods than to travel on black highways or to stay at home.

— John Muir

Chapter 4
Hiking Navigation

To be oriented in the wilderness is to be aware at all times of your exact location and altitude. Before leaving for any wilderness trip, you can begin to acquire this orientation by carefully studying good topographic maps, planning your route thoroughly, anticipating possible difficulties, estimating travel time according to the weather and the abilities of the hikers, and talking with people who know the area. Every hiker should be interested in the how-to of map and compass — you never know when you may suddenly have to rely on your knowledge of them if you become separated from your group or lost. Also, even if you never hike on anything but a well-traveled path, you'll probably find your trip more interesting and rewarding if you can figure out just what it is you're seeing as you go along; navigation can be fun!

4.1 Equipment

Compass

There are many different types of compasses on the market, some of which can be used for hiking navigation, and others with too many added features to be of practical value. Experience has proved that the simple "protractor" type is the most satisfactory, it is recommended that you buy one if you expect to do extensive hiking. These compasses are of transparent plastic, have a rotational baseplate, and can be bought at most sporting goods stores. The two makes most readily available are Silva and Suunto; they are identical in operation and nearly so in price. Be sure to choose a model that is liquid-filled — the liquid damps the needle swing, making the compass readings more rapid and accurate. All except the least expensive models have luminous needles and points for night use; this is a handy feature, for it means you don't always have to turn on your flashlight to read the compass, and thus lose part of your dark adaptation. If you are on a tight budget, cut your expenses some place other than in buying a good compass. It will last a lifetime and could turn out to be the cheapest life insurance you ever bought.

Maps

Any sufficiently detailed map will do, but the topographical maps prepared by the U.S. Geological Survey (sometimes called "topos," "quadrangles," or "quads") are the most accurate, detailed, and usually the most up-to-date maps available. The maps most used come in two scales: 15-minute, in which 1 mile equals about 1 inch and the whole quad covers an area of about 13 x 17 miles; and the 7½ minute, in which 1 inch equals about 2000 feet and the whole quad covers an area of about 6½ x 8½ miles. (In this context, "minute" indicates the amount of the earth's surface covered by the map; that is, it is a measure of space, not time. There are 60 minutes in a degree. One degree covers about 70 miles in latitude or longitude at the equator.).

U.S. Geological Survey maps may be purchased in local sporting goods stores or ordered from the USGS Federal Center, Denver, CO 80225 for areas west of the Mississippi, or from USGS, 1200 S. Eads St., Arlington, VA 22202, for areas east of the Mississippi.

To keep your maps readable and in one piece for longer, keep them either rolled up in cardboard tubes or laid out flat in artist's portfolios or between pieces of cardboard when not in use. On trips carry maps in waterproof, transparent cases. You can also mount maps between sheets of clear adhesive plastic to prevent them from becoming sodden and unreadable in wet weather.

Miscellaneous Equipment

Take a pencil and some paper to keep notes with , especially on longer trips or when the visibility is likely to be poor. Be sure your pencil does not affect the compass needle. Even some wooden pencils with metal tips can drastically change a compass reading if held near the needle.

4.2 Using Map and Compass

There are several different systems for using a compass, most of them too complex to be of practical value to the hiker. The system described here, however, is the simplest available and has been successfully used in the field for many years; with it, everyone can learn to navigate any terrain — desert, mountain, forest — proficiently and confidently.

Map Reading

Symbols: Maps attempt to convey the features of the area by certain conventional symbols. The following colors are typical: brown for land features, blue for streams and lakes, white for glaciers, green for vegetation, black for buildings, red for main roads, dotted lines for trails, thin double lines for jeep trails, and so on. A sheet containing a description of all the map symbols is available at places USGS maps are sold.

Elevation

The vertical relation between map areas is shown by contour lines. Because a contour line is essentially a water-level line it must ultimately form a closed curve, but it does not always do so on a particular map. Contour lines never intersect, although at cliffs they may appear to do so because only the top edge is visible. A closed contour line represents a horizontal cross-section of land at the elevation of the contour; hence, a set of contours at successive elevations gives a family of cross sections. A circular conical hill will be shown as a system of equally spaced circles, concentric if the hill is symmetrical. A dome-shaped hill is similar, but its circles are not equally spaced and are closer together where the slope is steeper. Tilted planes are shown as nearly straight parallel contours, spaced equally only if the slope is constant.

When looking at a new topo map one can best learn what it is showing by determining which contour patterns identify the ridges and spurs (sloping ridges), and which show the valleys and draws. (See Illustration 6.)

Do this by first identifying where the highest ground lies. In a mountainous area this is quickly done by locating a peak. If no peaks are shown, then determine which is the higher ground by reading the elevations given on the contour lines.

Because a contour line is the same as a water-level line, a succession of contour lines will form a V- or U-shaped pattern pointing *uphill* for a draw or upsloping valley. A similar pattern pointing *downhill* denotes a spur. A spur is usually always seen between two draws.

In steep, mountainous country the V and U patterns will be sharply defined. In a rolling terrain, where the draws may be broad and shallow and the spurs wide, the patterns will be very loosely formed over a broader area.

Profiling: When a new route for an outing is laid out, distances alone are not indicative of the territory. Wherever a route crosses a contour line, the elevation above the point of beginning for that segment can be read. The plotting of elevation vs. distance will give a visual profile of the plotted trail (see Illustration 6). To save space, such plotting usually exaggerates the vertical scale five- or ten-fold.

6. Identification of Spurs and Draws

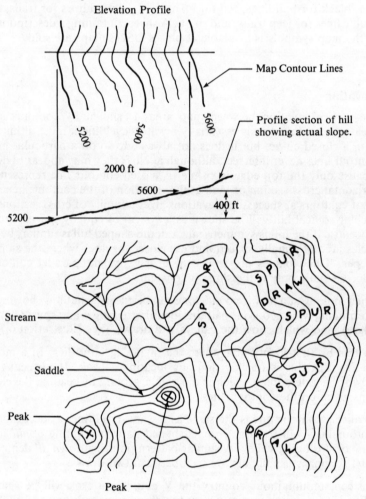

Elevation Profile

Map Contour Lines

Profile section of hill showing actual slope.

5200 5400 5600

2000 ft

5600

400 ft

5200

Stream

Saddle

Peak

Peak

SPUR
SPUR
SPUR
DRAW
SPUR
SPUR
DRAW

V- or U-shaped patterns pointing *downhill* are spurs. Similar patterns pointing *uphill* are draws. A stream also indicates a draw.

Measuring Your Pace

"Pace" is the number of steps taken to cover a unit of distance. The unit of distance may be either 1/10 mile or 100 meters. The standard method is to count each landing of one foot only (not each step). When measuring your pace, walk normally, and concentrate on your count. It's best to count your pace while wearing your hiking boots.

You need to be able to measure distances on the map to correspond with pacing measurements on the ground for dead reckoning navigation when landforms are not visible. To measure distance on a topo map, refer to the linear graph scales in the bottom margin. There is one in miles and one in kilometers. A method for making a convenient measuring instrument is to apply a strip of adhesive tape on the front edge of your compass baseplate, marking it in graduations of either 100 meters or 1/10 miles from the scale on the map (be sure to use a pencil or a pen with waterproof ink).

When pacing distances you need to devise a method for keeping track of how many units of distance (100M or 1/10 mi) you have covered. Tick marks on the map is one suggested method. Practice in the field will show that keeping track by memory alone is very difficult and unreliable.

Adding Magnetic North (MN) Datum Lines to the Map

Because we are using the simplified form of compass navigation, only magnetic north (MN) will be used for reference. The use of true north (TN) is not necessary. You can add MN datum lines to your map by the following simple procedure (this should be done before going into the field):

1. In the lower left-hand corner of the topographic map you will see a diagram giving the angle of MN declination from true north. You need to add MN datum lines to your map at the angle given on the diagram.

2. By using your compass as a protractor, you can draw your first MN datum line. Set the bearing arrow index mark at a degree point on the dial equivalent to the declination angle. Carefully align one of the grid lines on your compass dial to the vertical borderline of your map (this borderline is true north). Draw a line on the face of your map along the edge of the baseplate; extend this line as far as needed with a straightedge. This is your first datum line.

3. Add additional datum lines to your map by (a) putting two marks on the edge of a strip of paper as far apart as you want your datum lines to be, (b) using your strip as a measuring tool to put two dots on the map near top and bottom (draw a circle around each dot to make it easy to locate), and (c) connecting the two dots with a straightedge, thus producing another MN datum line parallel to the first (see Illustration). If you have a ruler you may find it more convenient to use it for a measuring tool rather than the strip of paper.

To add more datum lines, always measure from the first datum line. The space between datum lines is arbitrary but should be approximately one-half the width of your compass baseplate. You may wish to omit drawing the lines in the area of the map which you will not be using.

7. Adding Datum Lines to Map

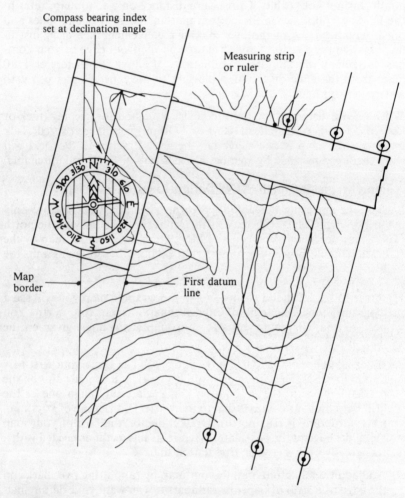

Compass bearing index
set at declination angle

Measuring strip
or ruler

Map
border

First datum
line

Definitions

Although the instructions given here are not highly technical, an understanding of correct terms is necessary. Below are some of the more common terms and their definitions.

AZIMUTH. Angular degrees read in clockwise direction on the compass in the horizontal plane.

BACK BEARING. Exactly the opposite direction from a compass reading. Add or subtract 180 degrees from your reading; use whichever figure falls within the 0-360 degree range or take the reading at the South end of the compass needle).

BEARING. The direction of a point relative to your position. You read the bearing in angular degrees in a clockwise direction on the compass dial (azimuth reading).

BEARING ARROW. The arrow on the compass baseplate. Same as "direction arrow."

DECLINATION. This is the angular difference between True North (TN) and Magnetic North (MN) on the earth's surface. This angle differs, depending upon geographical location.

DEVIATION. Errors in compass readings due to external effects; can be compensated for with complex procedures we are not concerned with here. Not to be confused with "compass error" caused by proximity of metal nearby when taking compass readings.

HEADING. The angle at which one is travelling. If you are hiking a compass course, your heading can be the same as your bearing if you are heading toward the point on which you took your bearing.

MN or NM. Magnetic North or North Magnetic.

TN or NT. True North or North True.

VARIATION. The same as "declination," but used in nautical navigation more than in land navigation.

YOUR POSITION. Where you are located, either on the map or on the terrain. Same as nautical term "fix."

4.3 Finding Your Way

Compass readings should never be taken near visible masses of metal or electric circuits. To insure proper functioning of the compass, observe the following suggested safe distances:

High tension power lines	50 yards
Vehicles	16 yards
Telephone lines and wire fences	10 yards
Ice axe, crampons, tools, another compass	1 yard

Also check the effect of your watch, belt buckle, pencil, or anything else on your person. Double check if you are navigating by dead reckoning.

Taking a Bearing on a Landmark

1. Stand looking at a landmark with your body squarely facing it. Hold your compass with the baseplate bearing arrow pointing directly at the landmark. Hold the compass level so that the needle swings freely.

2. While holding the compass steady with the bearing arrow still on target, rotate the compass dial to align the zero point (N) with the *red* end of the compass needle. This completes taking the bearing.

3. With the compass in any convenient position, the bearing can be read, in degrees, at the bearing arrow index point. Remember that all bearing readings are given in Magnetic North reference. Example: "140 degrees MN".

Note: When using the compass to take a bearing on a landmark, the zero or N point on the compass dial is *always* pointed directly to MN — never in any other direction (see illustration 9). The needle is not needed to position the dial to zero MN when the compass is placed on the map, because this is done by aligning the dial grid lines with the MN datum line.

Plotting a Bearing on the Map

After you have learned to take bearings from your position to landmarks on the terrain, try plotting a bearing on the map, as follows.

1. Take a bearing on a landmark on the terrain. The landmark must be one you have previously identified on the map. (It is not necessary to read the bearing in degrees for this operation.)

2. Without changing the dial setting, place the compass on the map. (The map may be in any convenient position when plotting a bearing.) Place the dial in alignment with an MN datum line, with the N in the northerly direction, and slide the compass up or down the datum line until the baseplate edge intersects the landmark on the map; simultaneously check the dial for alignment with MN datum line. Remember not to change the dial setting during this operation.

3. Hold the baseplate firmly against the map and draw a line through the landmark, extending it back away from the direction of the bearing arrow. The extended line will pass through your position on the map (see Illustration 8).

4. To find your exact position, pick out another landmark on the terrain at about a right angle to the first and transfer its bearing to the map, as in #3. Your exact position on the map will be where the two lines cross.

Note: During positioning of the compass on the map, the compass needle can be disregarded and the map can be in any position. It is best to have the map folded so that you can reach under it and press it against the compass baseplate.

8. Plotting a Bearing on the Map

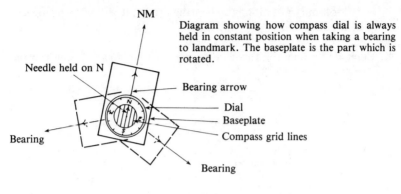

NM

Diagram showing how compass dial is always held in constant position when taking a bearing to landmark. The baseplate is the part which is rotated.

Needle held on N

Bearing arrow

Dial

Baseplate

Compass grid lines

Bearing

Bearing

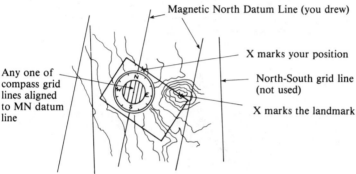

Magnetic North Datum Line (you drew)

X marks your position

Any one of compass grid lines aligned to MN datum line

North-South grid line (not used)

X marks the landmark

Diagram showing placement of compass on the map. Compass needle is not needed, and therefore not shown.

Locating a Landmark on the Terrain

After locating your position, try locating a landmark on the terrain by following the same procedures in reverse, as below.

1. Pick out a landmark on the map.

2. Line up the edge of the baseplate through the landmark on the map and through your position, remembering that the bearing arrow must point in the direction *away* from your position on the map.

3. Hold the baseplate firmly against the map and rotate the dial so it is aligned with an MN datum line (and with the N in the northerly direction). The bearing arrow has now been set; remove the compass from the map.

4. Hold the compass with the bearing arrow directly in front of you and square with your body (as in Illustration 9). Rotate your whole body

47

until the compass needle centers on N (*do not turn dial*).

5. Now look outward along the bearing arrow; it will be pointing directly at the landmark.

9. Compass Position for Taking a Bearing on a Landmark on the Terrain

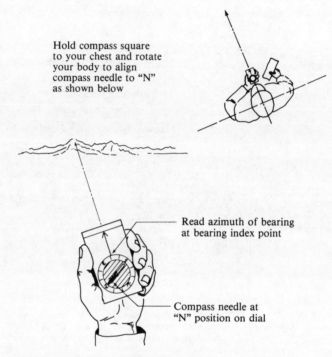

Hold compass square
to your chest and rotate
your body to align
compass needle to "N"
as shown below

Read azimuth of bearing
at bearing index point

Compass needle at
"N" position on dial

Giving Your Position in an Emergency

You may at some future time find it necessary to transmit to a second party information on your position in order to get their help. In daylight conditions with good visibility, proceed as follows:

1. Take a bearing on a landmark which is identifiable on a standard map. Write down the bearing in degrees.

2. Take a second bearing on another landmark which is at as broad an angle as possible to the first. Again write down the degrees.

    Example: Your position would then read — "From our position, bearing to Mt. Hood 140 degr MN, bearing to Mt. Hix 235 degr MN."

In case of darkness or bad visibility, you can give the necessary readings by taking the bearings on your map, *if* you know approximately where you are. Write down the degree readings in the same manner as above.

The bearing readings when transmitted verbally would enable a remote party to plot your position on a map so that assistance could be directed to your location.

When writing down readings always use the word "degree" or "degr." The symbol or little circle denoting degrees can often be misread as a zero. It is considered good practice always to write degrees in three digits as "014 degr" but this is not mandatory if the word is used and not the symbol.

Note: There is a procedure for giving your position in bearing readings *from* the landmark *to* your position. This is called giving a back-bearing and is done by adding (or subtracting) 180 degrees from your compass reading. You add if your reading is *less* than 180 degrees and subract if it is *more* than 180 degrees.

Although converting your compass reading into a back-bearing reading is in itself a simple exercise, in time of stress and possibly bad weather it is an additional step which can cause errors. It is for this reason that you should give your degree reading as read from your compass and state that it is *from* your position and *to* the landmark.

Dead Reckoning

When poor visibility or darkness make it difficult or even impossible to find your way by using landmarks for guidance, use your compass to determine your heading. This practice is commonly known as "dead reckoning."

To navigate in this manner, choose a route on your map by marking a series of one or more objective points. Then connect these points successively with a straight line. If you plainly number each point consecutively, you preclude the possibility of making a 180-degree error when taking a compass bearing on the map. The procedure for using dead reckoning is as follows:

1. Assuming you know approximately where you are on the map, mark this point and number it "zero". Mark your first objective point and number it "1."

2. Using your compass as a straightedge, draw a line on the map connecting these two points. This is the first leg of your route.

3. Take a compass bearing on the map from point zero to point 1. (It is not necessary to take a degree reading.)

4. Measure the length of the leg in tenths of a mile. As previously stated, you should have a strip of adhesive tape added to your compass for this purpose (see "Measuring Your Pace" in Section 4.2).

5. Since you now have the bearing of your first objective, take a compass sighting (aligning N on the dial with the needle and noting the direction of the bearing arrow). For an intermediate target pick out some discernible object in your line of sight such as a tree, bush, or boulder.

6. Walk toward the target you have picked, checking your heading by your compass in areas where the target is not visible, as when crossing a gully. *Concentrate* on your pace count. At the end of each 1/10 mile unit, start your count again. Keeping track of your pace count by making tick marks on the leg line on the map is recommended.

   If your objective point has no identifying feature on the terrain, as in a snowfield, your pace count will be your only means of telling you that you have achieved that approximate position.

7. If you need to navigate a second or third leg in order to reach your final objective, repeat the above procedure.

When proceeding on a compass course, try to observe landforms and features shown on the map (streambeds, knolls, saddles, spurs, draws, etc.). Identifying such features is very helpful in maintaining a correct heading and distance measurement. Fold the map to a manageable size and hold it in position so that the leg you are following is pointing in the direction of your heading. It is also good practice to hold the tip of your thumb on your position while you are walking and trying to relate landforms on the terrain with those shown on the map.

When your "sense of direction" and your compass do not seem to agree, recheck your procedure and always trust your compass. A compass will be reliable except in areas of vast mineral deposits.

White-Out Condition

In the case of a complete white-out situation when it is impossible to distinguish any usable sighting features on the terrain, the dead reckoning procedure can be varied as follows.

1. If you are alone, follow the heading indicated by your compass bearing arrow, keeping track of distance by pace count. With some practice, surprisingly good results can be obtained by this method.

2. If you have a companion, you can use the following two-person system.

   — One person advances first and is guided by the compass holder's voice to either right or left as may be required to stay on course.

   — When the advance person reaches the maximum distance possible under the limitations of the conditions, that person should stop and wait for the other person with the compass to join them. Both people keep a pace count.

Note: It is very important that the compass holder keep a steady "beat" on the verbal contact with the advance person, and that the advance person stop immediately when voice contact is lost.

Taking Bearings With True North Reference Index

All of the foregoing instructions have been based upon navigation using only Magnetic North as the basic reference index. As stated previously, this keeps everything simple and the chance of making errors is minimized.

There are times, however, when directions are given in bearings from TN as well as from MN, as in some guide book instructions for climbing or cross country routes in wilderness areas. The following procedure enables you to take such bearings in a simplified and direct manner, without the often confusing and time-consuming need for adding or subtracting the number of degrees of MN declination. The same simple protractor compass is used. It is not necessary to use one which has an adjustment for declination. The following example illustrates the procedure:

You are required to take a bearing 110 degr TN. The MN declination for the area is 14 degr.

— Set the bearing arrow index on the 110 degr point on the dial.

— Holding the compass to your chest with the bearing arrow normal, rotate your body as required to align the needle to the 14 degr point on the dial. You now have the required bearing 110 degr True North (see Illustration 10).

If you expect to frequently take bearings with the TN index, a small square of colored scotch tape can be permanently placed on the face of the compass dial as shown in the illustration. Although this is not necessary, it helps you to take bearings more quickly and reduces the possibility of error.

4.4 Compass Substitutes

There may come a time when you find yourself without a compass but in need of knowing your general direction. That's the time when it's good to know some of the "before compass" ways of direction finding. Remember, though, that the compass substitutes mentioned here are just that — compass and topographic map are far more reliable.

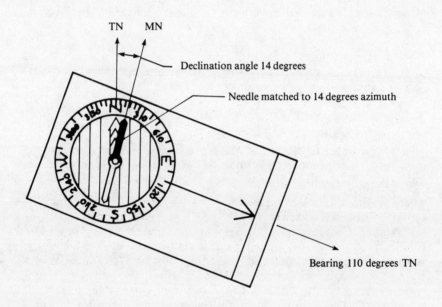

TN   MN

Declination angle 14 degrees

Needle matched to 14 degrees azimuth

Bearing 110 degrees TN

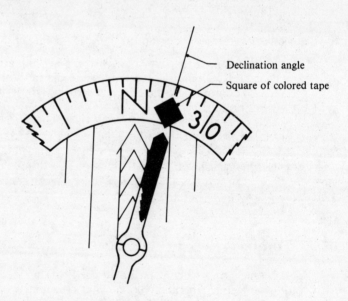

Declination angle

Square of colored tape

10.   Taking a Bearing with True North Reference Index

52

Sun

When visible, the sun can be helpful in approximately determining the north-south direction. In general, at its highest point it is due south; near mid-March and mid-September (the equinoxes) it rises in the east and sets in the west; near mid-June it rises northeast and sets in the northwest; near mid-December, it rises southeast and sets southwest.

Sun and Watch

Hold your watch with the hour hand pointing to the sun. In this position, the true north-south line passes through the mid-point between the hour hand and 12 o'clock (during daylight saving time use 1 o'clock). Before noon, read backward to find the mid-point; after noon, read forward. The accuracy of this method is probably plus or minus 10 degrees.

Straight Stick and Shadow

Put your stick in the ground, slanted toward the sun, so that no shadow is thrown. When a shadow appears, it will mark an approximate east-west line (you can do this at any time of day).

Polaris (the North or Pole Star)

Find the Big Dipper; project a straight line from the two stars on the opposite side of the dipper from the handle. Polaris is the first bright star along that line at approximately five times the distance between the two stars of the dipper.

4.5 Good Advice

When you are in the field at the time of year when a snowstorm may suddenly come upon you, it is always a wise practice to have a fix on your position at all times. When things "start to go bad" it may be too late to see a good landmark on which to take a bearing. Likewise, one should always have a "safety bearing" before crawling into the sleeping bag at night. This is particularly important when you have been prowling around in the dusk looking for the best place to establish camp, and paying no particular attention to which way is north. If you wake in the morning engulfed in a blizzard you will know which way "home" and safety are, *if* you remembered to set your compass the night before.

As an added safety precaution, you can take a sight on Polaris, if visible, and tie a rag in a tree or bush up off the ground, to mark its direction.

If you depend entirely on your compass setting, write down the bearing you will follow in the morning. Do not depend upon your memory alone.

All of this extra caution may seem unnecessary. However, the wilderness can be unforgiving: practicing good judgement on the side of safety is always better than becoming another statistic.

Chapter 5
Weather

Even though you can't do anything about the weather, you can consider its possible changes when planning a wilderness trip. You should avail yourself of the best forecast possible before leaving on a trip, and should also familiarize yourself with the principal weather elements, the basics of how weather forms, and the most common indicators of weather changes. This chapter certainly won't turn anyone into a weather expert (are there any?), but it may help you begin to understand the dynamics and some of the indicators of weather change.

5.1 Weather Elements

Temperature

In most areas, the difference between day and night temperatures averages 10 to 30 degrees F. The highest temperature occurs at about 2 PM and the lowest just before sunrise. Elevation also has an influence — for every 1,000 feet of elevation the temperature drops an average of three degrees F; on windy days the average drop can be as much as five degrees per 1,000 feet. Using these averages, you can forecast approximate expected maximum daytime and minimum night temperatures. Then you can equip yourself with proper clothing, sleeping bag, food, and shelter.

Humidity

Air contains varying amounts of evaporated water in gaseous form. This water vapor and the temperature determine the amount of humidity, usually expressed in percent by the weather people. The higher the temperature, the more vapor is required to produce a given percent of humidity.

When the moisture in the air reaches the saturation or supersaturation point, condensation occurs. Light condensation is called "mist"; more dense condensation is called "fog." Clouds are high altitude fog. If water in the air condenses when the temperature is above freezing, it rains; if it is below freezing, crystallization occurs and it snows. If rain passes through layers of air below freezing it becomes hail. Wet snow or wet hail is sleet.

As noted above, warm air can hold more water vapor than cold air, so when warm, humid air comes into contact with cold objects, condensation occurs. (As when your warm and humid breath flows over the night-air-cooled flaps of your sleeping bag, causing a cold, unpleasant sogginess.) The same phenomenon occurs if incoming moist air is blown over cold objects. If the objects are above freezing, dew forms; if below freezing, you get frost. Both dew and frost form—they do not "fall."

Winds

In clear daytime weather air tends to rise, due to the heating of mountain or foothill slopes by the sun, creating a "valley breeze." On clear nights the hills become cooler as their stored heat radiates into the air; after they become sufficiently cooled, they then cool the air, which becomes heavier and slides down into the valleys, creating a "mountain breeze." This process results in a temperature inversion and is the reason why on clear nights the bottom of a valley is the coldest place to camp; just a short way up the sides of the valley it is considerably warmer.

Clouds

The presence of any cloud indicates that a body of air has cooled below its dew point, resulting in some of its vapor condensing into liquid or solid form. Clouds are classified by both their appearance and their attitude. Those with a billowy appearance are "cumulus," while those which are layered belong to the "stratus" family. Clouds found from 20,000 to about 35,000 feet are "high" clouds, or "cirrus." You may be familiar with the feathery, upturned ones called "mare's tails," which are usually made of ice crystals. The more wavelike, patchier forms of cirrus are "cirrocumulus"; weather watchers have named this distinctive kind of a sky a "mackerel sky." When the sky has a filmy appearance and the moon and/or sun have haloes, you are seeing "cirrostratus."

Clouds found from about 8,000 to 20,000 feet are the "middle" clouds. "Altocumulus" resemble cirrostratus, but are denser; they may actually cover the sun and moon, and even if they don't they do produce a much smaller halo (a "corona"). "Altostratus" clouds come in sheets or as a dense veil that damps sun and moon brightness without producing a halo or corona. If these clouds thicken rapidly, rain is usually on its way within a few hours.

Clouds found from the earth's surface up to about 8,000 feet are "low" clouds. "Stratus" clouds (not to be confused with the stratus family) form in low, homogeneous sheets. When these clouds are thick the sky appears dull and heavy; when thin, the sky appears hazy. Stratus clouds never produce anything heavier than a drizzle, though. "Stratocumulus," as the name implies, are billowy clouds which form in a layer; they often have dark undersides and bright upper edges. Though stratocumulus clouds won't rain on you, they can change on short notice into ones that can: these are "nimbostratus," which are dark and low, and often have clear indications of rain falling from them.

Then there are the clouds which do not fit into any of these categories, but manage to base themselves at any elevation from sea level to about 14,000 feet and then tower to 40,000 feet or more. The "cumulus" cloud (not to be confused with the cumulus family) forms during the day from rising surface-warmed air; it usually indicates fair weather and disappears at night. When this cloud becomes exceedingly impressive, look out—for it can quickly turn into the "cumulonimbus" and thence into a formidable thunderhead which may bring torrential rain, lightning, snow, and/or hail. You've no doubt seen this cloud's characteristic, and unwelcome, "anvil" shape on a trip or two.

With some experience you can learn to read the clouds accurately now and then; but don't bother to get too confident—you'll soon find that very similar or nearly identical clouds can be produced by quite different weather conditions. In any case, as with changing winds, the *sequence* of cloud formations gives more information than a single cloud type, however accurately identified.

11. Cumulus, Stratus, and Cirrus Clouds

5.2 How Weather Forms

Temperature, humidity, and wind combine to form weather. Changes in the combination may affect only a small, local area or a very large region. It is a fact that air, a gas, expands when heated; it thus becomes lighter (fewer molecules per unit area) and rises. When cooled it contracts, becomes heavier, and falls. Wind is the result of both these processes. The earth's atmosphere is a mix of gases (oxygen, nitrogen, carbon dioxide, etc.), suspended solids (dust, smoke), and water (in liquid, solid, and gaseous forms—fog, clouds, rain, snow, vapor). Warm air can hold more water than cold, so when heated it sucks up moisture; the percentage of the total amount of water air can hold is the "relative humidity." When air is cooled, its capacity for holding water vapor decreases and the vapor condenses into fog, clouds, frost, snow, rain, etc. The "dew point" is the temperature at which water vapor ideally condenses; it varies with barometric pressure.

The ultimate source of all weather is the sun. The sun is assisted by the earth's yearly circuit of it, the tilt of the earth's axis with respect to its orbit (which causes the seasons), and the earth's daily rotation on its axis (which causes days and nights and prevailing winds). Of the solar radiation reaching the earth, only about 17% is absorbed by the atmosphere; about 43% is reflected back out into space; and the remaining 40% is absorbed by the earth's surface and re-radiated as long-wave heat. This means that the atmosphere is mostly warmed from the bottom up rather than from the top down. The proportion of solar energy reflected as compared to that absorbed and changed to heat varies with the earth's surface. For example, clouds may reflect up to 75%, water from 4 to 40% (depending on where the sun is), snow up to 75%, and a forest only about 5%.

Local Weather

If you are in the mountains, you may notice that during the course of the day the "valley breeze" brings hot air up from the valley. If it is humid, the large quantity of air rising rapidly gets cooled, causing condensation and heavy local clouds. By mid-afternoon this quantity can be sufficient to cause a local storm with thunder and lightning. Skill in recognizing this short-lived condition will make interrupting your trip unnecessary. The duration of such a thunderstorm is short, and clear weather usually returns soon. Incidentally, this is the reason why you should cover equipment left in camp, regardless of the existing weather conditions when leaving camp.

In the west, "lows" and "highs" travel from northwest to southeast, instead of west to east (as in the east), so if a storm approaching from the Gulf of Alaska passes us toward the southwest, the wind before the storm will be from the south and will swing around to north by way of *east*. If a storm from the Gulf of Alaska passes us on our northeast side, the wind will swing around from south to north by way of *west*. Thus, an observer can keep track of the progress of a storm by watching the wind change.

An approaching "low" is indicated by increasingly lower clouds and possible precipitation. A sign of the passing of the low and probably the end of the disturbance is the presence of rising clouds or their breakup into isolated caps over higher mountains. Very often lows occur in series, which means that the disturbance may recur.

Large-Scale Weather

Air Masses: The earth's air current patterns have their beginning at the equator, where the proportionately greater heating causes hot air to constantly surge upward and outward toward the poles. Near the poles, air cools and begins to descend (at around 30° latitude). The line of collision between this colder air and the warmer air around latitude 60°, along with seasonal heating differences and the proximity of oceans and land masses, creates the giant interruptions in prevailing air movements that we call "weather."

High pressure areas ("cells") can occur wherever air cools and descends, but most of the large ones ("air masses") begin in the artic and drift south. In a high pressure cell air flows down and out from the center, and is modified by the earth's rotation into a clockwise spiral. In the troughs between high pressure cells, air flows from all sides, and is deflected by the earth's rotation, thus setting up a counter-clockwise spiral—a "low." Within a high, conditions usually become somewhat stabilized and "good" weather results. But because lows consist of air from two highs which usually differ in temperature, the weather generated is often turbulent and unstable—that is, "bad."

Fronts: When a warm and a cold air mass meet, local conditions will cause air from the colder, heavier mass to periodically surge under the warmer; the latter must then whisk around to fill the partial vacuum behind the advancing cold air. Because the two are parts of a rotating cell, a warm front is always followed by a cold front. Due to the cold front's relatively rapid pace (around 30 mph) and the warm front's relatively slow one (about 15 mph), the latter's longer lead time and many approach warnings make its coming more predictable. A cold front can be upon the unprepared hiker or climber in a matter of a few minutes. Don't be surprised, then, if a cold front quickly succeeds a warm one! A cold front wedges under the warm front and ground friction slows the under part, causing the upper part to fall forward, making for a very steep leading edge and little advance warning.

Of course not all bad weather comes from fronts. The meeting of air and earth in local features such as mountains, ocean, large lake, and/or valleys, as well as air masses, causes turbulence.

Fronts are often difficult to identify with any degree of accuracy. A fast warm front and a slow cold front are quite similar in cloud warnings, with local distortions further confusing the predictions. The best way to find out the general weather situation before a trip is by viewing the nightly TV satellite report. This information, along with a minimum of theoretical information and a little practice in guessing airmass movements by observing clouds and winds, will allow an informed group of hikers to become pretty accurate weather guessers.

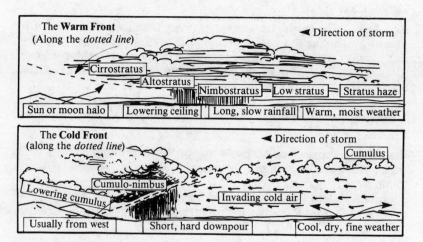

There are two major types of weather — that caused by *warm* air and that caused by *cold* air. Each type has its own kind of clouds. The warm air mass specializes in *stratus* clouds, the cold air mass features *cumulus*.

12. Cold and Warm Fronts

Fog: A fog is a cloud on the ground, with some fogs being the lower extensions of clouds created by two air masses in contact. Other fogs are the result of air-ground contact (as already discussed in "Local Weather"). Sea fog, for instance, occurs when warm, moist sea air moves over relatively colder land. Upslope ("adiabatic") fog indicates a stable air mass and, thus, good weather; it usually forms in the evening as upslope daytime winds continue while the mountains are rapidly cooling. Ground fog ("radiation fog") forms at ground-air interfaces where air temperature falls to the dew point.* Moist surfaces and clear skies predispose an area to this type of fog.

* The dew point is the temperature at which water vapor ideally condenses; it varies with barometric pressure.

5.3 Mountain Weather

Mountains normally experience more severe weather extremes than the surrounding lowlands. Local storms can occur that are confined to only a small region of a mountain range. When going into a new area, contact friends, forest and park rangers, and sporting goods store employees to find out about the extremes of weather which can occur in their area. For several days before a trip, check TV and radio weather satellite reports. You can also write the State and Federal weather services for historical weather data.

Plan equipment (including emergency equipment) and escape routes for the most extreme conditions. Don't be misled by optimistic forecasts so that you leave necessary emergency equipment behind. Storms can move 1,000 miles a day, so even weekend weather can be unpredictable. Weather is a major factor in mountaineering accidents and fatalities.

Thunderstorms and Lightning

Lightning kills over 600 people each year in the U.S., mostly in rural areas. Lightning storms are most common in mountain areas. Minimize your chances of death or injury by learning the basic facts about lightning.

The many lightning-struck trees you see in the mountains should be convincing testimony of the importance of being in the right place at the right time during a thunder and lightning storm. Thunderstorms occur almost everywhere, but due to the presence of mountains you may not be aware of a storm's approach until you hear the sudden sound of thunder. The approximate location of a thunderstorm can be estimated by the rule of thumb that every five-second interval between a visible streak of lightning and audible thunder means a mile in distance. If the intervals become shorter, this indicates the storm is approaching.

Lightning Discharges and Strike Locations: Thunderstorms generate lightning—that is, electrical discharges of enormous voltage but relatively low current. The voltage (electrical potential) of a cloud may become very large because the cloud is made up of such an immense number of small, electrified particles. A solid body, by comparison, carries its charge on the surface only.

Whenever the difference of potential between two clouds, between a cloud and the ground, or between two parts of a cloud exceeds the amount necessary to overcome the resistance of the air separating them, a discharge occurs. Due to the high voltage, these lightning discharges will be very erratic and no rules of thumb regarding when they will occur can be formulated.

Lightning between clouds is of little importance, unless you happen to be in a cloud — which can sometimes be the case, especially if you are in the mountains. Discharges from a cloud to the ground are common and dangerous. Such discharges have two parts: the lightning bolt and then diffusion, which disperses the current into the ground over a wide area.

The most highly probable targets for a direct lightning strike are tall objects reaching above their surroundings — for example, a mountain top,, a ridge, a rise in a ridge, broken peaks and ridges, a single standing tree, a limited group of trees, or a tall tree extending above the tree canopy in a wooded area. Other possible targets could be individuals or pack animals traveling on an exposed dome or flat area, tall boulders on such an area or on the side of a mountain (particularly if sharp-edged), or the sharp top edge of a vertical cliff. The latter are common strike areas in mountain valleys, especially when the clouds are hanging low.

The diffusion after the strike follows natural leads until the current is fully dispersed. Such leads may be cracks in the cliffs (particularly if filled with vegetation), small streams, grassy areas, debris at the base of cliffs, or splits in mountains.

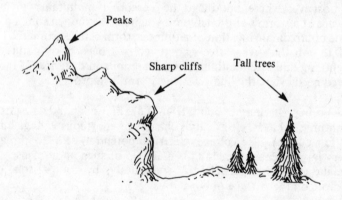

13. Lightning Strike Attractors

Recommended Precautions During an Electrical Storm: During the electrical part of the storm, avoid standing in or crossing exposed areas; that is, do not make yourself the "tall object." A depression is safer, but avoid any small stream in it. Climbers should take care not to be in a precarious position or rapelling. Tall objects offer a certain amount of protection to objects located at a distance of one to two times their height.

Recesses in vertical cliffs or entrances to a cave are dangerous because a lightning bolt can arch across the opening. Caves usually develop from seepage through an old split in the mountain and as a rule are wet and not safe. The center of a spacious cave, if dry, is a safer place than along the walls. An easier-to-find safe location is 50 to 80 feet from the face of a cliff or between and below the top of two flat boulders.

In the open, a sitting position or a low crouch with the feet close together is recommended. When feet are apart you are apt to feel a tingle; diffusing currents can enter through one foot, traverse the body, and go out the other foot. Sitting on a coiled rope with feet pulled in close is considered safest. As a further precaution, place any large steel objects at a distance from you. Because storms usually travel quickly and ordinarily only the head of the storm is involved in heavy electrical discharges, the waiting period should be short.

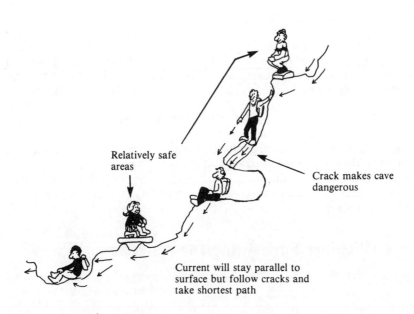

Relatively safe areas

Crack makes cave dangerous

Current will stay parallel to surface but follow cracks and take shortest path

14. Ground Current Paths

Sometimes you may enter a cloud-covered ridge with no thunderstorm in sight, but a while later find that the clouds are becoming turbulent. Soon an ice axe or the zipper on your parka (if metal) may buzz and an eerie blue light may become visible. This is a sure sign that the air is "loaded." If the electrical potentials are different in various parts of the cloud an electrical discharge within the cloud can occur. Such discharges have occurred even when the air was not turbulent. In either case it is safest to retreat altogether from ridges and peaks immersed in clouds when signs of static electricity appear. If there are indications that the cloud may recede, go to a safe location to wait — preferably on the side of a nearby couloir, but certainly off the ridges. Because moisture carries the charge, most of the static electricity will recede with the cloud.

Effects of Being Hit by Lightning: A direct hit by a lightning bolt can be fatal. Injuries caused by diffusion (or a direct hit) include leg and skin burns, singed hair on body or head, paralyzed limbs, amnesia, muscular spasm, and unconsciousness. Passage of electricity through the body, as in a direct hit, is most to be feared because this can actually cause the heart, brain, and/or lungs to fail. The body can better survive current going from one foot to the other through the legs, as with diffusion. For first aid procedures in case of electrical shock, see Chapter 9.

Mountains as Small-Scale Weather Makers

As mentioned before, not all bad or good weather comes from fronts; local geographic features such as mountains cause vertical currents which can exaggerate the instability of whatever air mass is presently enveloping them. Mountain ranges are obstacles in the paths of fronts. When the fronts rise to cross the ranges, atmospheric pressure decreases and the air mass expands. On the other side of the range the air mass flows down, compresses, and warms. These distortions of fronts, which are more marked when the front is small compared to the mountain range, often result in mountain weather which varies from peak to peak, valley to valley, and even couloir to couloir. In short, it is weather which may not at all fit the most recent forecast you may have heard. Despite this seeming unpredictability, there are some weather regularities and warnings you can learn to identify and use with some ease, though not with unerring accuracy.

5.4 Weather Forecasting for Amateurs

As Mark Twain once said about the weather, "There is only one thing certain . . . there is going to be plenty of it." But even Mark Twain was not entirely right; weather predictions can often be made with some degree of success, if you know what to look for. Knowledge of weather origins and experience can allow wilderness travelers to narrow the range of weather possibilities. Checking with the Weather Bureau before a trip gives a general idea about the short-term prediction for major air mass movements in your area of interest. You can also check with the "locals"; most areas have their own weather peculiarities which it pays to know about. Once in the middle of a trip, however, be it short or long, weather guessing suddenly seems to become more difficult. It then seems impossible to tell whether the clouds and winds are indicative of air mass weather or caused by local conditions. Despite this inevitable uncertainty, there are still a few weather signs which have some value even in the mountains. For example:

— Red sunsets, sunrises, rainbows, an indistinct horizon (usually grey) are "indicators" of high humidity in that area. They could mean rain if they are in the west. They should mean dew or frost.

— Yellow sunsets or sunrises and sharply outlined horizons are indicators of low humidity, and often predict good weather.

— A small ring around the sun or moon, called a "corona," and a much larger ring, called a "halo," are caused by moisture in the air and can be signs of a coming or departing disturbance.

— Thunder is a more immediate warning that beyond what you can see there is a disturbance in progress. If lightning is visible you may be able to estimate the distance of the disturbance as described in Section 5.3.

— Cloud movement high above the mountains is one of the best weather indicators. If all clouds move continously in the same direction, you may be under the air masses passing from a "high" to a "low" and probably will not experience a weather change.

— If clouds move in different directions and are increasingly lower, a "low" may be close by.

— Weather will probably remain clear if: the barometer stays steady or rises; wind is from northwest or west, steady and gentle; there are no or few clouds; fogs and mists burn off early.

— Rain or snow may occur if: the barometer drops; a south wind becomes stronger while clouds move in from the west; a north wind moves west and then south; a ring around the moon is followed by thickening and lowering clouds; the west is black.

— Better weather is usually in the offing if: the barometer rises; clouds rise steadily; winds shift from south to west to north.

In spite of their contrariness, weather changes make a positive contribution to the beauty and challenge of the wilderness environment. Keep that in mind next time you're trying to pitch your tent in a storm!

Chapter 6
On the Trail

Wilderness today is at a premium. It can remain wild and unspoiled for future generations to appreciate and enjoy only if protected and cared for by those who use it now. It is imperative that today's wilderness visitors adopt and practice low-impact wilderness ethics* in using these unspoiled areas. We, as today's travelers, must minimize our impact as much as possible in order to insure that those who come after us can have the same opportunities we enjoy. The primary objective of every back-country traveler must be, as far as possible, to LEAVE NO TRACE. Only in this way can we justify using the wilderness for recreation.

When we, as wilderness travelers, are on the trail and in camp there is much we can do to assure that we will leave a minimal trace. Many of the measures needed to keep our backcountry clean and unscarred are discussed in the two chapters covering trail and camp skills. As you practice these skills and acquire them, you'll undoubtedly experience a deep sense of satisfaction and personal achievement. Many find knowing that they have traveled through the wilderness leaving no perceptible trace is a way of being in harmony with the natural world.

6.1 Packing for the Trail

There are, of course, as many ways of packing a pack as there are backpackers; probably no two people do it exactly alike. Be that as it may, there are still a few principles of packing that almost all backpackers can agree upon, and these are the ones we'll discuss here

---

* Described briefly in Section 1.2.

(with a few gratuitous, sometimes contested, methods thrown in for good measure).

Let's assume, then, that you've already made your list, planned gear, food, clothing, fuel, and luxuries, and assembled all the items in one place. You have also checked them off the list one by one, making sure at the same time that each item is in good working order, and are now ready to put them in your pack. But you're wondering whether there are any "easiest," "most efficient," or "most convenient" ways to do same. (If you are an old-timer and already have worked out a packing method that suits you, you might want to skip this section.) So, where do you start? It would seem logical to begin by categorizing the items, perhaps as follows:

Backpack

Permits (Wilderness, Fishing, Fire)

Ten Essentials

Emergency

Repair and Maintenance Kit

Clothing

Cooking (including 2-3 lbs stove and cookware/person)

Food (1½-2 lbs/person/day)

Sleeping

Shelter (tent — 3 lbs/person, or tarp — 1 lb/person)

General (frequent use)

General (infrequent use)

Special Equipment (rock climbing, etc.)

Luxuries (camera, binoculars, field books, etc.)

Water (1 lb/pint)

Stuff Bags

To Be Left in Car

Next, you might weigh the whole pile. Most people find they hike most comfortably when their pack and all that's in it does not exceed 20-25% of their normal body weight. Of course, on long trips you may not be able to begin with this comfortable minimum.

Most hikers find it convenient to use marked stuff bags in storing their categorized gear in the pack; then there aren't a lot of small, loose items to elude you in times of need. When actually putting these bags in the pack, there are several important things you'll need to consider — for example, weight distribution, how often you'll want to get at an item, when you'll want certain items, and whether you'll need to separate certain things.

Weight Distribution

The consensus on this subject is that for walking on a good trail, it is best to have heavy objects packed high and close to the back. This keeps most of the weight on the hip belt and off the shoulder straps. Unfortunately, keeping the weight high also may cause the pack to sway as you walk, impairing your balance, especially when crossing streams or walking in narrow places. For this reason, if you're planning to do any cross-country walking, boulder-hopping, scrambling, rock climbing, or skiing, it is best to pack the heavy items low and close to the back. Be careful to balance the weight — don't put all your water and fuel on one side and all your clothes on the other.

Packing Little- and Frequently-Used Items

Obviously, it wouldn't be a good idea to pack your chapstick, sunscreen, and toilet paper at the bottom of your pack, and your extra sunglasses in an easily accessible pocket. It might be a good idea to put many of the items you hope never to have to use in a single stuff sack and pack them where they aren't easy to get at, thus freeing up more accessible space for those items you use often. Outside pockets are good candidates for storing frequently used items, such as lunch, water, first aid kit, windbreaker, sunscreen and chapstick, extra socks, bug repellent, hat, handkerchief, shorts, moleskin, etc.

Packing in the Order Items Will Be Used

This consideration is not quite the same as the previous one. For example, it might be a good thing to sort out all of a day's food each morning or evening (if you haven't already arranged it that way), put it in a sack of its own, and pack it near the top of the top compartment, near the cooking equipment, so that it will be easily accessible when you stop to make camp each day. This saves time — the cook can begin dinner while the rest of the party sets up tents, etc. If you always read for a few minutes before falling asleep, you might pack the book in the top of your sleeping bag's stuff sack. If you make your own stuff sacks, a convenient rest stop compartment could be the end of a slightly-longer-than-usual foam pad stuff sack. You can make it large enough to hold wool shirt, windbreaker, watchcap, mittens, snacks, or whatever. (This arrangement is particularly handy on top of a windy pass.)

Keeping Items Separate

Ordinarily, cooking fuel and water are packed in outside pockets, where they are both easy to get at and some distance from your food and clothes in case of leakage. Tent stakes, poles, or other sharp objects should be packed in such a way that they can't poke holes in the pack, your down jacket, food bags, etc. Fragile items should be carefully padded, wrapped, packaged, or wedged so they can't be crushed. For example, you can usually find a cooking pot that will exactly accomodate your stove and will thus keep it from being mashed. The pot should be protected from the stove's possibly gassy smell by encasing the stove in several layers of plastic bags.

After a few trips you'll work out the bugs and design your own variations on the packing theme. Whether you pack at home or at the trailhead, you can hasten the process by keeping notes on how your arrangement worked out during your trip. Soon packing will become almost automatic, and on the trail you'll be able to find even that extra pair of sunglasses in no time flat.

6.2 Getting to the Trailhead

Most hikers get to the trailhead by car. This is not necessarily a matter in which you have any choice, though. In the west, for example, few forms of public transportation go anywhere near a trailhead. Exceptions are the Greyhound Bus service to Yosemite National Park and the shuttle bus service from Mammoth Lakes to Devil's Postpile. If you are fortunate, from time to time you will be able to take advantage of charter bus trips which some organizations are able to arrange. It is possible, of course, to take a bus or train to an area within 50 to 100 miles of a trailhead, and then hitch hike the rest of the day. Unfortunately, this is an option not open to sensible women, unless they are traveling in a group. Some hardy souls who have lots of time and energy manage to bike to trailheads. Concealing your bicycle isn't too difficult unless you're traveling in the desert.

6.3 Walking

The act of walking is something we seldom think about, but the trail is often quite different from your usual city sidewalk (though in popular areas, trails are sometimes as broad and smooth as a freeway). In hiking with a pack—even just a day pack—such things as pace, rest stops, and blisters suddenly seem to take on great importance.

Pace

What do you need to know about "pace"? Experienced hikers will tell you that efficient hiking requires a steady, rhythmic pace. When going uphill, shorten the length of your step, but maintain the rhythm. Don't go as fast as you can (you won't go far), but don't loiter. When walking, do not lift your feet any higher than necessary. Swing your feet over obstacles. Adjust your pace and rhythm to the slowest member of the group. (When forming a group, it's a good idea to avoid great differences in stamina.) Don't exceed your strength—exhaustion causes accidents.

After about a half hour on the trail, stop to remove excess clothing and adjust pack straps, boot laces, and so on, if necessary. Go on at a pace which the first lap indicated could be maintained comfortably. Always observe the surroundings and trail for orientation purposes; consult the map often and identify prominent landmarks. Part of the fun of being on the trail is knowing what you're seeing. Stop to rest at regular intervals rather than waiting until you or someone else in your group is exhausted. Stand or lean against a tree or rock when resting, but not for too long or you'll cool down and have trouble getting started again (two to seven minutes is usually sufficient).

For a longer rest stop, perhaps for lunch, remove your pack, loosen tight belts or straps, and put on protection against wind or cold. Eat and drink lightly. Several short rests seem to work better than one long one (except for lunch). This is because your muscles can get rid of about 30% of the waste products of exercise (mostly lactic acid) in this time, but 15 minutes more rest will only eliminate about 5% more. Some people don't even stop for lunch, but nibble often along the way. Those who do stop for lunch feel the loss of rhythm is more than compensated for by the opportunity to take photographs, nap, munch unhurriedly, or whatever. The choice is yours.

The Rest Step

Most people find that a comfortable pace on the trail is a steady one, with long strides (one long stride takes less energy than two small ones covering the same ground). When you're going up a particularly long and/or steep slope, you'll probably find the "rest step" helpful. In using this step, you pause briefly every time you begin a new step, when the forward foot is on the ground but not yet weighted. The sequence of motion is: (1) lift left leg, move it forward and place it, unweighted, while keeping the weight on your right foot, (2) pause, rest left leg, (3) shift weight to left leg and move right leg forward, repeating same sequence for this leg. It sounds very simple, but you'll find that unless you practice the step until it becomes automatic you'll get out of rhythm. Do not practice the step on level ground; on an inclined surface it's easy to see how well it works.

Rhythm

The importance of a rhythm is that it enables the body to equilibrate and thus to function most efficiently. There's a rhythm for every speed, weight of pack, altitude, and degree of conditioning. You'll have a faster speed at a lower altitude, a slower one for going uphill at altitude, and a slower one yet if you are carrying a heavy pack and/or are in poor condition. If you're in at least fair condition, you probably know the feeling of working hard to get up a long hill, of breathing hard and sweating profusely, and yet, paradoxically, feeling perfectly comfortable, able to look about and enjoy the view or even chat with a companion. When you feel this way you've usually found your rhythm and your body has had time to equilibrate. At times you feel you could go on this way all day, which may be true, depending on the continued cooperation of a well-conditioned and well-fed body.

Blisters

Sore feet and blisters are usually caused by improperly fitted or insufficiently broken in boots, tender feet, wrinkled or wrong-sized socks, or too much soaking of feet in cool streams. Blisters never come on suddenly — they give you considerable warning ("hot spots"), so there's really no excuse for letting them become serious problems. It'll save you and your group a lot of time and trouble if you'll just stop and take preventive measures before your feet become too painful to walk on comfortably. Most hikers know just where their trouble spots are, and so can actually put on moleskin *before* any hot spots or blisters develop; this seems like the most sensible method. For advice on applying moleskin, caring for blisters, and breaking in boots, see Section 3.3.

Energy

Every hiker eventually finds the best ways of keeping their energy level up on the trail. Most find that frequent nibbling on complex carbohydrates* — rather than on straight sugar, protein, or fat — is effective. Others prefer to stick to the "three squares." If you prefer the latter method, you'll be more comfortable if you allow at least an hour for digestion before embarking on strenuous activities such as steep hills. Strenuous activity requires that your blood be available to keep your muscles well-supplied with energy. After eating, your blood rushes to your digestive system to give it a hand, and thus is not as available for hard work elsewhere. Indigestion and cramps may be the result if you choose to eat and run.

Remember to drink plenty of water, even when you're not particularly thirsty. You'll be sweating much more than usual, and sometimes your thirst doesn't catch up with your perception of it until you're already

* See Appendix E for a suggested list of trail foods containing complex carbohydrates.

quite dehydrated. Nausea, excessive tiredness, and headache can be some of the unpleasant signs of dehydration. If the weather is very warm and/or the trail quite difficult, you may find that an occasional buffered salt tablet will keep you from feeling exhausted from too quick a loss of body salts (electrolytes) in perspiration. People who are accustomed to strenuous hiking in hot weather – or just plain strenuous hiking – usually don't need salt tablets, because their bodies have adapted to the stress; others just don't seem to require extra salt; and still others find salt tablets indispensable. If you do take salt tablets, be sure to drink at least 10 ounces of water for each one you take; the tablets may cause indigestion if they don't have enough liquid to dissolve in.

Shortcuts

Building trails is expensive, as is the repairing made necessary by rain, melting snow, and storms. However, damage to trails is also caused by careless and thoughtless hikers who try to save time by cutting switchbacks or creating their own trails. The erosion which results is just as expensive to repair as that caused by Mother Nature. In a word, DON'T shortcut! Also, don't hesitate to tell or remind shortcutters of these expensive facts (tactfully, of course).

6.4 Going Cross-Country

Sometimes, when a trail leads only part way to your destination, you'll have to travel cross-country. Before starting into the untrailed area, make a visual survey of the region ahead by viewing it from some suitable vantage point. Map out a route free of major obstacles and then follow it (you may have to do this several times). We are assuming, of course, that anyone who goes cross-country is well-versed in the art of hiking navigation (see Chapter 4 for details).

Cross-country travel is usually slower and rougher than trail travel. It helps to have sturdy boots to protect your ankles and the bottoms of your feet from bruising. Also desirable is a soft pack or internal frame pack which rides close to your back and thus to your center of gravity, rather than an external frame pack which may lurch from side to side when you're scrambling over rocks or trying to cross a swift stream. In any case, pack all your heaviest items near your back and the bottom of your pack. Make sure angular objects are properly padded with soft items so you won't be able to feel them through your pack.

Brush

When entering a high brush area, secure all loose items of clothing or equipment which might catch on anything and get lost. When there is no way around the brush, change leader occasionally; leading in brush is tiring. Following ridges, rock slides, game trails, and stream beds is easier than bushwacking. In spring, particularly, there may be quite a few ticks about; gaiters may keep the little devils from crawling up your pant legs; insect repellent at wrists, neck, and ankles may help, too. One advantage of shorts and short sleeves is that you can see the critters better and get rid of them quickly. There's no substitute, though, for stripping off each night and checking yourself and others for them. (See Section 9.5 for advice on how to get rid of ticks if they get too attached to you.)

Stream Crossing

If no bridge is available, look for a suitable spot to cross, such as stepping stones or logs across the stream. If you find no easy route, you'll have to wade. If the stream is particularly deep and/or swift, you may even have to change your route or objective. In spring, the streams fed by snowmelt may be considerably lower in the early morning, due to nighttime freezing temperatures at higher altitudes. Don't wade barefoot; wear your boots and change socks on the other side. Some hikers carry an old pair of tennis shoes for stream crossings and "camp shoes." Tennies can be treacherous if the soles are too slick, so either choose a pair with some tread left or glue a layer of thick wool "fisherman's" felt on the bottom of the sole (don't use water soluble glue!). A stout staff placed downstream of you, giving a "third leg," can turn a precarious stream crossing into a safe one. When crossing, undo your pack's waist belt so that you can slip out quickly in case you need to. Then stand sideways to the current, put your feet wide apart, and take short steps, moving one foot at a time. Test your new footing before shifting your weight. Shallow, fast-moving water is usually safer and easier to cross than deep, slow-moving water. Think ahead. What would be the worst that could happen if you were swept off your feet? Could you get ashore downstream, or are the banks too steep? Is there a waterfall nearby? Be prepared for all forseeable eventualities.

What about using a rope to get across? Unless you are a group of experienced climbers, about the only use of a rope you should consider would be stringing one across, tying it to a sturdy anchor on each side (not a person), and using it for a handline. Then only the first and last person would be unprotected; the first could go across without a pack in order to secure the rope and the last could ferry his/her pack across before bringing up the rear with the rope. Do not tie the rope *on* to anyone! If a person with a rope tied on to them should fall in   deep, swiftly moving water, the current might hold rope and person under water, whereas a person without a rope would probably be able to stay on top of the water.

If you get more than your feet wet when crossing, eat some carbohydrates and start hiking hard—you'll be surprised at how fast you'll warm up and your clothes will dry. In cold weather, however, stop and change to dry clothes. If your body cannot cope with both wet clothes and cold air, you may become hypothermic. (See Section 9.4 for advice on hypothermia prevention and treatment.)

Scree, Sand and Talus

Loose sand and small rocks (scree) often collect on slopes, particularly below chutes and couloirs. The angle at which this debris comes to a standstill is between 30 and 45 degrees. Because the internal friction is low, the slightest disturbance will start it moving, though not so easily near large rocks or on the edges of vegetated areas. These scree and sand slopes, although not dangerous, are difficult to hike up because your feet slip before they eventually hold (two steps forward, one step back . . .); however, sometimes, these slopes are ideal routes of descent. Gaiters will help to keep rocks and sand out of your boots.

"Talus" is the debris from continuous rockfalls caused by weathering and crumbling of the higher peaks and rocks. These rocks accumulate at the base of the cliffs or spill over to the slopes below. Because these fragments are larger and more sharp-edged than scree and sand, the internal friction is greater and the angle at which the rock debris comes to a standstill can be greater than 45 degrees. Some talus rocks do not end up in a balanced position, so walking over them can be very precarious. Sometimes the material is so very delicately balanced that the slightest disturbance can start a rock avalance. Do not travel in the fall line of a companion!

Snakes

As for snakes, there is no substitute for watching where you put your hands, feet, and posterior. Snakes, as you probably already know, are more active on warm nights, and mornings and evenings of hot days. Because snakes have no temperature-regulating mechanism, their body temperature rises and falls with the ambient temperature. This "cold-bloodedness" makes them sluggish when it's cold or very hot, and active when temperatures are middling. They like warm rocks and warm bodies on cold nights — and who can blame them? (See Sections 9.3 and 9.5 for more information on snakes and what to do if preventive measures fail and someone gets bitten.)

Hiking Navigation Off the Trail

Here's where you really get to use those hiking navigation skills from Chapter 4 that you've practiced. Finding the easiest, most direct route to your destination is one of the most pleasurable challenges of wilderness traveling. It's pretty hard to get lost when you're reaching your destination on a trail, but as soon as you step off the trail, losing your way becomes a real possibility. You should never step off the trail or accompany a cross-country group until you know exactly what you are doing when it comes to navigating. Practice *on* the trail until it comes automatically to you; don't just assume that you can pick up the necessary skills easily as soon as you step off the trail.

6.5 Low Impact Pointers

When you are traveling on trails, take care to camp only where others have camped before you, stay on the trails, and confine your activities to the smallest area possible, not extending the area of already-used sites. Once off the trail, however, some of these good habits need to be temporarily exchanged for others suited to untouched country. For instance, try not to walk single file, thus starting a trail, but spread out your impact over a larger area (when walking on rock this usually doesn't matter). Try not to camp in fragile areas such as the timberline, meadows, or near eroded slopes. Don't build cairns or leave ducks unless absolutely necessary. Most hikers like the feeling that they may be the first to walk through an area, and if they keep seeing ducks it's pretty hard to have that feeling. Use a stove rather than building fires. In other words, take only pictures and try very hard not to leave any footprints!

Chapter 7
In Camp

Long before you arrive at the point when you begin looking for an appropriate campsite, you will, of course, have given careful consideration to each item you have in your pack. Each piece of equipment and clothing and every bit of food should perform a function that makes it worth the energy expended to carry it on the trip. With each trip you make, the lightness and simplicity of your "kit" will improve; experience will prove that a minimum of equipment can provide bodily comfort and the simplest of foods can be turned into healthful and delicious meals. Another thing you will soon learn is that good campsites are found, not made. As with equipment and food, less is more. If you're not satisfied unless your campsite has all the comforts of home, why bother to leave home? If, on the other hand, you're interested in feeling at home in the wilderness, on its own terms, then you'll have no trouble finding as many excellent campsites as you could possibly need — and all within the limits of the low-impact wilderness ethic.

7.1 Choosing a Site

One of the most important aspects of low impact wilderness travel has to do with campsites: their appropriate choice, setting up, managing, and breaking. No matter what the regulations are — and they vary from place to place — once you have complied with them you can't go wrong by adopting camping practices of the lowest possible impact. These practices will differ with the type of camp site you use, of which there are two main kinds — the pristine site and the site clearly marked as an often-used area. The latter have paths, bare ground, perhaps even fire rings. These camps are preferable to untouched ones because most of the damage has already been done. If you choose an untouched site (which usually isn't necessary unless you are traveling cross-country), your responsibility is great. You should make every effort to leave the land just as you found it, a task easier assigned than carried out.

An acceptable already-used site will be at least 200 feet from lakeshore, stream, and trail. It will also be a safe site. This means it should be free from possible rockfalls and snow avalanches, away from dry stream beds (which rainstorms can turn into raging rivers in the space of a few minutes), above cold air passageways such as gullies and valley floors, out of the wind, and out of the way of branches which could part company with their parent tree during a storm. If you're really clever, you'll also arrange for the site to be in an area that gets the last sun of the day and is one of the first to get sun in the morning. A campsite like this makes it easter to get an early start! In areas where bears are known to prefer people-food to more natural food, look for an appropriate tree (preferably two) to hang your food bag from at night and when you are out of camp. (See Section 8.6 for details.)

Remember, too, that cool air flows downward at night, settling in basins and bringing night breezes to gullies and ravines. A camp high on a hill or even on a small rise will be several degrees warmer than a lower one. In high summer you may prefer a lower camp, in late fall a higher one. However, if you want to drive away mosquitoes, a gully with a cool breeze can take on quite a charming air.

It's convenient to have water near your campsite, but not necessary. You can fill your canteens and water bottles late in the day and then be free to camp at that perfect view site which just happens to be a mile up from any water. If you must camp near water, take care to disturb the waterside as little as possible. Do not wash with soap *in* the stream or lake, do not move rocks around for your convenience, and crush as little vegetation as possible. This is particularly important in desert camping, because the few watering spots are vital to the area wildlife. You can wreak havoc in the lives of many animals by casually camping too near their water.

If you must use an untouched site, choose ground where foot traffic does the least damage to fragile vegetation. Never camp in meadows or on other fragile vegetation; even the weight of a sleeper, not to mention trampling and stake-pounding, can harm these areas. Try to choose sandy or rocky areas. Camp well back from lakeshore and stream. Although it's OK to move a few *small* rocks and sticks for your tent or bed site, do not rearrange the natural landscape for fireplaces and bedsites. Rig tents or tarps with lines tied to rocks or trees. Never cut boughs for poles or a mattress; do not put nails in trees or dig hollows or trenches. Locate your shelter so water will drain away naturally. When breaking camp, try to erase all evidence that you were there.

Be a considerate neighbor. Don't crowd other camps or sleeping areas. Camping some distance away from trail and water will help protect your and others' privacy. Most wilderness travelers seem to prefer a solitary camp, even if less than perfect, to a more well-populated spot. Even if you like company, don't just blithely assume that everyone else does too. Try to stay out of earshot of the nearest neighbors and keep in mind that sound carries very well across open areas such as lakes and meadows. Leave your radio and pet at home. Enjoy yourself, but do it quietly.

7.2 Water

Whether you are on a trip in the mountains or in the desert, the availability and quality of water is a major consideration. Although in the mountains you will usually find water along the trail, distances between readily available sources may be great in either summer or winter. Even when water is plentiful and potable, it is sensible to carry a minimum of a pint of water at all times. In the desert, of course, you need to carry much more. Remember to fill your water container/s before you start on the trail.

Water should always be drawn upstream from any trail crossings, to guard against possible contamination. Do all your bathing, clothes washing, and pot scrubbing well away from the shores of lakes and streams; do not return the dirty water to its source. Use soap only if absolutely necessary; avoid detergents. After cleaning fish, be sure to bury the entrails ashore rather than throwing them back into the water. Water drawn from backcountry sources should be considered contaminated if it is not moving, looks "dirty," or is located near or downstream from heavily used trails such as the John Muir or Pacific Crest. Be suspicious of streams with excessive amounts of algal growth.

Flowing or standing water in populated or well-used areas should be considered questionable and treated. Twenty minutes of boiling is adequate treatment, but because this uses up precious fuel it is easier and more economical to use chemical tablets such as Halazone, Potable-Aqua, or Globaline for water purification. Keep these tablets in airtight containers and replace them every other year. Read the directions carefully and be sure purification is complete before the water is mixed with beverage powders or crystals.

Stationary water should be checked for any visible impurities. If camping near a lake, it is best to locate its source or outlet and take your water from one of the points where water is moving. You will also find that impurities in the water are less on the windward shore of a lake. In glacial lakes you will see a greenish-gray discoloration of the water which is due to the mineral dust of glacial action; this dust can be partly removed by settling.

With the heavy use of what was once truly wilderness, it is becoming increasingly difficult to be certain of the purity of any water supply. Water dripping from a spring and water flowing across your path from an inaccessible upstream area are generally safe. If you question the habits of the people at the campsite above you, treat the water.

Water, of course, is for drinking. Always keep in mind that people who are exerting themselves only slightly more than usual still need at least two quarts of water a day. Part of the water comes from solid food and the rest you have to drink. If you are exercising strenuously on a trip you may need a gallon a day or more. When you exercise vigorously your thirst mechanism often lags behind your body's actual needs, so be sure to drink more and also more often than you feel like doing — or you may become dehydrated without knowing it. Dehydration can cause headache, loss of energy, cloudy thinking, and nausea.

7.3 Sanitation

Human Wastes

Use existing latrines whenever possible. If there is no latrine, go far from camp, water, and trail. Nature has provided a system of "biological disposers" (bacteria) in the top six to eight inches of soil; these work to decompose organic material, including human waste. Keeping this in mind, use your boot heel or small plastic trowel to dig a hole no more than ten inches in diameter and no deeper than eight inches. Keep the soil intact if possible. Fill the hole with loose soil and tramp on the sod. Cover everything completely. Heavy spring runoff carries with it a great deal of silt and soil, and also any uncovered and non-decomposed human waste. This is one of the ways wilderness water sources become polluted. Therefore, state law now directs that every back country latrine site must be located at least 150 feet away from the nearest water source and away from all dry watercourses. Pack out or burn all toilet paper.

Garbage

Burying garbage is no longer acceptable; in fact, it is now illegal. The practice was formerly promoted by conservation groups as a substitute for littering, but is now no longer appropriate due to the great increase in the number of wilderness users. Put candy wrappers, foil, orange peels, or whatever, in your pocket while traveling; do not throw them on or off the trail. In camp, if you build a fire, burn everything that will burn. Aluminum foil (including foil-lined papers), cans, and bottles do *not* burn. They will not decay in your lifetime. Do not burn plastic; some plastics give off poisonous or corrosive fumes when burned. Whatever you packed in, you can pack out! Garbage is not only non-degradable and unsightly, it also trains animals to become camp robbers.

Animals and Your Food and/or Garbage

Animals should not be molested or disturbed in any way. The back country is their home and you are the visitor. None of them will harm you unless provoked. Do not encourage them by leaving your food within their reach. In bear country, especially in central and northern Yosemite Park and along the lower elevations of the John Muir Trail, suspend your food at least 15 feet above the ground and away from limbs and branches (see Section 8.6 for information on how to do this). In non-bear areas, you can avoid most problems from chipmunks and other rodents by suspending your food a few feet above ground and three to four feet below overhanging limbs. It is also wise to keep your food separate from your pack at night and to use a special stuff bag for the food cache.

Dishwashing and Cleanup

Dishes and pots should be cleaned after each meal. It's always easier to clean dishes while food is still soft, so don't make it more difficult for yourself by letting food harden or freeze overnight. Dirty dishes also attract unwelcome animal guests. Hot water helps cut grease. A plastic scrubber is lightweight and handy—the "Scotchbright" variety works best. An extra bandanna can be used for drying. Individual dishwashing is very simple; soap isn't necessary. In larger groups, though, it's best to use a little pure soap and scald the dishes with boiling water to prevent any possible spreading of colds, etc. Water used for washing dishes or self should be poured out some distance from camp, several hundred feet from any water, and among stones or in a brushy area.

7.4 Bed and Shelter

When selecting a bed site, just as for the campsite itself, look for a high, level spot, preferably without vegetation. This will be easy in most often-used areas; in pristine areas, your impact will be lowest if you still follow this rule. Remove small rocks and branches that would damage an air mattress, foam pad, ground cloth, or sleeping bag; spread your ground cloth and pad over the area. Do not dig hip or shoulder holes. In cold or wet weather more protection from the damp is needed; this is the time a light-weight two-person tent is handy. If the weather is not too wet, you can rig a tarp or ground cloth as a shelter or lean-to, as noted in Section 3.6. Tarps and tube tents are most useful in mild weather, when there is little chance of a big storm or excessively low temperatures; they are of little help in difficult conditions, though they can be lifesavers in emergencies.

In warm weather it is good to have the cooking area some distance from the sleeping areas, but in cold weather it's handier to have the cooking area close to the sleeping bags or tents. Sometimes you may even decide to cook while still in your sleeping bag or tent if your tent is properly equipped with a cook-hole and is well-ventilated.

If the weather is good and the mosquitoes few, you probably needn't bother setting up a tent, but have merely to find a relatively level, well-drained spot to throw your ground cloth and sleeping bag on (if dew is likely to be a problem, try under a tree). Because each member of the party will probably look for a more or less private area, this dispersion can lessen your impact on the site. If you are putting up a tent, the same considerations apply. With a tarp or tube tent you may also need shelter from the wind and rocks or trees for anchors.

Although there are many different kinds of tents, you usually begin the pitching operation (after putting down your ground cloth) by staking down the corners of the floor, then inserting the poles, anchoring the guylines at each end, staking down the pullouts on the tent sides, and, if necessary, pitching the tent's fly for rain protection. Sometimes you can replace stakes by tying the cords to large stones, trees (taking care not to girdle them), or logs. Most lines tend to stretch and grow slack after being put up, so it is helpful to be able to adjust them without repitching them. This can be accomplished by using manufactured gripping devices (available in camping goods stores) or by tying a knot that will grip under tension and slide when you loosen it. The clove hitch and tautline hitch are both easy to use and effective.

When going to bed, make certain that boots are turned upside down so that moisture will not collect in them. If not sleeping in a tent, place your pack (without food) at the head of the sleeping bag so that it is accessible in the morning; protect the pack with a waterproof cover. A pack at the head of your sleeping bag can serve as a head rest and wind protection. In bear country, of course, your food and anything that might smell of food should be strung up out of the bears' reach (see Section 8.6 for how to do this). If it is a clear night, you will be drier without a waterproof cover over your sleeping bag, because your perspiration will then be able to pass through the bag into the surrounding air. Have a flashlight close at hand.

Sleeping Miseries

If, despite generally good planning, you find yourself with a sleeping bag and/or shelter that doesn't keep you warm, here are a few tips which might help you be a bit more comfortable:

— Move under a tree or beside a bush and put your head downwind so cold air can't get into your bag as easily.

— Exercise before going to bed or do isometrics inside your bag.

— Eat some protein before going to bed (this helps keep you warm when you're sleeping).

— Wear more clothes to bed, especially a wool hat (the head is the body's champion heat-loser).

— Put more insulation under you (your pack, a parka, a rope, etc.) and/or over you (a breathable tarp, extra clothes, etc.).

— Keep your clothes and bag as dry as possible (synthetics will keep you warm when wet, but down won't).

Cold isn't the only problem you may encounter on your nights in the wilderness; the mosquito can also provide a degree of uncomfortableness that borders, on occasion, on the unbearable. If you find yourself under siege, you can try:

— a lot of repellent

— a netted tent

— a head net

— lacking the above, a handkerchief or sweater to breathe through

— moving into a downslope breeze

7.5 Fires

Many hikers look forward to the pleasure and good companionship created by a campfire. However, in most wilderness areas campfires are forbidden, and in most others a fire permit and sometimes special equipment, such as a spade, are required. The negative impact of campfires is very great; fires often make fertile ground infertile for many years and use up downed and dead wood which should be left to return its organic matter to the soil. This wood is an essential link in forest ecosystems. In an area where fires are permitted, where there is plenty of downed and dead wood (by law, it must be *both*), where fire pits or areas already exist, and when you know what you are doing and exercise extreme care in doing it, the luxury of a small campfire need not make you feel guilty.

Conserve wood. If you can't break it using your hands, feet, or a rock, you have no business burning it. Never break or cut standing wood, living or dead; snags are part of the forest setting and are homes for many species of animals. Never build fires near trees, meadows, or against a rock where they will leave long-lasting scars. Do not build fires on vegetation, duff, or against logs or roots where it may spread.

Fires are dangerous; never leave one unattended. When breaking camp, drown your fire completely, stir the ashes, and drown it again, until cold to the touch. Bury ashes and charcoal; cover all traces.

7.6 More Low Impact Pointers and Reminders

— When camping at a well-marked site, make use of the ground that is already bare. Don't increase the bare area.

— Use gas, kerosene, butane, or propane stoves for cooking.

— Keep your group small. Impact on the land can be reduced by traveling in groups of no more than eight to ten people and camping away from other groups.

— Try to travel in little-used areas.

— Be as invisible and inaudible as possible. Camp in an unobtrusive place off the trail. Radios and pets do not belong in the wilderness.

— Remember that smoking in the wilderness, as everywhere else, is unnecessary and unhealthful. In the wilderness it can also cause unnecessary fires.

— If camping in an untouched area, confine your activities to unvegetated ground. Try not to walk repeatedly over any piece of ground (use different routes). As much as possible, walk on rocks, dry soil, or duff. Wear no-tread camp shoes so that ground compaction will be minimized. Compaction interferes with air and water moving through the soil and can make it essentially sterile.

— Remember that the best campsites are found, not constructed.

— Pack out all your garbage and trash.

— Use the wilderness without consuming it!

Chapter 8
Food and Cooking

Whether a mountaineering trip is successful or not depends a lot on the physical condition of the hikers — and physical condition depends a great deal on proper nutrition. Therefore, as any sensible hiker knows, it is important to plan meals and snacks very carefully for any trip, regardless of how long or short, strenuous or easy. The foods selected should first be nutritious, second, as light as possible, and last, but certainly not least, delicious. Careful consideration should be given to each item before it goes into the pack. Each piece of cooking equipment and package of food must perform a function that makes it worth the energy expended to carry it. It matters not whether you are most interested in taste, cost, or ease of preparation — nutrition and weight are still prime considerations. Once these requirements have been met, you'll find there are almost infinite possibilities, and no rules. As long as your meals and snacks are hearty, they can be fancy or plain, easy or hard to prepare, tailored for meat-eaters or vegetarians, natural food oriented or supermarket specials. If you have a mind to try out new recipes on the trail, however, be sure to try them at home first. And be sure to take plenty of familiar foods; it's quite amazing how incredibly delicious even the simplest old favorites taste on the trail. A bit of practice will make it clear that it really isn't difficult to plan meals that are nourishing, delicious, light, and relatively inexpensive. You just have to think ahead.

8.1 Nutritional Necessities

A balanced diet is composed of protein, fats, and complex carbohydrates. Adequate amounts of vitamins, minerals, roughage (bulk), and water are also needed. On most trips of at least moderate strenuousness, approximately 3,000 to 5,000 calories per person per day are needed, though the actual amount depends on individual needs.

Even when you are not exercising much, your body burns about 15 calories/day/pound. On the trail you may burn 20 to 30 calories/pound, depending on the amount of work you are doing and the temperature (you burn more calories in cold weather). On the average trip you'll probably feel the most vigorous if your caloric input matches your output, and if those calories are made up of about 65% carbohydrates, 20% protein, and 15% fats.

Complex Carbohydrates

Complex carbohydrates are your basic running fuel; they are easily digested, give quick energy, keep the muscles working smoothly, and provide bulk and fiber. They don't stick with you all day, but you can keep munching. Carbohydrates provide about 100 calories/ounce. Some **typical complex carbohydrate foods** are: all whole-grain products (breads, cereals, cookies, rice), dried fruits (or fresh), some vegetables (beans, potatoes, winter squashes). Simple carbohydrates also give quick energy, but are burned so fast that they can give you an energy slump if you eat them alone. Some **typical simple carbohydrate foods** are: jams, sugar, honey, most candies, products made of refined (enriched) flour (bread, cookies, etc.).

Proteins

Proteins are your staying power; they burn more slowly than carbohydrates, maintain body tissues and rebuild muscles, and keep you warm when not exercising (eat them before going to bed). Proteins also provide about 100 calories/ounce. Some **typical high protein foods** are: cheese, milk, eggs, fish (tuna, salmon, sardines), nuts, lean meats, legumes (beans, split peas, etc.).

Fats

Fats are your basic stored energy source; they are digested even more slowly than proteins. Your body often calls fats up in case of emergency (cold weather, lack of food). Fats are a very concentrated energy source, providing 200 to 250 calories/ounce, which makes them especially good for trips in cold weather when you need to eat many more calories than usual. Some **typical high fat foods** are: butter, nuts and nut butters, cheese, eggs, fat meats, oil.

Vitamins

Vitamins are necessary for the enzyme functioning which leads to proper absorption of food and the transformation of food components into energy. This energy fuels our muscles, maintains body tissues, repairs injury, and keeps us thinking clearly. Without appropriate amounts of vitamins you cannot make the best use of your food or the best use of your body—as in strenuous hiking. Because this is not a course in nutrition, only the vitamins which seem particularly important for somewhat strenuous outdoor activity will be mentioned.

Vitamin A is essential for good night vision, something one often needs when traveling in the wilderness. Some **vitamin A-rich foods** are: carrots (you guessed it!), sweet potatoes, cantaloupes, winter squash, papaya, apricots, nectarines, broccoli, peaches, and tomatoes. Fortunately, most of these foods dry well.

Vitamin B-complex (thiamin, riboflavin, niacin, pyridoxine, cobalamin, folacin, pantothenic acid, biotin, choline) is required at several stages of carbohydrate, protein, and fat metabolism; it is also necessary for protein synthesis, energy release, and hormone production. Some **vitamin B-complex-rich foods** are: milk products, brewer's yeast, tofu, soybeans, whole grains, spinach (and other dark green vegetables), beans (all kinds), cantaloupe, oranges, bananas, nuts, sweet potatoes, strawberries.

Vitamin C is a wound-healer; it is also necessary for fighting infection. Some **vitamin C-rich foods** are: papaya, oranges, cantaloupes, strawberries, red peppers, broccoli, green pepper, cauliflower, and tomatoes.

Vitamin E assists in proper muscle functioning during strenuous exercise; people who suffer from muscle cramps after or during exercise are sometimes benefited by vitamin E supplements. This vitamin also seems to speed healing of injuries both when taken internally and when put on externally. Some **vitamin E-rich foods** are: wheat germ and wheat germ oil, walnuts, filberts, almonds, spinach, sweet potatoes, blackberries, and safflower oil.

Minerals

Minerals (calcium, magnesium, sodium, potassium, iron) perform many functions in the body; those we are primarily concerned with here have to do with efficient muscle function under strain, the blood's oxygen-carrying ability, and fluid balance.

Sodium and **potassium** concentrations in the blood and other body fluids help regulate the passage of nutrients into body cells and the carrying away of waste products. Strenuous activity which results in sweating can unbalance the concentrations of these minerals in body fluids, which in turn can lead to exhaustion, headache, fluid retention, dizziness, muscle cramps ("heat cramps"), and/or nausea. In addition to replacing these minerals by eating foods rich in them or by taking buffered salt tablets (which have the advantage of balancing the sodium with the potassium—table salt is a sodium salt only), it is also necessary to replace the fluids lost. This can be done by drinking up to a gallon of water a day when exercising strenuously in warm weather. Some **sodium-rich foods** are; salt, soy sauce, cottage cheese, oatmeal (if salted), corn, tomato juice, cheddar cheese. Some **potassium-rich foods** are; winter squash, lima beans, spinach, black beans, papaya, cantaloupe, raisins, split peas, dates, potatoes, oranges, bananas, milk.

Calcium is required for efficiency of muscle contraction and muscle stamina, both of which are important when hiking. Some **calcium-rich foods** are: milk products, sesame seeds, broccoli, tofu, whole-grain corn tortillas, carob.

Magnesium is essential in energy transfer, and works closely with calcium in keeping the muscles in good order. Without enough magnesium, calcium can't do its job properly, and vice-versa. Some **magnesium-rich foods** are: beans, whole wheat, peanut butter, sesame seeds, cashews, green beans, spinach, avocadoes, bananas, blackberries, dates, oranges, dried figs, milk.

Iron is essential to the enzyme systems which carry oxygen; even a very slight iron deficiency can make hiking at altitudes of over 5,000 feet a chore, so it pays to eat iron-rich foods regularly. Some **iron-rich foods** are: liver, prunes (also good for another common trail affliction), beans (in general), lentils, spinach, dried peaches, split peas, tomato juice, pumpkin seeds, wheat bran, winter squash.

Roughage/bulk (fiber)

Roughage is necessary for proper elimination; it is often missing in the diets of hikers who use highly processed rather than whole trail foods. It is questionable whether these usually expensive foods are quicker to prepare on the trail than whole food meals. What is not uncertain, though, is that many people who eat these highly processed foods are soon afflicted with one of two complaints: constipation or a form of "nature's revenge." The do-it-yourselfers who emphasize whole foods seldom have these problems, because their diets provide roughage. Some **fiber-rich foods** are: wheat or other whole grain bran (you guessed it again), prunes, raisins (and most other dried fruits), whole brown rice, beans, rolled whole oats, whole grain bread and pasta (actually, whole grain anything), apples (ever wonder why the "apple a day"?), vegetables.

8.2 Planning Trip Meals and Snacks

The kind and amount of food needed on a trip should be determined accurately in order to reduce the weight carried and yet provide delicious and nourishing meals. No matter what kinds of foods you decide to take on your trip, keep in mind that it takes twice as long to cook food at 5,000 feet than at sea level and three times as long at 10,000 feet.

You probably noticed that there are quite a few foods which appear in several categories of Section 8.1. These might be good ones to make a regular part of your trail food list — for example: whole grain anything, beans, dried fruits (particularly papaya, apricots, raisins, figs, dates), winter squash (dried), milk (spray-dried), cheese, nuts, broccoli and spinach (dried), tomatoes (dried), bananas (dried), eggs, cantaloupe and blackberries (dried), brewer's yeast, tofu (dried), fish, lean meats (dried), wheat germ, safflower oil, sesame seeds. For more complete lists of complex carbohydrate-, protein-, and fat-containing foods, along with a suggested seasoning and beverage list, see Appendix E.

Complete planning is essential. Much of the meal-preparing for a trip takes place before you leave home. You can't run to the mini-mart in the wilderness! Some of the essentials to consider in planning include:

1. How many are being planned for? Is each hiker to be self-contained or is there to be a group or central commissary arrangement? Usually weight and labor are less for each person if the trip is planned so that several people share food and equipment (for example, 2 to 3 people per stove).

2. What are the energy requirements and tastes of the people in the group? The best way to find this out is for everyone to participate in the planning.

3. What kind of a trip is being planned? Planning for a 2-day trip is far less complicated than planning for a 2-week trip. The longer the trip, the more critical the weight of food becomes. The more strenuous the trip, the more critical the energy level of the food becomes.

4. Where is the trip to take place? Will there be clean water available near the campsites or the trail, or will you have to pack in all your water (as on many desert trips)? If water is to be at a premium and the trip is relatively short, you may consider taking more fresh foods than you usually would.

5. What weather is expected during the trip? Summer and winter trips offer different challenges in meal planning and preparation. Frozen water and snow take extra time and fuel to melt. Stove operation on snow is different than on bare ground.

6. What kind of a trip is this? Is the goal climbing a peak? Is it a leisurely hike on flat terrain? Does it cover a few or many miles? Simple, easy-to-prepare meals are essential if the days are long, strenuous ones and camp is likely to be reached after dark by tired hikers. Longer time for meal preparation is sometimes appropriate if the day has been easy and the cook enjoys being creative.

7. How much food will each person (or group) need to carry? The answer to this question depends somewhat on the answers to some of the previous ones. In general, though, the average person on an averagely strenuous trip probably won't eat more than 3,000 to 5,000 calories/day (though probably somewhat less the first couple of days). This figures out to about two pounds of lightweight food per person per day—give or take a little for individual differences.

Where to Buy Trail Foods

Once you've answered these essential questions, you're ready to proceed to the next step: working out the actual meals and snacks, keeping in mind that you need foods that taste good, are light, will keep, are relatively easy to prepare, are economical, and, most importantly, are nutritious (that is, which satisfy carbohydrate, protein, fat, vitamin, mineral, fiber, and calorie requirements). You can shop at the supermarket, at mountaineering specialty stores, at natural food stores, ethnic specialty stores, or what have you.

Mountaineering or other sporting good specialty stores usually stock only freeze-dried meals and snacks; unfortunately, many of these contain highly processed ingredients and additives of questionable safety, so read labels carefully. These foods are also expensive, compared to doing it yourself.

Natural food stores often carry dried or dehydrated items in bulk at prices considerably lower than any of the other stores, including the supermarket (when you buy items in bulk, you don't pay for unnecessary packaging and advertising). Some bulk items you may find in natural food stores are whole brown rice, granola and granola ingredients, bulgur wheat, rolled oats, many kinds of beans and grains, spray-dried milk, honey, polyunsaturated oils, trail mixes, nuts and seeds, sesame burger mixes, soups, spices, etc. Such stores also have items you may not find elsewhere, such as high-protein crackers, a large selection of dried fruits, high-protein drink mixes, high-protein candy bars, herb teas in bulk or bags, and so on. Most items of these sorts which are suitable for backpackers do not contain the questionable additives; however, it pays to read the labels here, too—quite a few manufacturers with less than admirable motives are invading the health food sector.

Ethnic food specialty stores may carry some of your favorite dried foods, such as falafel and hummous, and spices which are difficult to find elsewhere.

At the supermarket you can find many items suitable for backpacking in weight, price, nutrition, and ease of preparation—if you are willing to read labels in order to avoid most of the unnecessary processing. Be especially careful of "instant" dishes; these often contain very low-quality ingredients, doctored up with all kinds of unhealthful colors and flavors. You can get along without these kinds of "foods" if you are willing to do a little ahead-of-time preparation yourself to make sure the food will taste like you want it to and be more economical to boot.

Dehydrating Your Own Trail Foods

A fairly recent development in the do-it-yourself preparation of foods for backpacking is the dehydrator. Not everyone owns one of these handy units, but almost everyone interested in doing much traveling by foot in the out-of-doors knows someone who does, so access is not usually difficult — just ask a friend to loan you theirs for a few days. Home-dehydrated food has many advantages. For example, such foods are far less expensive when you dry them yourself than when a company does it for you and sells it through a distributor (they all have to have their cut). Also, foods which are dehydrated retain more vitamins and minerals than foods processed at higher temperatures. If kept dry, dehydrated foods will keep for a long time without refrigeration. Almost anything can be dehydrated, and when pre-cooked before dehydration even beans and rice take little preparation time in camp. Many dehydrated foods can be eaten dry, for a tasty snack. If you own or borrow a dehydrating unit, be sure to read and follow the directions carefully — they will tell you how to choose, prepare, cut, dry, and store many different kinds of fruits, vegetables, meats, poultry, fish — even candy, soups, desserts, fruit bars, sauces, and gravies.

8.3 Eating on the Trail

Meal Suggestions for the Trail

All in all, you'll probably be most satisfied with your trail meals and snacks if you stay away from highly processed foods and get a bit closer to the basics, such as: whole grains, fruits; vegetables; homemade desserts, candy, and main dishes; personally concocted granolas and trail mixes; spray-dried instead of "instant" dry milk; homemade beef, chicken, and fish jerkies; high-protein, whole-grain breads, crackers, and cookies. Putting together your own food, to your own taste and that of your group, is not only enjoyable but cheaper.

Breakfast: This meal should include plenty of complex carbohydrates and some protein. For example, a quick breakfast might consist of some or all of the following: granola or other whole-grain uncooked cereal, whole grain bread or crackers with nut butter and honey, fruit juice, dried fruit (perhaps rehydrated overnight), and dried milk (mix with cereal and add water). A more leisurely breakfast could include some or all of the following: a hot drink (tea, coffee, hot carob or chocolate, Pero or other cereal beverage, etc.), pancakes or eggs, toast with nut butter and honey or jam, cooked whole-grain cereal (oatmeal, familia, cream of rye, etc.), milk, and fruit.

Lunch: For many hikers, lunch is a movable and continuous feast. Regularly spaced nibbles — , and, for some, an additional light lunch — during short rest breaks seem to work best in keeping the energy flow constant and the stomach happy. Except for a fairly substantial, high-carbohydrate breakfast before breaking camp (which gives the meal time to digest a bit before you hit the trail), a moderately heavy meal before hiking means many people feel lethargic. A high-carbohydrate, low-protein and low-fat selection of nibbles will keep your energy level high without slowing you down. Some possibilities for lunch/snack items could be: sandwiches, whole-grain cookies and crackers, cheese (not too much), honey or jam, trail mix (not too many nuts), dried fruit, freeze-dried fruit juices (juices made from these crystals not only taste better, but usually don't have unnecessary additives), fresh fruits and/or vegetables (first few days), homemade jerkies (small amounts), lots of water.

Dinner: Here's when you'll consume most of your protein and fat calories for the day—and you'll have time to properly digest them. After a long day, when all one wants to do is crawl into the sleeping bag, dinner is still essential to restore the salts, liquid, and calories lost during the day and to provide the fuel to keep you warm during the night. Dinner is a pleasant, social time when the day's experiences are reviewed and the next day planned over cups of soup and tea. Dinner should include, first, some hot drinks (unless the weather is hot) such as soup, tea, or bouillion. The main course is often a "one-pot" effort, heavy on the protein.

Some of the more popular ingredients for one-pot meals are some mixture of the following: dehydrated whole potato flakes, cheese, whole-grain noodles, split peas, lentils, canned or dehydrated tuna or chicken, freeze-dried or dehydrated beef, fresh or dehydrated vegetables, dried milk, soup mix, nuts and seeds, bulgur wheat, beans, whole brown rice, raisins or other dried fruit, hot chili spices, sesame salt, soy sauce, italian spices, curry, salt, honey, garlic, onion flakes, oil, pepper, bouillion cubes (for stock), and so on. Serve the one-pot meal with bread (good for scooping up the last of it), crackers, biscuits (if the cook is feeling energetic), and any spread of your choice. Dessert can be whole-grain cookies, hot or cold rehydrated fruit (made into upside-down cake if the cook is still feeling ambitious), trail mix, candy (this can be made before the trip), hot pudding (ingredients put together before trip), etc. Follow with more hot or other drinks. Salads and vegetable dishes are also welcome. Beans, rice, split peas, etc. should be pre-soaked.

Eating and Drinking on the Trail

It's a good idea not to change your diet too abruptly when you go out on the trail. An abrupt change of diet can lead to constipation, diarrhea, gas, nausea, or just plain "no appetite." Don't be alarmed, though, if you find your appetite a bit less hearty than usual the first couple days of a trip; it will pick up pretty soon, and by the end you'll probably be eating quite a bit more than you usually do.

Also keep in mind that you will be losing more minerals than usual in your sweat. You may notice an increased desire to salt your food, so go ahead — this will replace the sodium. To replace potassium, which is just as important as sodium, try eating dehydrated bananas, apricots, raisins, nuts, and eggs. You don't lose much calcium and magnesium in your sweat, but your muscles have an increased need for both when you are exercising more strenuously than usual; in proper balance these minerals help keep your muscles from cramping. To replace calcium and magnesium, drink milk, eat green vegetables. You can also take supplements of calcium and magnesium if you think you aren't getting enough of these minerals.

Some people find the buffered salt tablets (which contain the proper proportions of sodium and potassium) helpful on strenuous trips or in hot weather; if you use these, be sure to drink at least 10 ounces of water with each tablet. Nowadays there are also powdered drink mixes formulated to provide the minerals lost in sweating; examine the labels carefully, though, because some of these mixes use chemicals of questionable safety to preserve them for long periods or to color and flavor them in ways the companies think consumers find attractive. If you do use these electrolyte replacement mixes, try diluting them with 2-3 times as much water as suggested. This often makes them more palatable and easier on the stomach.

All that sweating you're doing on the trail isn't just using up minerals and energy-producing foods, it's also using up a lot of water. Even if you don't usually drink much water, make an effort to drink frequently and long — you'll be much more comfortable. Headache and furry mouth are not the companions you want on the trail. Besides, the water on the trail is sometimes purer and tastier than that you are used to in the city! (See Section 7.2 on how to purify the water if it is contaminated.)

Above about 7,000 feet many people find that it's best to eat most of their protein and fat for the day at a time when they will not have to hit the trail for several hours. Protein and fat, as mentioned before, take longer to digest — which means you not only do not get your energy out of them right away, but that your digestive system, while busy with them, is hogging more than its share of the blood you need to carry nutrients to your muscles. When you then start exercising vigorously, the blood rushes to your muscles without carrying much energy with it, and your digestive system is left without the blood necessary to digest the food you've just given it. Result: indigestion, possible nausea, possible muscle cramping, tired feeling, etc. Below 7,000 feet your body can usually han-

93

dle this protein/fat situation pretty well, but at higher elevations your body is having to cope with the altitude, too, so it will probably help you to keep feeling energetic if you stick to eating mostly carbohydrates whenever you're going to be on the trail soon (unless the ground is pretty flat).

8.4 Stoves and Other Cooking Equipment

Wood is no longer an acceptable cooking fuel source except in emergencies. Below the timber line, dead or downed wood (the only kind hikers are allowed to use) is becoming more and more scarce. New regulations requiring hikers to use their own stoves (butane, propane, white gas, kerosene, liquid petroleum) are intended to decrease human-caused disturbances by allowing organic matter to keep its rightful place in the energy cycle. In some areas of extreme fire danger, even stoves are forbidden and hikers must use cold foods.

Small liquid- or gas-fueled stoves provide a reliable source of cooking heat. When operating properly, these stoves leave no soot on cooking utensils. Because stove models frequently change, you should test as many as possible and talk to people who have used them on the trail before purchasing one.

A stove can be a boon or a bane to the hiker, and even a danger to the unwary or careless. Which stove is best for you depends on preference and intended use. Some factors to consider are weight, compactness, type and weight of fuel, safety, stability when cooking, heat output under different conditions, burning time per ounce of fuel, cost of stove and operation, and availability of fuel. The most common and available fuels are butane, propane, liquid petroleum (LP), gasoline (white gas or Coleman fuel), kerosene, alcohol, Sterno, and charcoal. Some stove manufacturers have several models, which may or may not use the same type of fuel. (See Appendix D for stove/fuel/time-to-boiling comparison chart.)

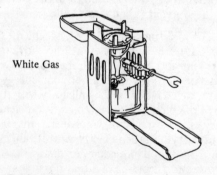

White Gas

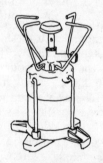

Propane or Butane

15. Backpacking Stoves

94

Stove Fuels

Butane stoves are probably the most convenient and easiest to operate; they have immediate maximum heat output and can usually be turned down to a simmer (which under certain conditions saves fuel). Propane stoves are similar, but have a heavier cartridge (canister). Both are higher in cost to operate than gas or kerosene stoves. Cartridges present a space problem and have to be carried out when empty. Butane doesn't operate well in cold weather unless a heat coil or reflector is used to carry heat to the canister. Propane freezes at a much lower temperature than butane and operates quite well in cold weather. Some butane cartridges (Bleuet, Gaz) must be left attached to the stove until empty, while most others can be removed and carried separately from the stove. Quite a few sporting goods stores do not carry butane cartridges for all types of stoves.

Hazards of Stove Operations

Butane Stoves: Butane stove refueling should be done very carefully. Although there is no liquid fuel to worry about, the cartridges for various butane stoves often attach differently. Read the directions on the cartridge carefully, noting whether the cartridge needs to be held upright or not, whether it can be removed between uses or must be left on until empty, whether it screws on (if it does, be careful not to strip the threads) or plugs in. After attaching the cartridge, listen carefully to see if there is any fuel leak; if there is, you will probably hear a faint hiss. If you can't do away with the hiss by tightening the appropriate connections, try another cartridge.

Gasoline Stoves: Gasoline stoves burn hotter but need priming unless provided with a pump attachment. Gasoline is readily available throughout the U.S. and is no more dangerous than most other fuels — it is very flammable, but evaporates rapidly when spilled. Most gas stoves are fairly compact, are more efficient than butane, and cost less to operate. Such stoves need to be insulated from the cold or snow so that the fuel tank will be warm enough for the stove to operate properly. However, the tank should not be allowed to overheat. If it does overheat (that is, gets too hot to touch with the bare hand) the vapor pressure may build up so much that it will force open the safety valve in the tank lid and transform your stove into something resembling a blow torch (it's wise not to hang over the stove while cooking). If the stove does not have a safety valve, you have a potential bomb on your hands.

Kerosene Stoves: These stoves also have a high heat output. Kerosene doesn't evaporate rapidly, which means that when spilled it will not readily ignite. A kerosene stove needs priming, but can operate directly on the snow without insulation (though it is a good practice to insulate any stove from the snow). Kerosene is not as readily available in the U.S. as it is abroad.

Alcohol Stoves: These stoves are lightweight and fairly stable in the wind, but heat and heat control are limited and the fuel cost is quite high. Alcohol burns clean, but it takes forever to cook a meal!

Tips for Successful Stove Use

All Stoves: Before going on any trip with a new stove, thoroughly test the stove at home, out-of-doors. If you have difficulty operating the stove, go back and read the instructions again. Sometimes there may be a small metal burr or chip in the fuel orifice which can be removed by using the cleaning needle. Once you have the stove lit (if it is gas operated), let it burn until it has reached its full heat output.

When situating your "kitchen" in the camp site, choose a level area out of the wind and out of the main line of traffic (or the cook may wind up with everyone's dinner in his/her lap!). Keep this area away from any other flames, fuel cartridges or bottles, and burnable equipment, trees, and bushes. Point the stove's safety valve away from people and flammable objects. If camping on snow, insulate the stove's fuel tank by putting it on a small piece of wood, foam, masonite, even a glove, and then putting a piece of foil or a pan lid between the insulating material and the tank.

Before lighting the stove, clean the fuel jet orifice. If the stove runs out of fuel in the middle of cooking, let the burner cool off enough to touch before refueling (some fuels will ignite if spilled on very hot metal). Do *not* check fuel level when stove is in use; refuel before beginning use. Immediately after shutting off stove, turn it back on for just a moment (do not light!) to blow out particles of carbon that may have fallen back into the orifice. If burner plate is red-hot, wait until it cools a bit before doing this—otherwise the stove could reignite.

A windscreen is helpful in windy weather, but if not used properly it can cause heat buildup which could result in the safety valve opening and the escaping vapor igniting—thus producing the "blow-torch effect." Cooking in the tent eliminates the need for a windscreen, but can be dangerous unless the tent is properly equipped with cook-hole and cross-ventilation. A flare-up or ignition of spilled fuel can engulf the tent and you in flames almost instantly. There is also a fairly high output of carbon monoxide gas, which could cause headache, nausea, or even asphyxiation.

Some stoves are not stable enough to accomodate large pots without a serious tendency to topple over (no need to describe the ensuing scene). Cooking for a large group is best accomplished on several stoves rather than trying to make do with one.

To diminish the high heat output of any stove so that it can be used for simmering, a heat-spreader or diffuser can be used. This is simply a piece of tin or asbestos put on top of the burner to keep the flame from making a hot spot in the center of the pan. The top cut from a tin can works nicely. A spreader wastes fuel, but allows a high heat output stove to be used for simmering.

Spare parts are available for some stoves, but not many. It's a good idea to have an extra orifice in your spare parts or repair kit. A cleaning needle is necessary for removing carbon or dirt particles from an orifice (unless your stove has a built-in one); a carbide lamp reamer works well if the orifice has been removed for cleaning.

And last but not least: *do not leave the stove when food is cooking!*

White Gas Stoves: For gas stoves, it's a good idea to have a spare gas cap for the stove as well as for the fuel bottle. A funnel or pouring spout is also handy (actually, indispensable). A small plastic bottle of alcohol and an eye dropper will help you keep a gasoline stove clean when priming (an empty mosquito repellent bottle works well).

Fill the tank before each use, leaving a small air space at the top; use a funnel or the pouring device supplied by the manufacturer (you'll spill a lot less heavy, precious fuel if you do). Wipe up small spills, but change your stove site if you spill a lot of fuel.

Follow manufacturer's instructions about pumping and/or priming. Light stove, allow priming flame to die back somewhat, then open valve to fuel tank slowly. Adjust flame to desired level, then remove metal valve key (if you have one) from valve so that it won't get so hot you can't touch it to adjust the flame. A few splutters and flares aren't unusual, but if the stove doesn't settle down in a few minutes, shut it off and start all over again.

Kerosene Stoves: Follow manufacturer's instructions for priming and lighting. If the flame is smoky or very yellow, shut off stove and prime and light again.

Butane or Other Cartridge Stoves: When lighting these stoves be sure to light your match first, before turning on the gas (a little miscalculation about how long you've had the gas on could cost you your eyebrows). To warm the cartridge if the weather is cold, put it in your sleeping bag with you at night or hold it under your clothes for a while before lighting the stove. Never shake a cartridge.

When the stove is in use, as with gas stoves, do not allow the cartridge to overheat to the point that you cannot hold it in your hand. Don't pile rocks around the cartridge or allow any hoses to get close to the flame.

Pack all cartridges out with you, and don't throw away any cartridge until it is empty. Never throw any cartridge into a fire!

Fuel Planning

White Gas: One-half cup white gas will burn 40 to 60 minutes under average conditions. Cold weather and the height of the flame you use (high or low) will affect the amount of fuel you use.

Kerosene: One-half cup of kerosene will burn 50 to 70 minutes under average conditions.

Butane and Propane: One ounce of butane (in a vapor-feed cartridge) will last 20 to 30 minutes under average conditions. Two ounces of butane (in a liquid-feed cartridge) will last 20 to 30 minutes. Most cartridges contain about six ounces of fuel.

Experience with cooking different kinds of meals on different trips at different altitudes will enable you to accurately guess how much fuel you will need for a particular trip. Until you have gained this experience, get some advice from more experienced friends and take a little more fuel than you think you'll need.

Other Kitchen Equipment

Pots, Pans, and Misc. Equipment: The number of people and the type of trip, whether you're planning for group commissary or individual meal preparation—all affect the size, type, and number of cooking utensils needed. A pint pot with lid is minimum pot equipment for one person. Empty cans and foil (for lid) can be used; be sure the cans do not have seams soldered with lead. For pots without handles, a light pot-grabber will prevent burned fingers. There are many varieties of nesting pots commercially available. A stirring spoon can be used for eating if there is only one person, but not for a group. For more than one person, a wooden spoon is handy, silent, and more efficient than a pointed metal spoon for stirring (just don't leave it in the pot while cooking). A small wire whip is indispensable for mixing dry milk, gravies, soups, etc. Many people like to take a small, light frying pan for eggs, pancakes, and so on.

Eatingware: The stainless steel "Sierra" cup, with slanting sides and wire handle, and a spoon are minimum equipment for eating. A second cup, a plastic one (marked for measuring), is a luxury. It can be used in meal preparation, and for meal and beverage at the same time. (Also, a plastic cup won't burn your lips when filled with a steaming beverage!) A pocket knife will take care of any cutting that needs to be done. A fork is handy but not necessary.

All-Purpose Containers: A couple of wide-mouth plastic bottles of different sizes (1 pint, 1 quart, or 1½ quart are handiest) have many uses. If you mark the bottles at ¼-cup intervals for measuring, they can be used for mixing powdered drinks, dry milk, juice crystals, and pancake mixes, and as canteens for carrying drinking and cooking water.

Food Bags: To protect foods from dampness and permit orderly packing, waterproof nylon, rubberized, or plastic bags can be used to carry and "string up" food items. Recycled plastic sacks can be used to separate meals or dishes when perfect seals are not required. Use new bags if leakage is a possibility. Ziptop bags can be used to carry water, soak items, or mix ingredients. Bags for stoves and fuel containers are helpful. It is recommended that all food items be kept segregated in one large, washable, coated bag in each pack.

Water Bags: Heavy plastic water bags with a nylon cover are easily available and very convenient for carrying cooking and dishwashing water (these bags usually hold two gallons). The nylon-covered bags are handy for supplying the camp with water; they save many a trip to the water source with smaller water bottles.

Canteens: There are many plastic bottles, flasks, and containers of almost any conceivable size available. Plastic containers are useful for carrying any type of liquid except fuel, which should be carried in metal containers. Avoid canteens with a very small opening, as they are hard to fill. Many clear containers contain harmful chemicals that can be leached into the liquids you fill them with. Metal canteens can give liquids an unpleasant flavor, but some are good fuel containers.

Meal Preparation

One-pot meals, with everything but dessert cooked in the pot at one time, are quick and easy to prepare. A second pot with boiling water will allow for soup or broth while the main dish is cooking, beverage after the meal, and hot water for cleanup of utensils and self. In planning and purchasing foods, keep in mind that buying the ingredients for creating your own lightweight meals is less costly and provides you with higher quality, better tasting food than many of the more expensive backpacking meals sold at sport specialty stores. Judicious use of condiments will help you vary your recipes. Each morning make sure to get that evening's meal into the top of the cook's pack so that no time is lost searching for ingredients when the dinner hour arrives.

8.5 Packing Food

No matter which food organization method appeals to you, you will have to do some measuring and repackaging of ingredients when preparing for your trip. Get rid of most original wrappings (if any), keep any directions, put most foods in plastic freezer bags (double-bag oil containers and powders even if they are already in a container). Canned tuna and sardines are of course kept in the original containers. Heavier and larger poly bags can be used for "day" or "meal" accumulations. While on the trail, as at home, save and reuse all plastic bags, twist-ties, and rubber bands.

Packing Food by Individual Meal

Using your menu and recipes, pre-measure and pack each meal in its own labeled plastic bag, along with recipe/s and dry condiments. Although this takes more pre-trip preparing, it saves time in camp; also, it's hard to run out of food with this kind of comprehensive planning.

Packing Food by Generic Meal Ingredients

Pack all "breakfast" ingredients in a single large plastic bag; ditto "lunch" and "dinner." Be sure to include recipes. Put all condiments in another plastic bag. Each day, consult the menu and select the appropriate ingredients and recipes from the bags.

Packing Food by Day

Sort ingredients and recipes by day (1, 2, 3, etc.) before going on trip. This method can be combined with the "by meal" method (if you are the methodical, time-saving type).

8.6 Protecting Your Food from Animal, Insect, or Other Marauders

Vigilance is the most effective means of protecting food from rodents, both human and animal. Raccoons, rats, and ground squirrels will chew through anything short of a tin can to get to food (leather thongs are one of their favorites). Food left alone in camp during the day may be ripped off by freeloading intruders—human or miscellaneous other animals, including the avian type (don't underestimate the birds!).

In remote areas, above timberline, or when snow camping, you usually don't have to worry about the fauna munching out on your carefully planned meals. However, if you are planning a trip in a medium- to heavily-used area it is a good idea to check around beforehand to see if you'll need to take any special precautions. In any case, always keep your camp spotless, storing away all food in your food bags between meals—and not in your tent!

If bears (squirrels, marmots, raccoons, porcupines, etc.) are a problem, you may need to hang your food (and sometimes your foody-smelling pack) from a heavy cord over a high horizontal branch or between two trees whenever you leave camp and at night. To accomplish this, tie a rock to one end of the cord, throw rock over branch, then retrieve rock and replace with your food bag (along with some pans as an alarm, if you wish); pull bag up until it is at least 15 feet above the ground, 10 feet from the nearest tree trunk, and 5 below the branch; anchor the end in your hand around something the bear would have trouble climbing up. You can also, instead, counterweight the free rope end with something that weighs about the same as the food bag and then push both up high enough that a bear can't reach them, but you can (with a stick).

If you know the bears are really hardened cases and no high, long, horizontal branches are available you may need to use two trees and two anchor lines, with the food bag being hung between. If bears do get to your bag, let them enjoy themselves; it's not worth risking an injury to argue with a bear over a little food!

16. Bearbagging

Chapter 9
Safety and First Aid

You can meet an emergency wherever you go — at work or school, at home, on a shopping trip, or on a wilderness trip. Usually you have easy access to medical attention. On a wilderness trip it is different: you don't have community resources just around the corner, but must provide the resources yourself — at least until you can get to a place where medical attention is available. Each group which goes into the wilderness should be prepared to provide a reservoir of equipment, training, and personal skills sufficient to meet its possible emergency needs.

The success and enjoyment of every wilderness trip depends on the physical well-being of each and every member of the group. In the wilderness, accident victims can only be sure of safe handling and treatment if all members of the group have a basic knowledge of first aid. The free courses on first aid given by the American Red Cross in most communities offer a good opportunity to acquire such knowledge. The main emphasis of such courses is on how to prevent further injury or possible death by providing emergency aid until professional aid (if necessary) is available. Mountaineering first aid differs from that taught in the Red Cross courses only in that it takes into account that medical care is often a long way off and that some temporary treatment may be necessary.

In the mountains and desert, as at home, you can take some commonsense precautions to help prevent serious trouble from developing and can also relieve many common miseries which do not usually require professional medical help. Most of the preparations you'll make to insure survival in an emergency can be made in the comfort and safety of familiar surroundings, when you are not under the stress of emergency.

This chapter will be made up of brief discussions of several common medical problems and miseries you may meet with in the course of your wilderness travels. The chapter is not intended to be a substitute for adequate first aid *training*; anyone planning to do anything more than casual day hikes should have such training. Whatever your level of expertise, though, keep in mind that the most important, yet most frequently neglected, aspect of good first aid is thinking ahead—preventing emergencies.

Most injuries and miseries can be prevented or avoided, but prevention requires thorough knowledge of the following: each person's physical condition and limitations, the kind of trip you are undertaking (with attention to weather conditions, altitude, time limitations, and training), equipment (with attention to adequacy and need for duplicating certain articles such as sunglasses, gloves, socks, etc.), and, last but not least, how to deal with emergencies that may arise. Each group member should have a first aid kit and know how to deal with common emergencies and miseries. This kind of preparedness cannot be overemphasized.

9.1 Safety—Preventing Illness and Accident

Know Your Group

Anyone affected by a chronic, serious, organic illness should not undertake strenuous wilderness trips unless under medical supervision. The exertion and strains involved might seriously tax such a person's strength and even endanger their life. Also, if professional medical care became necessary, reaching it would present a problem not only for the person but for the whole group. If you know any member of a proposed trip party has an illness of this sort it is important to call this to the leader's attention.

A group member who is suffering from any temporary indisposition (such as upset stomach, diarrhea, an infection, bronchitis, or even a cold) just before a trip should notify the leader. Colds and bronchial troubles, as well as many other passing physical problems, are likely to be aggravated by increased altitude. Also notify the leader if you have recently had a moderate to severe illness, operation, or injury, even if the latter are healed.

The leader should prepare a detailed roster of the people in the group—including names, phone numbers, addresses, emergency notification phone numbers, useful medical information, etc. Even simple information like this may be hard to assemble in the crunch of an emergency, when struggling with the problem of an injured or ill companion.

Plan Ahead

Physical conditioning is a must for safe participation in wilderness outings. The degree of conditioning necessary will depend on the strenuousness of the trips you are planning to participate in. (See Section 2.1 for conditioning details.)

A tetanus immunization or booster shot is recommended if you are going to spend any time along trails or in camps where stock has been.

Plan evacuation routes to places likely to have medical facilities (or at least a phone). Pick some fallback points for each leg of your route. Look up and list phone numbers of area sheriffs, park rangers, and mountain rescue teams. Each person should keep this information with them at all times, so that if an emergency should occur each will be free to concentrate on handling it in the best way possible and will not have to waste precious time assembling information they should already have.

If you are carpooling, all riders in your car should know where to find an extra key and be able to drive your car in an emergency.

Do Not Go Into the Wilderness Alone

Regardless of how experienced you are, accidents can happen—even to you. You increase your chances of dealing successfully with emergencies if you are not alone, providing your companions are sensible, relatively experienced hikers.

Know Basic First Aid Techniques

Anyone who goes beyond the end of the road—and thus beyond immediate medical attention—should be able to deal competently with such major emergencies as breathing failure, cardiac arrest, snakebite, bleeding, shock, heat stroke, and fractures; and with such minor emergencies (relatively speaking) as frostbite, infected wounds, heat exhaustion, burns, altitude sickness, sprains, sunburn, snowblindness, poison oak, blisters, nausea, vomiting, diarrhea, ticks, and so on.

Carry the Ten Essentials at All Times (and Know How to Use Them)

Before going beyond the end of the road, you should know how to use your map and compass and, of course, your first aid kit. (See Section 4.2 for map and compass instructions.)

Let Someone Know of Your Plans and Expected Return

Prepare a detailed itinerary showing your route and timetable. Give this well-documented list to a responsible person, along with written instructions on what you want them to do with it in case you do not return as planned.

Know Some Distress Signals

Learn the ground-to-air and ground-to-ground emergency code distress signals. You can use the waterproof matches from your Ten Essentials to build signal fires, etc. Know how to use your signal mirror. Always carry something large and bright colored, like a yellow tarp or orange pack.

Be Properly Equipped and Trained

In addition to the Ten Essentials, you should have with you whatever equipment is appropriate to the trip you are taking (warm clothing, shelter, enough food, etc.) You should also be competent in any special skills needed for the trip — for example, belaying.

Formal training in first aid and cardio-pulmonary resuscitation (CPR) is available in most communities. Such training is not usually aimed at the wilderness traveler, but it nevertheless should be considered a necessity for anyone who plans to do more than a little day hiking. By learning proper emergency first aid you are better able to help others and yourself in an emergency.

Formal training in using the map and compass is not as easily come by as first aid and CPR training, but fortunately this skill lends itself to self-study and practice. The compass works the same way in the city as it does in the wild, and familiar surroundings give you a chance to recognize mistakes and correct them without endangering yourself or others.

First aid, CPR, and proficiency with map and compass are the minimum skills needed for safe and enjoyable travel in the wilderness. Several members of any group should be qualified in these matters.

Each year people die in emergencies that could have been avoided or because they did not do the right thing after the emergency occurred. Not all accidents can be prevented, but if you are properly equipped, trained, conditioned, and have observed the precautions mentioned above you will be able to deal competently with almost any emergency.

9.2 First Aid Kit

Every hiker, climber, and backpacker should have her/his own first aid kit and know how to use it. Each item should be hygienically packed and clearly labelled for easy identification by other users. When administering any drug, be sure you are (1) giving the proper kind, and (2) giving the kind you intend. To avoid giving improper medication it is absolutely essential that all drugs in your first aid kit be adequately marked. Check before every trip to see that your first aid kit does not need replenishing. Some minor items are necessary only in certain kinds of weather and can be removed if out of season. Certain other items may have to be periodically replaced—for example, snakebite antitoxin, some antiseptics, antibiotics, water purification tablets.

Your first aid kit should contain the following:

Triangle bandage
Large absorbent sterile dressings
Adhesive tape (the paper kind is best)
Bandaids
Moleskin
3-inch roll "cling gauze"
3 ″ x 3 ″ sterile gauze pads
Ace bandage
Sting-kill swabs
Non-prescription antibiotic salve (e.g., Neosporin)
Betadine or other antiseptic (Zephirin)
Phisoderm or hydrogen peroxide
Tylenol
Buffered multiple mineral tablets (salt tablets)
Antihistamine and decongestant, non-prescription
Small scissors
Safety pins
Tweezers (tapered to point)
Small pliers (needle-nose)
Single-edge razor blades
Snakebite kit
Biodegradable soap
Cotton Swabs
Needle
Poison oak lotion (e.g. Cortaid or Rhulitol)
Water purifier (Globaline, Potable-Aqua, Halazone)
Kaopectate (for diarrhea)
Your own medications, if any
Moisture-proof container (to carry above items)

9.3 Mountaineering First Aid

The injuries and ailments in the following section are, on the whole, of a serious nature and the treatment they require is somewhat difficult. Professional help is usually needed. However, because such help is often far away when you are in the wilderness and immediate treatment of some kind is imperative, you do need to be able to give temporary aid in such emergencies.

First aid is defined as "the immediate and temporary care given the victim of an accident or sudden illness until the services of a physician can be obtained." When you are in the wilderness first aid skills are extremely important, because if you are injured or ill you will have to depend on the knowledge and skill of your companions; if your companions are the victims, they will be dependent on you. In order not to fail them, or yourself, don't just assume that you have already picked up all the knowledge that is necessary. Take a Red Cross course in first aid and study this section, which draws heavily on the statements and illustrations presented in the textbook on first aid issued by the American Red Cross.

When an emergency occurs, think first — then act! But above all, *do no harm*. Again, the following are moderately severe to severe illnesses and common accidental injuries, along with brief outlines of their appropriate treatment. These outlines are *not* meant to be a substitute for a first aid course!

Life-Threatening Conditions

Breathing Failure: When a person has stopped breathing as a result, for example, of a lightning strike, concussion, shock, severe hypothermia, or asphyxiation due to drowning, artificial mouth-to-mouth respiration should be applied immediately. To give artificial respiration:

1. If possible, put the person on his/her back and clear the mouth and throat of foreign matter including loose or false teeth. Artificial respiration can be performed with the person on their stomach, if necessary.
2. Tilt the head so the chin is pointing up and pull the jaw into a jutting-out position so that the tongue will not obstruct the airway.
3. Pinch the nostrils closed to prevent escape of air (keep the neck extended with the same hand that is on forehead).
4. Open your mouth wide and place over person's mouth (or mouth and nose in small children).
5. Breathe into the person until you see and feel the chest expand.
6. Remove your mouth and let the person exhale, pressing down lightly on the chest if necessary. Repeat this cycle at a rate of 12/minute for adults and 20/minute for children. Continue until help arrives or the person begins to breathe on their own.

Cardiac Arrest: To properly perform cardio-pulmonary resuscitation (CPR) you should take one of the courses offered by your community. However, if you find yourself in a situation where CPR is necessary and no one else has had any training, follow these instructions (remember, just four minutes after a person's heart stops beating, the brain cells start dying — so don't delay):

1. Put the person on his/her back.
2. Put the heel of your hand 2 to 3 fingers above the base of the

person's breastbone.

3. Place the other hand on top of the first — don't let your fingers touch the chest.
4. Smoothly depress the breastbone 1½ to 2 inches. This compresses the heart against the spine. (For children use only one hand and apply less pressure. For babies, use only two fingers.)
5. Apply pressure 60 times/minute when two rescuers are present. Use 80 compressions/minute when one rescuer is present.
6. Continue until normal heartbeat is restored or until medical help arrives.

Note: It is absolutely necessary to administer artificial respiration at the same time, as follows —

If one person is administering CPR, use 15 compressions and then two breaths.

If two people are administering CPR, use five compressions and then one breath.

17. Artificial Respiration

Shock: Shock may occur with any serious injury or illness. No matter what the cause, first aid for shock is essential. Shock is the result of impaired circulation of blood to body tissues; its symptoms are weakness, pale, moist, cool skin, thirst, feelings of faintness, nausea, perhaps vomiting, and dilated pupils.

Injuries must receive first attention. Control bleeding with firm compression, keep airway clear to ease breathing. Then give first aid for shock whether symptoms are present or not.

To improve return of blood to the heart keep person lying down with the head slightly below the feet (or raise feet and legs if injuries permit). If there is a head injury or if breathing difficulty increases, the head should be slightly raised. Maintain normal body temperature (98.6°F).

In mountain accidents, even in summer, maintaining normal body temperature may require applying external heat, as a person in shock may be unable to produce sufficient body heat even when in a sleeping bag. Any injury in the mountains which results in shock may be followed by hypothermia due to heat loss and fall in body temperature, even when the weather is above freezing. External warmth must be provided to restore normal body temperature! This can be done with carefully padded hot water bottles, heated rocks, or by direct skin-to-skin contact with other people. Any warm liquid, including coffee or tea, but not alcohol, can be given if the person is conscious. Above all, the person should be treated with kindness and consideration and not bothered with many questions or additional worries.

Bleeding: In any injury involving serious bleeding, immediate action is essential. Tear or cut off clothing if necessary in order to determine the extent of the wound. Work fast. Loss of 2-3 pints of blood at one time can be fatal.

The bleeding may be from an artery (strong spurts) or from a vein (slow, steady flow). Have the person immediately lie down, elevate the injured area higher than the heart if possible, and apply firm, direct pressure to the wound. Most hemorrhages, whether arterial or venous, can be stopped by direct pressure on the wound with compresses. An elastic bandage, snugly applied, is ideal for keeping pressure on the compress.

If you know the pressure points, you can act quickly even before the wound is located or compresses and bandage are ready. Although stopping bleeding by using pressure points is only a temporary measure, it can substantially reduce the loss of blood.

A tourniquet should be used *only* for major arterial bleeding — for example, injury to the leg's femoral artery. If a tourniquet is used it should not be loosened and must be tight enough to stop bleeding until medical help is available. Again, if the limb actually needs a tourniquet, a major artery has usually been cut; loosening the tourniquet in this situation will not allow blood to flow to the rest of the limb to prevent gangrene — it will only allow more bleeding and the person will bleed to death slowly instead of quickly. Though an extremity can be lost if deprived of its blood supply, this is preferable to loss of life. Never cover a tourniquet; write "TK" on the person's forehead to call the situation to the attention of medical personnel when they become available.

In summary, when an accident occurs, the following actions should be taken immediately, as needed:

18. Pressure Points (P) and Tourniquet Placement (T)

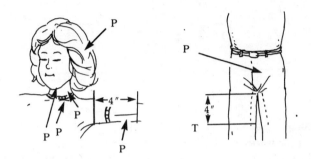

STOP BLEEDING – Apply direct pressure on bleeding area and, if possible, elevate the injured part. Do NOT apply a tourniquet unless it is a life or death situation.

RESTORE BREATHING – Clear the mouth and throat of any obstruction and open the person's airway. Give mouth-to-mouth resuscitation.

RESTORE HEARTBEAT – Perform cardio-pulmonary resuscitation (CPR).

TREAT FOR SHOCK – Shock may follow or accompany any injury or moderately severe illness. Symptoms are cool, clammy skin, shallow breathing, rapid and weak pulse, and feelings of nausea and/or faintness. Keep the person warm and calm. If there is no chest injury, elevate the legs slightly. If the person is conscious and has no abdominal injury, give warm fluids. *NOTE: Never give any substance by mouth to an unconscious person!*

Once you have accomplished the above, do a thorough examination of the person from head to toe. There may be multiple injuries. Do not move the person until the extent of injuries is determined, unless absolutely necessary to save the person's life.

Common Injuries

Lacerations: Wash the lacerated area with soap and water; apply antiseptic if necessary and bandage. If the wound becomes red, warm, swollen, and tender, clean wound and change dressings frequently, soak in warm salt water (or apply warm salt water compresses), and elevate. Gaping wounds may require butterflies – which you can make with adhesive tape – and/or pressure dressings.

19. Butterflies Cut from Adhesive Tape

Contusions: These injuries often cover large areas, such as the side of a leg or a whole buttock. The damage to the outer layers of the skin may be minimal, with the damage being done to the deeper tissues. Contusions usually swell, due to seepage of blood and lymphatic fluid from damaged vessels. Cold packs or even immersion of the part in cold water will help keep the swelling down and hasten clotting. If the contusion is large, cold can be applied fifteen minutes on and fifteen minutes off for a couple of hours before resuming mild activity. For small contusions, apply cold for 10 to 15 minutes two or three times a day. After a couple of days, warm compresses will hasten clot absorption if applied for 15-20 minutes two or three times a day.

Fractures: Simple fractures are usually recognizable by loss of function, presence of lacerations or cuts, pain, swelling, and deformity. In other cases, however, a fracture may not be apparent and can only be determined by x-ray. Consequently, care should be taken in diagnosis; a suspected fracture should be carefully watched for developing evidence of injury. This is particularly true when a pain-killer taken by the patient has perhaps made him/her unaware of further damage from a non-detected fracture. If there is any doubt, treat as for a fracture. Never test for a fracture by having the person move.

In some fractures the broken bones may extend through the skin and the limbs may be deformed. This type of fracture is called an "open fracture." Because there is serious danger of infection, the broken skin should be washed with soap and water (if feasible) and covered with a sterile dressing. Do not push a protruding bone back! Splint in place. Cool tissue to reduce swelling.

Broken bones and their fractured ends can be immobilized by using splints, pads, and bandages, which can be improvised if necessary. A pain killer is sometimes needed. Patients with fractures of the pelvis, ankle, femur, tibia, fibula, spine, and/or serious head or knee injuries cannot be evacuated by walking. The danger of further harm is too great. Stretchers should be used. Patients with fractures of the forearm, upper arm, shoulder, ribs, fingers, or jaw can, with aid, walk out after splints have been applied.

If at all possible, splints should be applied before moving the person in order to prevent further injury. To immobilize a fracture properly, be sure to splint the joints above and below the fracture, too. Don't fasten the splints so tightly that they cut off circulation.

Ankle sprains are often difficult to tell from fractures — when in doubt, splint, leaving shoe in place, but taking out laces.

Head and Spine Injuries: These injuries are usually caused by falls or falling rocks. Before any attempt is made to move the injured person, try to determine the extent of injury so that further injury can be avoided.

Serious head injuries can be identified by certain symptoms: the pupils of the eyes are not of equal size or do not react to light; there is bleeding from the ears, nose, or throat; the person may be disoriented as to time and place; there may be loss of muscle power and sensation; there may be complete loss of consciousness. Never administer pain-killing drugs when head injuries are suspected, as drugs can mask symptoms.

Fractures of the spine and neck from a fall are very common. Often there may be no symptoms and the fracture is discovered only later by x-ray. Any person injured in a fall should be treated as for fracture of the spine if there is the slightest question of that possibility.

You can identify a fractured neck by localized pain and spasm. There may also be loss of sensation or of motor power, such as inability to move fingers or toes. Check for possible loss of feeling, first with your hand and then with a sharp object. Move the person as little as you can, but if they must be moved turn them gently, keeping body in line with the neck. Do not sit the person up or bend their spine or neck if you suspect an injury to either of these areas. When in doubt, evacuate the injured person by stretcher or helicopter — do not attempt to walk them out.

Dislocations of Major Joints: These injuries should be treated as fractures. Do not manipulate joint; splint in place, do not try to relocate; treat for shock; get medical help.

Damaged Ribs: Ribs are sometimes damaged in climbing, skiing, or hiking accidents. If damaged ribs are suspected, examine for other injuries, treat for shock, have the person rest for a while, then have him/her spit. If the spit is clear of blood, apply three tight bandages across the chest, one above the damaged rib or ribs, and the other two below. Adhesive tape may be used. The bandages should be applied and tightened while the person exhales. The tight bandages may hinder breathing somewhat, but they will help prevent further harm caused by shifting rib sections.

Broken Lower Arm

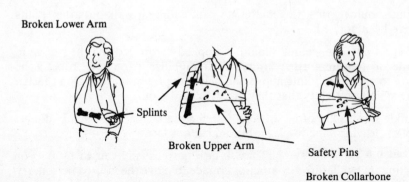

Splints

Broken Upper Arm

Safety Pins

Broken Collarbone

Fractured Elbow

(bent)   (straight)

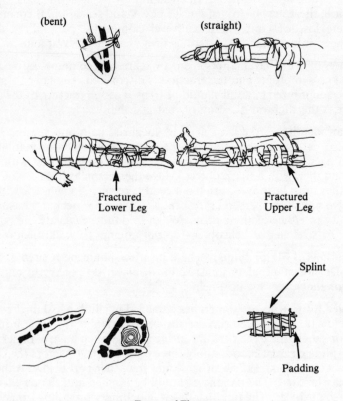

Fractured
Lower Leg

Fractured
Upper Leg

Splint

Padding

Fractured Fingers

20.   Typical Fractures and Treatment Suggestions

21. Taping and Bandaging Damaged Ribs

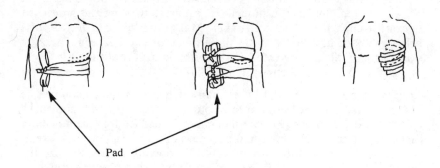

Pad

Sprains and Torn Muscles: Sprains are often caused by slipping or by a misstep. You can usually avoid slipping and wrong steps by watching where you step on the trail and by lacing your boots snugly. Ankle sprains may be treated by applying cold compresses and by appropriate use of ace bandages or taping. Beware of wrapping or taping too tightly, as this may affect circulation. Have the person stay off the foot for at least one-half hour after wrapping.

Fractures of the ankle cannot be ruled out without an x-ray; they are not necessarily more painful than a sprain. If there is any question, the ankle should be treated as for a fracture and not walked on. If a sedative is taken to relieve the pain, care should be taken in using the ankle; in the absence of pain, the person may do more damage.

Torn muscles are caused by overstretching. Applying heat will relieve the pain but if there is swelling — which indicates broken blood vessels — use of cold will hasten clotting and minimize damage. Use Ace bandages or tape for support. Have the person rest for 10 to 12 hours before resuming even mild activity. If there is any doubt whether the injury is a torn muscle or a fracture, treat as for a fracture. It may be necessary to carry the person out, depending on which muscles are affected.

Uncommon Injuries

Snake Bite: If you do not know what type of snake was responsible for the bite, you can be sure it was a venomous species if discoloration, swelling, and/or intense pain appear at the site of the bite within ten minutes after the bite. As little as three drops of venom from a poisonous snake can kill a person if it enters the circulatory system. Treatment must start immediately.

To prevent spread of the venom, the person bitten should avoid any physical activity. Have them lie down and try to keep them calm, quiet, and cool. Using a handkerchief, belt, or similar material, apply a constricting band (not a tourniquet) on the heart side of the wound and two to four inches away from it. This constricting band is not meant to cut off circulation, like a tourniquet—it is meant to slow the spread of poison through tissues near the skin. Make sure you can feel a pulse below the band and that you can slip a finger or two between it and the skin. If the swelling progresses, move the band to stay ahead of it. Treat the person to avoid the onset of shock.

Keep the area of the wound lower than the heart. If the person can be gotten to medical help within a few hours, don't use the "cut and suck" treatment; it can do more harm than good. If medical treatment is more than a few hours away, and symptoms develop, the "cut and suck" treatment can be used—with extreme care. To do this safely, sterilize the sharp razor blade or knife from your snake bite kit by using a match or disinfectant, and cut through the fang marks lengthwise relative to veins, arteries, bony structures, and skin grain. The longer the time interval between the time of bite and treatment, the deeper the cuts will have to be—but no more than ¼ inch deep and about ½ inch long. Get the cuts to bleed freely by applying the suction cup from the kit or by using your mouth. Using your mouth will not endanger you if the skin in the mouth area is not cut or exposed by infection (cold sores, etc.). However, you should spit out after each suction. If suction does not draw out any blood, loosen the band for a few seconds.

Give the person plenty of water to drink. Do not give coffee, tea, or alcohol! Treat for shock if it develops. Evacuate the person as soon as possible.

Hikers and climbers can avoid snake bites by being alert and watching wear they put their feet, hands, and posteriors. Snakes are more prevalent in the deserts and lower mountain regions. Walking in single file lessens the exposure, but each member should be alert. Be careful of hidden rock ledges and do not put your hands anywhere you haven't looked first.

Anti-venin is available; its efficiency lasts, on the average, for five years *if refrigerated*. Do not rely on anti-venin unless the expiration date is known—and you know how to use it. Use of anti-venin is preferable to cutting. However, anti-venin should be used with great care because many people are allergic to it. The allergic reaction can be fatal in 20 minutes — far more quickly than the snake bite.

Lightning Strike: Treat for cardiac arrest with CPR if necessary. Treat for shock.

Uncommon Illnesses

Pneumonia: Because pneumonia has an incubation period, a hiker or climber may be surprised by its unexpected appearance in a critical stage. At high elevation the onset of pneumonia can be very sudden, generally beginning with a severe chill. The person's temperature and respiratory rate may rise quickly; there is usually a hard, dry cough, with sharp pain in the chest. The person will look ill and his/her face will be flushed.

If any member of a group suffers from the above symptoms at a high altitude, steps should be taken to get them to a lower elevation immediately. Altitude aggravates pneumonia to the point where it could be fatal. In the meantime, the fever can be somewhat reduced by aspirin or Tylenol, taken with plenty of fluid and preferably not on an empty stomach. The person should be kept warm. If they appear very ill, outside help should be obtained and the person evacuated as quickly as possible.

Appendicitis: Appendicitis should be suspected when anyone experiences pain over all or part of their abdomen, nausea and vomiting, and tenderness in either the lower right or left quadrant of the abdomen.

Apply cold compresses to the affected area and, above all, do not give any laxative. This is an illness for which a speedy trip to medical attention must immediately be planned. In the meantime, do not give the person any food or water and have them rest quietly until they can be evacuated.

Heat Stroke: This malady can be fatal; fortunately, it is a much rarer occurrence than heat exhaustion. Heat stroke symptoms are much different from heat exhaustion symptoms, so there is no excuse for confusing the two (see Section 9.4 for description of heat exhaustion). A person with heat stroke will have hot, red, dry skin, and may be irrational and/or incoherent. The treatment for heat stroke is to lower the person's body temperature. You can douse them with water, even immerse them in a lake or stream if necessary or cover them with wet cloths (keep changing them). If immersion is not feasible put the person in the shade, but preferably not on the ground, which may be hot; keep the head higher than the rest of the body and massage arms and legs gently to increase the flow of blood and heat loss. Early symptoms of heat stroke are headache, dizziness, nausea, and dryness of skin and mouth. Do not give aspirin, as it interferes with the body's temperature control mechanisms.

Heat stroke is thought to result from continuous and heavy sweating which causes the sweat glands to "wear out" and shut down temporarily. When this happens, the body is no longer cooled by evaporation, its temperature rises above the range in which you can function properly (rectal temperature above 104 degrees F), and the temperature-regulating mechanism in the brain may even be damaged if the symptoms are not recognized and treated in time. If you are hiking in hot weather that stays hot even at night, you may become a candidate for heat stroke unless you take care not to overdo. To ward off heat stroke: rest frequently in the shade; cool yourself with water whenever possible; drink more water than you think you need; take in plenty of sodium, potassium and magnesium; and wear a light-colored hat that shades your head, face, and neck from the sun.

A person afflicted with heat stroke may be more susceptible to it after recovering, if their heat regulating mechanism has been damaged. Anyone who suffers heat stroke on a particular trip should not try to complete the trip, but should rest until feeling well again and then return home in easy stages (not alone!).

9.4 Common Miseries Caused by Heat, Cold, and Altitude

The ailments and inconveniences discussed in this section are usually brought about by your own negligence and ordinarily can be taken care of by simple means, unlike the injuries and illnesses discussed in Section 9.3.

Heat and Sun Injuries

Heat and sun ailments can be prevented by proper adaptation. This requires several days of graduated activity in a hot environment and adequate fluid and salt intake. This may mean up to 6-8 quarts of water and 3-5 grams of salts (potassium, sodium and magnesium) with extreme exertion. Salts as well as water must be replaced if problems of nausea, bloating, dizziness, confusion, and clumsiness are to be avoided. If you must hike or climb when it's very hot, take buffered multiple mineral salts when profusely sweating, protect your head from direct heat, drink lots of water, take rests in the shade, and go for a swim or dip as often as possible. These preventive activities will help keep your body functioning in its proper heat range of 98 to 99 degrees F. If your body temperature is allowed to go much above this range — as when you are hiking hard in hot weather — your heat regulating mechanism may stop working properly, and you may wind up with heat stroke or heat exhaustion.

Heat Stroke: Heat stroke is a medical emergency. Immediate treatment is required. This is a much greater problem in the backcountry than in the city. (See Section 9.3 for details.)

Heat Exhaustion: This is the most common heat misery. However, if you pay attention to its shock-like warning signals it need not be a dangerous one. If you are working hard on a hot day and begin to feel faint, perhaps nauseated, and notice that your skin is pale, cool, clammy, and sweaty and that your heartbeat is a bit fast and irregular — stop what you're doing immediately. Go and rest in the shade, lie down if possible, and loosen your clothing, drink plenty of water, and do nothing until you feel better. Once you've recovered, you can resume your activity, though you should take it easy for a while. Be sure to keep your water and salt intake up, for heat exhaustion is caused by diversion of blood flow from the brain to the skin and excessive loss of body water and salt through sweating.

Sunburn: This misery is caused by the sun's ultraviolet rays — the short ones which are not filtered out by the earth's atmosphere and which are present in ever-larger numbers the higher you go in the mountains. At high elevation or when these rays are reflected from snow, fog, granite, or light-colored sand, their effect is even greater than under ordinary conditions or at sea level. The higher the altitude, the thinner the atmosphere and the less protection it gives you from sunburn, skin aging, even skin cancer. A light to moderate overcast does not protect you from these rays. Use a sunburn preventive, wear a wide-brimmed hat, and stay covered up with loose, light clothing.

Sunburn preventives with an oil or petrolatum base are more lasting than those with an alcohol base. Para-amino-benzoic acid (PABA) provides good screening, but the alcohol base preparations require frequent applications. The best protection is offered by opaque zinc oxide or titanium dioxide grease. The former is good for use on the nose and lips, which is important for those susceptible to recurrent fever blisters. "Sunscreen" and "suntan" preparations are not synonymous. "Suntan" preparations are often just oils, which give *no* protection against sunburn. Many "sunscreen" preparations are now numbered according to their strength, from "2" to "15", with "15" being the strongest. The stronger the preparation, however, the greater the chance of allergic reactions, skin irritation, and staining (clothes). A strength of "6" seems a good compromise. "6" will protect you for about six hours in the sun and for about three hours if you are in the water and in the sun.

If you have a mild sunburn, you can use your sunburn preventive as a salve; if you have been careless enough to get a severe sunburn, bicarbonate of soda paste or a compress wet with strong tea or boric acid solution (one teaspoon to one quart of water) can help relieve pain.

Snowblindness: This is one of the most serious and painful of all sun-caused miseries — and one of the easiest to prevent. It is actually a sunburn of the cornea of the eye. This condition may come on suddenly or give warnings such as burning eyelids or scratchy eyes, headache, or spasms of the eye muscles. A snowblind hiker or climber is in extreme misery and may force the delay or cancellation of a trip. Fortunately, though the pain may be severe and long-lasting, the damage is not usually permanent.

The best cure for snowblindness is prevention. Wear sunglasses or goggles whenever hiking or climbing on highly reflective surfaces (snow, ice, light sand, light rock), even on cloudy days, and carry an extra pair of sunglasses for emergencies.

First aid treatment for snowblindness is cold compresses and darkness. Do not use topical anaesthetics, as they may injure the inflamed cornea.

Cold Injuries

Hypothermia: Like heat stroke, hypothermia can kill—in fact, it is the most common cause of death in the mountains. In hypothermia, your body is struggling to maintain its equilibrium in a situation where heat is being carried away from the body faster than the body can replenish it—usually by cold wind and/or damp clothing. Just as in heat stroke, the body's heat-regulating mechanism can break down as it tries to right the situation by conserving as much heat as possible for your vital organs: heart and brain. This breakdown can take place in temperatures well above freezing when you are not prepared for it. In fact, most hypothermia cases develop in air temperatures between 30 and 50 degrees F. You may think you are doing fine when your activity is the only thing preventing you from going into hypothermia. If exhaustion forces you to stop moving, even briefly, your rate of body heat production will instantly drop by 50% or more, violent and incapacitating shivering may begin immediately, and you may slip into hypothermia in a matter of minutes.

The moment your body begins to lose heat faster than it can produce it, you are undergoing "exposure". Exposure drains your energy reserves; the only way to reduce or stop the drain is to reduce the degree of exposure. If exposure continues until your energy reserves are exhausted, your temperature will slowly drop to a level incompatible with life. As body temperature drops, judgment and reasoning are impaired. You may not even be aware anything is happening to you.

The best way to avoid hypothermia is to stay warm and dry. When clothes get wet, some lose a great deal of their ability to insulate. Cottons, polyesters, and down lose almost all their insulating value when wet, whereas wool retains about 60% of its insulating value. Minimize heat loss by wearing breathable garments close to your body, outer garments which are windproof and trap warm air between layers of fibers or air cells, mittens and hat to decrease heat loss, and water-repellent outer clothing when it's raining. You can also optimize heat gain by keeping your calorie intake high—this enables you to generate heat through muscular activity and to shiver without rapid exhaustion. Put on rain gear before you get wet. Put on wool clothes before you start shivering. Beware of the wind; a slight breeze carries heat away from bare skin much faster than still air. Wind drives cold air under and through clothing and refrigerates wet clothes by evaporating moisture from the surface.

If you cannot stay dry and warm under existing weather conditions, get out of the wind and rain. Fix a hot drink. Build a fire, if necessary, to get warm. Concentrate on making your camp or bivouac as secure and comfortable as possible. Never ignore persistent or violent shivering; it is a clear sign that you are on the verge of hypothermia. Make camp while you still have a reserve of energy, allowing for the fact that exposure has greatly reduced your normal endurance.

Think hypothermia. Watch yourself and others for these symptoms:

1. Uncontrollable fits of shivering.
2. Vague, slow, slurred speech.
3. Memory lapses, incoherence.
4. Immobile, fumbling hands.
5. Frequent stumbling, lurching gait.
6. Drowsiness.
7. Apparent exhaustion, inability to get up after a rest.

The hypothermic person may deny he or she is in trouble. Believe the symptoms, not the person. Even mild symptoms demand the following immediate, even drastic treatment:

1. Get the person out of wind and rain.

2. Strip off all wet clothes

3. If the person is only mildly hypothermic:
   a) Give them warm drinks, preferably sweet (no alcohol). Never give food or liquid to an unconscious person.
   b) Get them into dry clothes and a warm sleeping bag.
   c) If necessary, use warm rocks or canteens as "hot water bottles."

4. If the person is semi-conscious or worse:
   a) Try to keep them awake.
   b) Put them in a sleeping bag with another person (both stripped). If you have a double bag, put the hypothermic person between two warmth donors. Skin-to-skin contact is the most effective treatment.

5. Build a fire to warm the camp.

Remember, this is a life or death situation. Hypothermia may be a new word to you, but it is the Number One killer of outdoor recreationists. Hypothermia is caused by exposure to cold and aggravated by wet, wind, and exhaustion. Hypothermia is the rapid and progressive mental and physical collapse accompanying the chilling of the body's inner core. THINK HYPOTHERMIA!

Frostbite: Frostbite is actual freezing of body tissue due to cold and impaired blood flow to the frozen part. This painful and serious condition is often found along with hypothermia because the body, in an attempt to keep its core temperature up, cuts down the blood supply to the extremities. The fingers, toes, ear lobes, nose, and cheeks — where adequate protection is hardest to maintain — are the most vulnerable. Frostbite may begin upon exposure of the skin to cold wind, especially if the skin or clothing is wet. For this reason it is important to keep the skin protected against cold winds and to keep clothing dry. Be sure that the circulation in your feet is not restricted by too-tight lacing of boots or crampons or by too many pairs of socks. Overexposure of the face and neck to cold can cause reflex loss of blood supply to the hands and feet. Fatigue and inadequate calorie and fluid intake also contribute to frostbite.

Early detection of freezing can prevent permanent damage and possible loss of tissue. Feelings of coldness and pain, followed by loss of sensation, are warnings of impending freezing.

First-degree frostbite occurs when the top layers of the skin freeze. The skin becomes white and frosty, but will still feel soft when pressed. At this stage you can warm the affected part by covering it with clothing and/or placing it on your own or a companion's warm and unexposed skin. If the parts affected are the feet, and they are still soft, the person can walk on them after the feet have been warmed up.

Second-degree frostbite is when all layers of the skin have become frozen, but underlying tissues still feel soft and have not become frozen. In second-degree frostbite, blisters form when the skin thaws. Treat possible second-degree frostbite the same way as first degree. However, if warm water is readily available (100 to 108 degrees F), immerse the part in it. Do not rub with snow or apply any pressure to warm the flesh, as this will increase damage to the tissues.

With **third-degree frostbite,** the part is marble-white, firm and board-like. Treatment should begin as soon as possible and be performed with the utmost gentleness. Again, do not apply any pressure or rub the part. Ideally, the whole part should be immersed in warm water (as above) until completely thawed and soft. After thawing, the part should be kept scrupulously clean, free of any overlying pressure from boots, blankets, sleeping bag, etc. Unfortunately, it is not always possible to provide this care in the field. If remote from optimal first aid, parts other than feet can be thawed by body contact. If the person must walk, do not thaw the feet, but hike out as quickly as possible. Once the feet have thawed, the person cannot walk because severe maceration of the injured tissue may result.

Prevention is the only real cure for frostbite.

Altitude Illnesses

Altitude Sickness: Altitude sickness is no fun, but it's usually not life-threatening and is over with soon, if you just take it easy. People who are not adapted to higher altitudes often experience "mountain sickness" if they try to do too much too soon after arriving at an altitude of something over 5,000 feet. The reason for this is that as the altitude increases, the amount of available oxygen decreases. Because the same amount of oxygen is required to produce energy at a higher elevation as is required at sea level, the body adjusts by increasing the rate and depth of breathing, thus decreasing the amount of work done per unit of time. If you try to do too much work per unit of time, the oxygen delivery systems (lungs, heart, and red blood cells) and waste product removal systems cannot keep up. As a result, you get out of breath and lose muscle power as you become oxygen deficient; lactic acid also builds up in the muscle cells and blood stream, causing acidosis. In acidosis, your body fluids become more acid than they should be, which upsets your normal metabolic processes and can cause nausea, headache, muscle cramps, vomiting, and a feeling of exhaustion.

The combination of oxygen deficiency and acidosis causes some of the potassium in the body cells to be replaced by sodium. This results in a shift of water into the cells, which causes them to swell and function poorly. Fortunately for most unknowing hikers and climbers who overexert in the mountains, the buildup of lactic acid is nearly balanced out by the alkalinity of forced deep breathing necessary for hill climbing. However, overexertion not only causes potassium depletion but also sodium, calcium, and magnesium depletion. These minerals are used in muscle contraction and are lost in sweat and urine. Such depletion can result in muscle weakness and cramping.

You can prevent or minimize altitude sickness, though, if you condition your body in progressive stages before a trip. While on the trip, maintain a slow, steady pace, one not causing gasping or painful heart-pounding. Eat carbohydrate-rich, easily-digested foods and drink more water than you think you need. Don't wait until you are thirsty to drink! (A drop in blood volume can cause shock, a marked increase in potassium loss through the kidneys, and a decrease in your ability to do muscular work.)

Also, keep in mind that the following conditions can influence how well and how quickly you will adjust to being physically active at altitudes over 5,000 feet:

1. Age, physical fitness, general health
2. Oxygen-carrying capacity of your blood (hemoglobin level)
3. Heart and lung capacity (do you smoke, have asthma or emphysema?)

4. Weight (are you overweight or underweight?)
5. Pace maintained
6. Kinds and amounts (calories) of food eaten
7. Amount of water consumed

Briefly, the major symptoms of altitude sickness are:

1. Loss of appetite, nausea, vomiting
2. Dull or pounding headache, faintness, unconsciousness
3. Listlessness, fatigue, drowsiness
4. Rapid pulse (over 100 while resting) and shortness of breath
5. Temporary visual loss
6. Nosebleeds and capillary bleeding in whites of eyes
7. Mental confusion and irritability
8. Insomnia

If you or any member of your group should suffer from severe altitude sickness, going to a lower altitude will help relieve the condition by supplying more oxygen. For mild altitude sickness, however, it is not necessary to go to a lower altitude if the affected person is allowed to rest (perhaps overnight), drink plenty of fluids, and eat carbohydrate-rich foods containing salt as soon as they feel hungry. When the person begins hiking again, they should take it easy, rest frequently, and be sure to drink and eat enough. Sometimes a buffered multimineral tablet taken with plenty of water relieves the symptoms of altitude sickness dramatically in a short time.

Cerebral Edema: This condition is fairly rare (luckily) and consists of a violent headache caused by fluids accumulating in the brain. The person with this condition may become incoherent, fall into a stupor, and eventually into a coma, which can be followed by death if they aren't quickly taken to a lower altitude.

High Altitude Pulmonary Edema: This condition results from an accumulation of fluid in the lungs and usually occurs at altitudes over 8,000 feet; it is not infectious. The symptoms are breathlessness, loose cough, wheezing, and rapid respiration. The breathing eventually becomes irregular and sounds bubbly, as if the person were breathing through liquid. Pulse and temperature are often elevated. The only known effective treatment is getting the person to a lower altitude or administering oxygen at the first sign of difficulty.

A person afflicted with pulmonary edema may say that their lungs feel tight, that they can't get their breath or can only breathe when sitting up. Eventually the person's lungs fill up with body fluids and their oxygen level gets so low that they fall into a stupor or coma. In any case, try to keep the person awake, have them sit up, make sure they drink plenty of liquid, and move them to a lower altitude as soon as possible.

Miscellaneous Minor Miseries

Blisters: See Section 3.3.

Headaches: These miseries have innumerable causes, many still unknown. If you often suffer from headaches, you will already understand some of the conditions which give rise to them. But remember that some causes, such as sinus infection, inadequate sleep, and indigestion, are aggravated by altitude. In the healthy individual, headaches at altitude are often either

— a dull pain in the whole head, possibly caused by dehydration, mild altitude sickness, and/or constipation (sometimes accompanied by nausea)

or

— pain in or around the eyes resulting from eyestrain or glare.

The latter type of headache can usually be prevented or cured by wearing dark glasses. In winter this kind of headache may signal the beginning of snowblindness. If the pain is very bothersome, rest the eyes (close or cover them) and apply cold compresses.

Muscle Cramps and Fatigue: These discomforts are a common problem among backpackers, hikers, and climbers. To help avoid fatigue, get a good night's sleep before each hike or climb and eat an easily digested, high-carbohydrate breakfast. Start out slowly; as you warm up, increase the pace to one you can hold all day. Rest stops should be short (two to seven minutes) to prevent stiffening up or cooling down. Meal stops should be considerably longer, allowing at least 30 minutes after meals before hiking and more than 30 minutes if the meal was substantial and the hiking ahead is strenuous. Snacks can be munched throughout the day while on the trail. Muscle cramps can be caused by poor physical condition and/or deficiencies of sodium, potassium, calcium and magnesium. Buffered multimineral salts help relieve cramping for some; be sure to take each with at least 10 ounces of water and perhaps a cookie or some trail mix. Once you've adapted to the altitude and exercise you'll probably have no need for these tablets. Many people never use them and get along just fine; others find them a great help.

Nausea: Like headaches, nausea has many causes; only the three most common causes of "mountain" nausea are included here.

1. **Altitude.** Because most of us live at sea level, our body metabolism is adjusted to sea level conditions. At higher elevations where there is less oxygen in the air, some people become nauseated. If this happens to you, stop, sit down, and rest; over-ventilate to increase blood alkalinity and counteract lactic acid buildup from exertion. When starting again, go at a slower pace. If this does not help, and

you do not feel considerably better in 24 hours, return to a lower altitude. You can usually avoid this condition by not attempting to gain too much altitude the first couple of days out, especially if you go from sea level to a trailhead above 5,000 feet and begin hiking or climbing up almost immediately. An overnight at the trailhead before beginning the trip is a big help.

2. **Constipation or Diarrhea.** The difference in your daily routine while on a trip may cause constipation or diarrhea, which may result in some nausea. For relief, keep your fluid and bulk intake up and pay attention to elimination. NOTE: if there is pain in the lower abdomen—either on the right or left side—along with nausea and vomiting of short duration, consider the possibility of appendicitis (see Section 9.3 for more information).

3. **Hunger or Digestive Upset.** When combined with heavy exercise and altitude, nausea may also be caused by hurried eating, eating too much protein and/or fat just before hiking or climbing, or insufficient food or water.

Dehydration: Your body's lack of water can catch you unawares because it takes a while—sometimes several hours—for your thirst to catch up with your body's needs. The first warning of serious dehydration is dark yellow urine. If you notice your urine darkening, or if you rarely have to answer the call of nature, increase your liquid intake immediately. Always carry plenty of water and drink it frequently while hiking. Loss of about 1½ quarts of water reduces your efficiency about 25% and can predispose you to altitude sickness, or at least a little nausea and a headache. Perspiration rate while hiking and climbing in hot conditions can be as high as two quarts per hour. Drink up!

9.5 Harmful or Annoying Plants and Animals

Black Widow Spiders

These poisonous spiders are most often found in old buildings, under rocks, in woodpiles, in hollow logs, and at the edges of fenced fields; their web is irregular. The female's round, shiny, glossy, black body with the red hourglass on the underside is easy to recognize. The male is smaller, thinner, and has white lines on his sides. The body (not counting the legs) is ¼ to ²/₅ inch long. The venom is a nerve poison and can produce a severe reaction, or even cause death, in some people. Others have a milder reaction, perhaps no more than swelling or redness at the bite; others have abdominal cramps or some degree of temporary paralysis. There is danger of death for about 5% of those bitten; most fatalities occur in the very young or the very old. However, this spider is not aggressive and usually tries to escape rather than attack. It can only bite through soft skin. If bitten, get medical help as soon as possible; in the meantime, apply cold to the bite in order to slow down spread of the venom.

Cactus

Many cacti have a great deal of natural protection — protection which can cause you painful injury if you are not careful. Many hikers swear that the ubiquitous cholla ("choy-a") cactus jumps out at them; one variety is even called "jumping cholla." If you brush against a cactus, a small branch (if it is cholla) or several spines may attach to your skin or clothes. Use a fork or comb to flick the branch or spines off; don't try to use your bare hands. After flicking it off, remove any remaining spines with needle-nose pliers or tweezers. Beware the cactus!

Mosquitoes

For the most part, mosquitoes are just annoying. In California coastal and mountain areas, where there are many breeding places, hikers usually practice mosquito control by means of netted tents and repellents. The most effective repellents contain N, N, diethyl-meta-toluamide. When the mosquitoes are particularly bad, it helps to pitch your camp in a windy area away from water. One mosquito, *Culex tarsalis*, is a carrier of encephalitis in California. It breeds in sunlit pools and is found at elevations up to a little over 7000 feet.

Poison Oak

This oak look-alike is actually not related to the oak at all, but to the eastern poison ivy. Unfortunately for the 50% of the population who are sensitive to its irritating oil, this is one of the West's most widespread shrubs, and is found at elevations up to 6000 feet. Learn to identify it so you can avoid it. Some poison oak climbs like a vine, some forms bushes; all have clusters of three leaves which grow out at different points along the plant's stem. That is, the clusters are "alternate" rather than "opposite." The plant seems to have more irritating oils in spring, though you can certainly pick it up on your skin and clothes even in fall and winter. In fall the bushes are easily recognized by their bright red foliage. The smoke from burning poison oak plants also carries the oils, so stay upwind of any fires in poison oak areas.

If you do come in contact with poison oak, and are sensitive to the oils, you will know it within a few hours. Your skin will itch, redden, and become bumpy or blistery. The irritation often spreads to other areas if you are not careful to wash your skin and clothes thoroughly with strong soap and cold water. Do not use an oily soap or any kind of oily cream, as these will only spread the irritating oils. Sometimes, if you know you have been exposed, you can minimize or head off the rash by immediately washing as above. Once you have the itchy rash, you can control the itching somewhat with various preparations: a wet paste of sodium bicarbonate (baking soda), cold compresses soaked with boric acid solution (one teaspoon to one quart of water) or strong tea, and/or "Rhulitol" or "Cortaid" — non-prescription items which are among the most effective of the over-the-counter lot.

Remember — "Leaves of three, let it be."

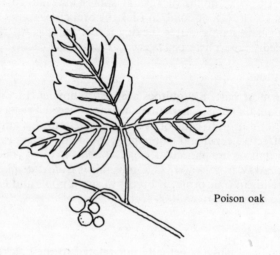

Poison oak

22. Poison Oak

Rabid Rodents, et al.

Any bite by an animal, wild or domestic, can be dangerous. One danger, tetanus, is easily averted by having an immunization injection and then a booster every several years. Anyone who hikes should keep their tetanus booster up to date. Infection can usually be prevented by keeping any bite or wound scrupulously clean; if this does not suffice, antibiotics can be used.

One of the dangers most to be feared from any animal bite is rabies: this disease is almost always fatal once it is allowed to develop. Unlike tetanus, you cannot be immunized against rabies before the fact. There is, however, a treatment which, if instituted within a few days of the bite, can stop rabies from developing in humans. This treatment, unfortunately, is far from pleasant.

If you are bitten by any animal which acts strangely (e.g., is too "friendly," too aggressive, acts "dopey," seems uncoordinated), try to capture and kill the animal and bring its body, or at least its head, to a laboratory which can perform the proper analysis to discover whether the animal was rabid. Do this immediately! Do not continue your trip! If you do not, you may have to undergo the unpleasant treatment mentioned above.

You will have less chance of being bitten if you do not feed, pet, or in any way encourage the animals you meet with in the wilderness. Ground squirrels, chipmunts, bats, foxes, coyotes, raccoons, skunks, and marmots are occasionally rabid: give them a wide berth.

Rattlesnakes

In California the only poisonous snake is the Western Rattler. The markings of these vary, but all have diamond-shaped heads and rattles on the end of their tail. Not all rattlers give warning by buzzing their rattles; in some areas of California so many of the "noisy" rattlers have been killed that the ones remaining are mostly "silent." Not many rattlers are found above 7000 feet, so the chance of coming across one in the Sierra is small. However, it's always a good idea to watch where you are putting your hands, feet, and posterior. Try not to put your hands on rock ledges you cannot see; look at the ground on the other side of a log before jumping over or putting your foot down. Check the shady areas under bushes at the side of the trail ahead as you hike.

Because rattlesnakes, like other cold-blooded creatures, have no temperature-regulating mechanisms, they maintain a comfortable body temperature by moving between warm and cool areas. In hot weather they usually stay in rock crevices or burrows during the day and come out at night to hunt small rodents and lie about on warm rocks and sand. In cool weather they stay in crevices and burrows during the night and come out during the warmer days. Unlike some other snakes, rattlers move slowly and often spend hours just lying in one place. When disturbed, they may buzz their rattles and coil to strike. When striking they can go no further than about half their body length and can rise only about one foot off the ground. Rattlers cannot "jump."

For information on what to do if someone is bitten by a rattler, see Section 9.3

Scorpions, Centipedes, and Tarantulas

The scorpion, an eight-legged relative of the spider, is mostly found at lower elevations in southern California, though a few have been found in Oregon and Montana. Two species found in Arizona have a sting which can be fatal, but the ones in southern California are usually only mildly venomous. In any desert region it is a good idea to shake out your boots and clothes in the morning and to be careful when digging in sand or moving rocks and logs. Scorpions sting with their tail, which they carry high and arched over their back; their venom attacks the nerves. If you are stung, cold packs can help the pain and slow the spread of venom.

Centipedes, like scorpions, live under rocks and logs. They too can inflict a painful sting. Millipedes are harmless look-alikes of centipedes. You can tell the difference by noting that the millipede's body is cylindrical and has two pairs of legs growing from each body joint, while the centipedes have a flat body and only one pair of legs at each joint.

Tarantulas are hard to mistake—they are large, furry spiders (three to four inches, including legs) which only move about in the open at night. During the day they are found under rocks and logs. Their bite is painful but not dangerous; infection is the only thing to be wary of. They are found up to about 7000 feet.

Ticks and Fleas

In California, ticks are found in almost all brushy regions and in some forested areas; they become less numerous the higher you go. Ticks are about ¼ inch long, with an oval, flat, brown or grey body; they are blood suckers which utilize a variety of hosts—some of which may be carriers of Rocky Mountain Spotted Fever. Fortunately, this serious disease can now be more or less successfully treated with antibiotics.

You and other warm-blooded creatures pick up ticks by brushing against bushes. Once they are on your clothes, they move around until they find some bare skin, where they painlessly attach themselves. Using repellents at wrist, neck, ankles, and waist can help discourage them. In heavily infested areas, wear long sleeves and long pants, button up your collar, and wear gaiters. It's also a help to strip off each night and examine yourself and others for these unwelcome hangers-on.

Unfortunately, ticks are hard to get rid of once they have become attached to you. Here are a few methods of tick removal some hikers have found effective: drench tick with repellent or solvent (alcohol, white gas); cut off the tick's air supply by putting grease (vaseline, butter) around it; apply heat to its backside, being careful not to burn yourself; use tweezers or needle-nose pliers to gently pull the tick out while grasping it as close to its head as possible and not crushing it (you don't want to force its stomach contents into your bloodstream). Remove any head and mouth parts left behind and wash the area thoroughly with soap and water; apply antiseptic.

Fleas are also bloodsuckers. In California, the ground squirrel flea and the chipmunk flea can both transmit plague to humans from infected wild rodents. The ground squirrel flea is found up to about 6000 feet and the chipmunk flea at higher elevations. You can reduce your chances of being bitten by these fleas by staying away from injured or ill wild animals and by not handling, feeding, or encouraging any animals you may meet with.

Yellowjackets, Bees, and Wasps

Most of us have no reaction to the sting of a yellowjacket, bee, or wasp other than a painful, itching bump. However, some people are violently allergic to the venom of these insects. If you are one of these allergic people, be sure to carry with you at all times whatever medications you need to counteract your reaction if you are stung when hiking or camping. Your companions will be unable to help you unless you take this precaution.

An allergic reaction to these stings is quite recognizable: the person will first appear to be in shock, with cool, moist skin, and feelings of faintness and/or dizziness. If the reaction is moderate, it may resemble an acute attack of hay fever and can be somewhat relieved by antihistamines; if the reaction is severe, the nose and throat may swell up so that the person cannot breath. At this point, an injection of adrenalin is often needed (this is why the person who knows they are allergic should always be prepared; adrenaline and a syringe are not regular parts of most hikers' first aid kits).

When stung by a bee, scrape the stinger off with a comb or knife blade to avoid injecting yourself with more poison from the venom sacs, which are attached to the stinger.

In California, the yellowjacket is the most common and annoying nuisance (with the possible exception of the spring mosquito): it is found at elevations up to about 8000 feet. Although yellowjackets may seem aggressive, in reality they are only looking for bits of food—and wherever you, the hiker, are there also is food. The one time when they will pursue you, though, is when you disturb their nest. Many nests are at ground level, so beware of hitting the bushes with your walking stick or poking it into holes in the ground. Yellowjackets retain their stinger and can sting you many times, unlike bees which can only get you once. Cold compresses, a paste of bicarbonate of soda, and/or "sting-kill" swabs (available at the drugstore) can help ease your misery after such an attack.

9.6 Good Advice

You may have been tempted to skip over these sections on first aid because you see nothing in them that seems of direct use in hiking or climbing. However, a person who plans to take up mountaineering seriously must be prepared to handle all of the emergency treatments outlined here. You may seldom or never be called upon to use this knowledge, but if you are not ready and competent when the need does arise, you will fail in your responsibility to your mountaineering companions. If you are unprepared, you may cause or be unable to prevent permanent injury to another person. This is a memory that is hard to live with.

Take a first aid course offered by the Red Cross; it will give much more information than the very condensed outline in this chapter. Such courses also give you practical experience and make you aware of those actions which can cause more harm.

Chapter 10
Search & Rescue

The difficulties associated with rescue operations make it important that you leave the details of your intended trip with family, friends, and/or park and forest officials. Also, if possible, every party entering the wilderness should consist of a minimum of three people. If a member of a two-person team is injured, he or she may have to be left alone for an extended time and more serious problems may arise in the rescue. Solo rock climbing is foolhardy.

This chapter is, of course, only a sketch of how to deal with wilderness situations requiring search and rescue. It is intended to alert you to some of the problems you may encounter.

10.1 On Being Lost

The old warning on railroad crossings told you to stop, look, and listen. In the wilderness, the same applies if you find that you don't know quite where you are. If you have been separated from the rest of your group for only a short time you may still be able to hear them; if not, try to follow in the last known direction. Stop often to call, then listen for a reply. Using a whistle is the least tiring method of generating your own noise. If you can't locate your group, but still feel lost, stop and think again. Consider the following — can you find your own way out by: (1) retracing your steps to the last place where you knew where you were? (2) climbing high enough to get your bearings? or (3) using map and compass to find your location on the map and then proceeding toward the previously agreed on objective (if it does not offer major technical difficulties)? Can you make it before dark?

133

If retracing your own steps is necessary, look for boot imprints, bent grass, etc. Mark your moves with an occasional duck so you will be able to return to the spot. If you are unable to determine your location on the map, if you have no map, or if you are injured, remain where you are. When you are missed, the others will look for you. The spot where they last saw you is the place where they will probably start their search. Conserve your energy, food, water, and strength. If you are in normal good health, you have ample reserve for nearly 48 hours of activity at normal output, even without food, unless the weather is very hot or cold. Do not start complicated exploratory trips within two hours of darkness if you do not have your pack.

If you must wait to be found, select a spot where you can be found easily and where you can wait in relative comfort. High open ground with shelter in nearby rocks or trees is best. Build a fire, if it is safe to do so, for warmth and/or signal. Mark your area to help searchers: use letters trampled in the snow, an arrangement of rocks, articles of bright or light-colored clothing spread out, or put your pack in a prominent place. Ration your food and water to last through the expected stay. When help is near, aid searchers with audible signals such as calls, whistles, or beating on a hollow log; a series of three signals means help is needed. If you have to be out all night, look in the darkness for campfires in the surrounding area and headlights on nearby roads; do not try to reach them at night, but mark their direction.

If you can't find your way out in cold weather, don't continue on until you become exhausted. Energy is heat; conserve it. Take shelter. Get out of the wind behind rocks or trees, set up a tent or tarp or make a snow cave. Keep warm. Protect your extremities: your hands, feet, ears, and head. Get off the snow if possible; if not, insulate yourself from it with a foam pad, branches, climbing rope, or pack. Put on dry socks and mittens. Sit on your feet or put them near the body of a companion to prevent freezing. Put your hands between your legs or under your armpits. Use a hand warmer. Build a fire. Eat foods high in energy—sweets, starches, fats. Make a hot drink. Don't eat snow; melt it before drinking. Unless movement is necessary to keep hands and feet from freezing, rest or sleep. Put on all available clothing. Get into a sleeping bag. Wrap yourself in a survival blanket (mylar). Do whatever is possible to mark your location so that searches can find you.

If you can't find your way out in hot weather, keep cool. Stop and think; analyze your situation. Heat emergencies usually result from car failure in desert terrain. How far is it to help? To water? How hot is it? In extreme heat stay in the shade (under the car if necessary). Scrape away the top layer of sand to the cooler layer underneath. Ration your water. Set up a desert distillery (see Section 14.3 for details). If you must travel, do so only in the cooler hours of the day or night. Avoid becoming exhausted or overheated. Take it easy — you'll make it. (See Section 10.6 on "Your Car Can Save Your Life.")

If, under any circumstances, you decide to attempt hiking out, leave a note in a visible place stating your direction of travel, time, name/s, etc. In general, try to follow water courses, as they lead to lower levels. It may be necessary to go around ravines or waterfalls. If the water course is very rough, follow an adjacent ridge. Visibility is better from a ridge.

Your "Ten Essentials" include both a compass and map of the area. With these you can generally find your approximate location by the methods described in Chapter 4 ("Hiking Navigation") and decide on the route best suited for walking out. Take frequent compass bearings of landmarks while walking. If you come out on your own, notify the nearest ranger so that any search for you may be discontinued.

If you expect to be the object of a search and walking out on your own is not possible, there is even more reason to conserve strength. Consider the best ways you can give the emergency signals under existing conditions and make the necessary preparations. Prepare a fire or smoke signal to get the attention of approaching airplanes or helicopters. Mirrors may also be used for signaling. When attention is obtained, indicate your distress by the standard signals as shown in Section 10.5

If through carelessness or accident you do not have a map or compass and you cannot rely on dead reckoning, you will want to find the direction to the nearest trail or settlement. Hike to the nearest raised point that affords a clear view at least in some directions, but preferably in many. Search the horizon for any indications of civilization. If you have binoculars, you may spot water or fire towers, windmills, or straight lines indicating highway banks. At night you may see automobile headlights flash up and disappear on a far off highway. If all these possibilities fail and you do not expect someone to search for you, then you will have to choose a direction arbitrarily.

It is important that you stick to your chosen route either by map, by sighting, or intuition, for seldom do people who are lost find their way out by walking aimlessly or in circles. To follow the general direction you have established without a compass, use some of the suggestions in Section 4.4 on "Compass Substitutes" to find the north/south/east/west directions. In the desert, an additional but less accurate indicator is that sand dunes run in the direction of the prevailing wind, which is northwest to southeast in the western United States. After establishing a fixed direction, maintain it.

None of these procedures is a substitute for being properly prepared with both equipment and knowledge of the area. The experienced mountaineering party is alert and curious, and while it may be temporarily confused it never will actually be lost.

10.2 Bivouac

A bivouac ("biv-wak") is a camp made with little or no shelter and usually used for only a short time, perhaps overnight. When you can't get back to your base camp before dark, you can bivouac. Depending on how well you plan ahead, a bivouac can be miserable, comfortable, or even a rather pleasant adventure. The better prepared you are when day-tripping from a base camp, the easier the bivouac will be. Always carry minimum bivouac gear if you think your day hike or climb could run into difficulties. (This includes summit attempts.) Minimum bivouac gear includes the items below.

For the mountains: (1) Adequate warm clothes, preferably down or polyester batt jacket, wool pants, mittens, and wool hat. (2) A closed-cell foam pad (e.g., Ensolite). A regular 54-inch pad ¼-inch thick is best, but some use two pieces one foot square by ⅜-inch or ½-inch thick. (3) Something that is waterproof to keep the rain or snow off—a tube tent, emergency plastic tent, plastic tarp, space blanket, waterproof bivouac sack, tent fly, or ground cloth. A bivouac sack is a surprisingly efficient "sleeping bag." (4) The Ten Essentials.

In the desert: (1) Plenty of water! (2) Wool shirt, cotton and poly long pants, and a windbreaker will usually be adequate unless the nights are still cold. (3) Closed-cell foam pad. (4) Ground cloth. (5) The Ten Essentials.

The decision to bivouac is based on your situation at the time. Do you have sufficient daylight to return to camp? Can you reach a place where it would be safe to travel at night? On warm, calm nights, you might elect to either keep traveling or to bivouac. On cold, rainy nights, you must bivouac before being overcome by exhaustion and hypothermia. What's your physical condition? A strong party might hike out; injured, sick, or tired people must bivouac. The terrain also is a factor to be considered. Above timberline, travel may be difficult and steep slopes almost impossible.

Be conservative in your decision to bivouac. If it looks like you won't make it back to camp because of any of the above reasons, make the decision and prepare your bivouac. Leave at least one hour of daylight to make camp and prepare and eat dinner.

Select a spot which is level, dry, and sheltered as much as possible from the weather. If you have a tube tent or similar shelter, you can select a relatively open site. If you must bivouac in just your clothes, burrow into the densest underbrush or thicket you can. Or make a big pile of leaves and get under it. Use whatever native insulation you can find. If you are not alone, sleep close to your companion/s.

If you're cold, flex your muscles until you begin to breathe heavily. Wiggle your toes. Don't swing your arms and legs, as this tends to force out the warm air around your body.

If you are uncomfortable and can't sleep, try lighting a fire. This will keep you warm for a while, but requires constant tending. Two parallel fires with you in the middle work if there is no wind, though this requires twice as much wood. Better to sit with your back against a vertical rock with the fire in front, reflecting off the rock. Eating a good hot meal before you turn in will help you sleep and will also keep you warm.

Psychological tricks can help pass the night. Note the stars' positions and estimate where they'll be at dawn. Count to yourself. Think of friends, job, and how lucky you are to be out in the mountains or desert. Think of all the songs you know. Before you know it the first grey light will appear and your bivouac will be over.

10.3 Search

What to Do If a Person Is Missing

If you are the leader, you are responsible for the safety of the group. You must not abandon any member. If an accident occurs or someone is lost, all else stops until the person is treated or evacuated or found. It is the leader's responsibility to account for all people on the trip.

When an emergency occurs, it is sometimes possible to get help from specially trained search and rescue personnel. In the U.S. this help is available through the law enforcement agency for the particular area. Generally, this means the sheriff, state park ranger, national park ranger, city police, or state police.

Rescue units are professionally trained volunteer teams who are equipped for mountain and desert search and rescue. They may be called by any responsible law enforcement agency to conduct a rescue operation. In many counties the sheriff's department is not geared for search and rescue operations, so they have a working agreement with local or regional rescue teams. In some cases the teams are deputized.

If a person is missing, first analyze the situation. How long has the person been missing? How are the weather and the terrain? Conduct a quick search of the area, making sure at least two people stick *together* while searching.

Night searches can be risky, especially if the night is cold and overcast. Every person searching at night must have a flashlight, and preferably a headlamp. Use voice signals to keep in contact. Calling or whistling from a high point is sometimes helpful.

If a few hours have passed without the person being found, send two people to get help. They should be given as much information as possible, including the name and description of the missing person, his/her physical condition, the area they were last seen in, where they were headed, and who to see at your base camp for more information.

The reporting party should contact the nearest official agency and give the required information and the telephone number or location where they can be reached. If possible, they should go to the sheriff's office or ranger station. Because the reporting party may then have to turn around and hike back to the scene, the people chosen to go for help should be in good physical condition.

While waiting for the search team you can send parties down trails or roads where the person might come out. This may save the search team time, if done early. Circle footprints of the missing person, if there are any, and keep people away from the area where they were last seen. Search teams use bloodhounds and trackers and it is less confusing for them if the area is kept clear.

If necessary, when the rescue team arrives, obtain an article of the missing person's clothing for the bloodhounds. Underclothing or socks which have been worn next to the skin are best. Do not touch the clothing; handle with a stick and put in a plastic or paper bag.

Keep the rest of the party in control, either by having them remain at base camp or assigning them jobs.

10.4 Rescue

Evacuating an Injured Person Without Outside Help

When an accident occurs, the first thing to do is give first aid. Often the injured person needs to be treated for severe bleeding and shock. See Section 9.3 for instructions on how to stop bleeding, restore breathing, restore heartbeat, and treat for shock. Do not move a person injured in a fall unless absolutely necessary to save his/her life.

Evacuating an Injured Person Without Outside Help

A major problem in evacuating an injured person is that of organization. If the party is sufficiently strong or if other groups are helping, evacuation can be attempted without outside assistance. If this is done, careful planning is important. The strength of the injured person, the weather, and other pertinent conditions must be considered in choosing the route to be taken and in making other necessary decisions.

Improvisation is often necessary for successful handling of an emergency evacuation. If it is necessary to transport the injured person on an improvised stretcher, it must be fabricated from equipment at hand. Climbing ropes, pack frames, skis, ice axes, and branches can be used as stretcher materials. When any combination of the above is padded with a sleeping bag, the result is a strong, comfortable carrier. Regardless of whether you use an improvised stretcher or a regular litter (which an outside party would bring), it is a good idea to tie the injured person securely into the unit to prevent further injury.

What to Do If Outside Help Is Required

If help is required, make a list of the following to send with the people going out for help.

— time and place of accident, nature of injury, condition of injured person

— name, address, and phone number of injured person

— number of people in assistance and their names

— amount of food and equipment at the scene

— terrain over which evacuation must take place

— special equipment or supplies necessary for rescue

— details for notifying families of members in group

Whenever possible, send two people out for help and always try to leave someone with the injured person. If the group is so small that only one person can be spared to go for help, they should not travel by night, except under ideal conditions. Signals to be used in case of an overflight in order to indicate any changes in the situation should be agreed upon with the messengers before they leave. The messengers should have change for a pay telephone.

The people going for help should mark their route on the way out so that they will be able to direct help to the injured person. When they reach the nearest telephone, they should notify the County Sheriff and the District Ranger, giving them the information above, in addition to the distance by road, trail, or cross country, and the probable time needed to reach the injured person. They should stay on the phone until assured by responsible rescue personnel that help is on the way. If possible, they should wait for the rescue party and guide them to the scene. Once a rescue message has been delivered, preparations for the use of pack animals or air rescue facilities are best left to local authorities.

Evacuation with Outside Help

The people remaining with the injured person have the task of preparing for evacuation while making the person as comfortable as circumstances permit. Of prime importance is marking the location so that is may easily be found by the rescue party.

When help arrives, explain the circumstances and follow the directions of the rescue operation leader. You may want to remain with the injured person; this is usually allowed. Check to assure yourself that the rescue team is treating the injured person properly. Give the operation leader your name and address so they can contact you for the accident report.

10.5 Using Distress Signals

Mountaineering clubs in the U.S. have adopted the old woodman's signal of distress for indicating that help is needed. Do not use this signal unless you or your party are in urgent need of help. The signal consists of three signs, audible or visible, repeated at intervals. Acknowledgment is by two signs, preferably of similar nature.

There is also an international distress signal, used in Europe, Canada, and Mexico. It consists of six signals of any type, audible or visible, given within one minute and repeated at one-minute intervals. The recognition is three signals within one minute, also repeated after one-minute intervals. Remember your distance from the observer. Consider also that under certain conditions — such as a nearby waterfall or heavy wind — audible signs will be insufficient. A large makeshift flag with much color contrast or smoke signals are usually easily seen.

Ground to Air Signals

The U.S. Coast Guard has adopted a set of 5 international "ground-to-air" visual signals to be used in communicating with an overflight. Several of these signals are important to a land party and are reproduced below. Although they are simple, they are easily forgotten if you don't use them often. Here are the signals you should use:

To produce the ground signals, prepare the area to be used ahead of time by clearing it of other objects. Prepare equipment to be used. Color contrast between signs and background is important. The size of the signs should be six to eight feet: two sleeping bags, liners, air mattresses, ground sheets, even people, may be used. You may give more than one signal, in which case preparation for a quick change should be considered.

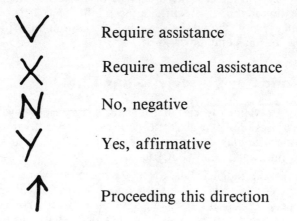

V — Require assistance

X — Require medical assistance

N — No, negative

Y — Yes, affirmative

↑ — Proceeding this direction

Helicopters may communicate with a ground party by loudspeakers or by blackboards on which words are written. Both airplanes and helicopters have a system of replying "yes" or "no", "message understood" and "message not understood":

— Dipping of wing or rotor to left and right . . . Message understood

— Steep banked close circle to left or right . . . Message not understood

— Short dippings of bow of aircraft . . . Yes, affirmative

— Short sideways skidding of craft to left and right . . . No, negative

Preparing for Air Rescue

Newer methods of rescue, such as helicopters, make possible much faster action than can be taken by a ground party. However, landing difficulties, wind, and poor visibility may prevent their use.

Airplanes require a landing strip which is fairly long, level, and free of obstructions; however, such an area is seldom available at higher altitudes or over uneven ground. Other possibilities are dropping of paramedics or materials to assist ground, search, or rescue parties.

If air rescue is a good possibility, ground personnel can be of great help by preparing for possible overflight. A blazing fire is visible from great distances. Before the first pass over the camp a smoke signal should be given to indicate the direction and intensity of the wind. Throwing water, wet logs, or green leaves on the fire will cause a mixture of steam and smoke, which will increase the fire's visibility. The smoke signals are of particular importance when cliffs or steep hills are nearby. A person in the ground party should be assigned to continuously observe the overflight for any communications.

10.6 Your Car Can Save Your Life

If you are traveling by car in isolated country and have a serious mechanical breakdown or accident, your car can be a fortress. Beneath its hood and within its steel body can be found materials for survival for yourself, your family, and your friends.

The average car radiator holds 6 to 21 quarts of water. If not contaminated by anti-freeze or some other additive, that is enough water to last four people for four days. Hubcaps cleaned with sand can pinch-hit for cups and signal mirrors. Your horn can alert rescuers as far as a mile downwind. Under the hood are four quarts of oil. A quart of oil, burned in a hubcup in the still air of the morning, spews a signal of smoke visible for miles. Lube oil can be used as a salve to protect your skin from the sun and wind. Windshield washer tubing can be an effective tourniquet. Door panels can become ground blankets, insulating you from frozen, wet, or scorching ground. Domelights can be used to focus the sun's rays for fire. The glove compartment door and sun visors can also double as shovels. Seat covers, floormats, and rugs can serve as blankets and clothing. One family, when their car was broken down on a little-used fire trail, carefully removed a sealed-beam headlight, leaving it wired to the battery. By directing its beams upward in wide sweeping arcs, they drew a rescue team's attention.

Many people have warmed themselves (and stayed alive) over a tire-fire. A little gasoline ignites a tire-fire. A hose from the engine can be converted into a siphon for getting gasoline from your tank. An average tire will burn three to four hours.

Drastic, you say, to destroy your car. A highway patrolman says, "Everything you need to stay alive, except food, is found in the average car, but few motorists, when up against it, think of the car as a survival kit. The first inclination is to set out on foot for help. Too often the person is beyond help when found a few miles down the road — from heat exhaustion or from the cold."

If your car breaks down in a remote area, don't panic — stay with it. Use your imagination to make it a lifesaver.

10.7 Good Advice

Don't panic when a person is lost or injured. As you go into the wilderness, keep in mind what you will do if something serious happens. The farther into the wilderness you go, the longer it will take you to get help and the more careful everyone must be to make sure no one gets lost or injured. If you are the leader, make sure that everyone has the Ten Essentials before they go on side trips. If you have inexperienced people in your group, explain the safety "ground rules" before you start any trip.

A great deal of time and expense are involved in removing an injured person from the wilderness, particularly from the high country. Most of such effort is voluntary, so if those who have been helped will make their appreciation known, by letter and in person, their rescuers may be more ready to give the same valuable assistance when it is next needed.

Part III:
CLIMBING
AND OTHER
CHALLENGES

Tahquitz Rock, Mount San Jacinto Wilderness Area, San Bernardino National Forest

I saw no mountains in all this grand region that appeared at all inaccessible to a mountaineer. Give me a summer and a bunch of matches and a sack of meal and I will climb every mountain in the region.

— John Muir

Chapter 11
Rock Climbing

Rock climbing is but one aspect of mountaineering. It is one of the skills — along with hiking and snow and ice climbing — that enables a person to climb a mountain. It has also developed into a sport which many people enjoy for its own sake. This chapter will give you the basic technical details of this phase of mountaineering. Even a minimum of knowledge and training in rock climbing will enable you to see many obstacles as enjoyable challenges rather than as limits on your wilderness experiences.

Some mountaineers feel rock climbing is the most interesting part of mountaineering and concentrate on climbing to the exclusion of other outdoor activities. Some of these people achieve a high level of skill. If you learn and use what is in this chapter, you can qualify as a safe companion for more advanced climbers and begin to gain experience in increasingly more difficult types of climbs.

Over the years, climbing methods and equipment have become more or less standardized, making it easier to learn what one should do and to understand the reasons why a particular practice is recommended. For example, if a novice climber understands the "why" of climbing signals, he or she will learn how to use them effectively. On the other hand, climbers who learn climbing in a haphazard, random way do not understand the reasons for these signals and continue using unsafe methods.

In most instances, rock climbing does not require more than moderate strength. However, it does require a certain tolerance for high-angle exposure. Whether or not you have this tolerance can be discovered only through practice. If you don't have it, you can develop it. Perseverance is often necessary, though. By far the most important requisite for rock climbing is the desire to do so. People of all ages, sizes, and sexes climb.

11.1 Climbing Classifications and Definitions

Classifications

Several different systems of climbing classifications have been standardized over the years. The one detailed here is the Yosemite Decimal System.

Class 1: Walking.

Class 2: Scrambling, occasionally using hands for balance. Good boots advisable.

Class 3: Easy climbing. Extensive use of foot and hand holds. Moderate exposure. Take a rope; some climbers may wish to be belayed.

Class 4: More difficult climbing. Holds are smaller. More exposure. Ropes, carabiners, chocks or friends, and slings necessary for safety. Use adequate belays.

Class 5: Holds smaller and climbing very exposed. Same procedures as for 4th class except that equipment is used more extensively to maintain the same margin of safety. Fifth class climbing is divided into categories 1 through 13; the higher the number, the greater the difficulty (5.1, 5.2, etc.).

Class 6: Artificial aid climbing. The climber's weight is supported by standing in stirrups that are clipped to chocks or pitons or attached to the rope. This is necessary because of the extreme steepness and smoothness of the rock.

Definitions

Below are a few short definitions of some words commonly used in climbing:

ANCHOR. A system of chocks, nuts, friends, slings, or pitons that secure the belayer and rope to the rock.

BELAYING. A system of protecting climbers by using a rope.

EXPOSURE. The combined effect of steepness and height.

PITCH. The distance climbed between belay positions; usually the length of the rope. Rock climbs are measured by the number of pitches.

RAPPEL. A method of descending on a rope.

11.2 Safety

There is no such thing as not falling when you climb, particularly in the more advanced classifications. Even if a climber does nothing to cause a fall, the chances are that sooner or later she or he will fall. Therefore, some means of protection must be used to prevent injury.

Belaying is one of these means of protection. The word "belay" is derived from a sailing term involving the large wooden pins mounted on shipboard. When a heavy sail was to be lowered, the lowering line was wrapped around the pins. The weight of the canvas was absorbed in the friction of the line around the pins. A single person could control the descent of a sail many times their own weight. The same method of handling forces is applied to climbing. When necessary, each climber is protected by being "belayed" by other members of the rope team.

When climbing, you should always be aware that rock pitches can be complicated and made more difficult by the weather. Rain or snow can make the rock slippery. Cold may necessitate wearing mittens; however, mittens make a safe grip much more difficult. Extra clothing for protection against cold makes a climber less secure in his/her moves. Weather or other disturbances may affect your night's sleep, your food intake, or may cause overexertion. If this is so, your performance and/or judgment as a climber can be impaired.

Dangers

The four main dangers to avoid in rock climbing are: falling, being hit by falling rock, being stranded, and climbing with people who don't know what they are doing.

To avoid being hit by (or hitting others with) falling rock:

— do not use routes where rockfalls are frequent

— wear a hard hat

— climb at times of minimum rock fall (for example, when there are few or no climbers above you or during the coldest times of day if melting ice will cause rock falls)

— learn to climb without dislodging rocks

— warn climbers below of falling rock

— at the cry of "Rock!" take cover and yell "Rock!" so that climbers below will be warned (if no cover is available and your head is unprotected, cover it with your hands or arms)

To avoid falling:

— climb with your eyes first; see the route and your sequence of holds to the next stopping place

— balance climb; keep the weight on your feet

— know how to use counterforce holds

— maintain three points of support on difficult rock; move only one hand or foot at a time

— use a smooth, rhythmic motion; do not lunge

— choose and test every hold carefully

— use short steps; these are safer and easier

— shuffle across narrow traverses; do not cross your legs

— wear proper footwear and have proper safety and climbing equipment

— learn your limitations and do not exceed them

To avoid being stranded:

— choose your route carefully to avoid cul-de-sacs or pitches beyond your ability

— never climb a pitch where you do not have the ability or nerve to descend if necessary

— never jump or slide down a pitch which you cannot climb back up if necessary

— while ascending, look down frequently to become familiar with the route and holds to be used in descending

— never attempt a step into a position from which you cannot move forward or back; to be caught "spread eagled" on a cliff or on knees in a cramped position is painful, tiring, embarrassing, and may even cost you your life.

— be sensible enough to turn back if the way becomes too difficult for your abilities and equipment

— carry the Ten Essentials for safety and emergencies

— be sure someone knows where you are climbing and when you expect to return

— never climb alone

To avoid climbing with people who don't know what they are doing:

— if you are a novice climber, make it your business to find out who the experienced climbers in your area are; take their advice

— do not climb with people whose attitudes toward safety practices are casual

— use your own judgment; if a practice which seems dangerous is recommended, demand to know why so that you can determine if it is safe or not.

Becoming Involved in Rock Climbing

If you want to become more involved in rock climbing, some reading will be helpful in learning the terminology and getting an idea of the techniques. However, there is no way to really learn to climb other than by climbing.

Experienced climbers recommend beginning by: (1) practicing knots and belaying until you know them thoroughly before setting out on any climb; (2) learning the basic moves so that you can start putting them together in various combinations on a wide variety of boulder problems; (3) getting a lot of bouldering practice; and (4) learning as much as possible about climbing gear and its proper use. For most people it takes many months of intensive practice to become a competent beginner who is qualified to participate in easy multi-pitch climbs. Don't be impatient; it takes time.

Be careful in your choice of climbing companions. Not everyone is adequately experienced or conscientious about safety. It is hard for a beginner to judge whether a climber is an expert or not. Climbing is a highly technical subject, and a novice climber can easily snow a non-climber with technical jargon. Most rock climbing accidents occur among the inexperienced. Keep in mind that rock climbing can be a dangerous activity if not practiced properly; it is not a sport to be taken lightly.

11.3 Equipment

Rope

The climbing rope is usually 150 ft. (45 meters) or 165 ft. (50 meters) long and has a diameter of 11mm, which provides suitable strength and handling properties. For glacier and snow travel, snow climbing, or extension of rappels, 9mm rope is sometimes used.

Modern climbing ropes are made of a nylon-like synthetic called "perlon." Perlon will stretch very little under a body-weight load, but will stretch by more than half its length to cushion a severe fall. The rope consists of an inner core and an outer sheath or mantle. The outer sheath is usually colored; different brands and models of ropes can be identified by the colors used. Twisted ropes are rarely used in modern climbing.

Ropes that are to be used on snow or ice come in waterproof versions (a wet rope is much heavier than a dry one and is much harder to handle). The problems that occur when the water in a wet rope freezes will be left to the readers' imaginations.

Proper care of climbing ropes is important. Ropes should be stored in a cool, clean, dry place and protected from oils, grease, and solvents. If a rope gets wet, dry it slowly, away from heat and out of range of sparks from camp fires. Never step on a rope—stepping on it can cause serious damage. Remember that the rope is your lifeline: treat it with respect.

Any permanent stretch resulting from loading a rope near one-third of its limit is reason to discard or destroy it. This may happen when stopping a serious fall or when you use a rope to pull a car in an emergency. Loss of resiliency makes a rope unsafe.

Inspect the rope before climbs and at regular intervals. Keep it in orderly coils for easier carrying and ready use. When the sheath of a rope become fuzzy or is torn or worn through, the rope should be discarded. A "soft" spot in the rope can indicate serious damage.

It is unwise to climb on a rope whose history is unknown to you or your partner. Do not climb with a borrowed rope and don't loan your rope to others. NEVER purchase a used rope; a brand-new climbing rope is a bargain when you balance the cost of the rope against the protection it provides. When a rope has done its duty, it deserves an honorable retirement.

24. Coiled Climbing Rope

Hammer

The climber is traditionally shown with hammer in hand, but advances in climbing technology have made this tool almost obsolete. Most climbers never use a hammer and those who do use one only do so on rare occasions. A beginner should save his/her money for other tools.

Pitons

Like the hammer, pitons are now rarely carried by climbers. There are many varieties (some of which are listed below), but the beginner can afford to ignore this item of hardware.

Angle piton: These are formed from a flat steel sheet and usually come six in a set, ranging from ½" to 1½" thick, and 4" to 6" inches long.

Ring angle piton: These are the larger units of the above class in which the eye is replaced by a ring welded in place. Useful for narrow places where carabiners cannot be inserted.

Bong-bong: These are also formed from sheet stock, with the smaller units being made from steel and the larger from dural. Used for cracks 2" to 6" wide.

Offset-eye pitons: These are steel forgings, up to 10 sizes in a set.

Vertical pitons: Steel forgings are preferred for these pitons, which are used for vertical cracks. Leg is 3" to 5" long. Place these with caution, selecting a spot where the crack is narrower above and below it.

Leeper piton: These are formed from flat sheet metal, are "Z" shaped, and come six in a set. Can be used in vertical cracks and in combination with other pitons.

Ring wafers: These are steel hand forgings having a welded ring. Can be used for narrow cracks that cannot take an angle piton.

All pitons listed above are only typical examples of some shapes and sizes available; they can be used for Class 5 and Aid climbing. There are additional pitons and other hardware which are intended for aid climbing only. Some of these are "rurps", "knife blade pitons", "cliff hangers", "long", "short", "flat", and "offset" "crack-tacks", "beat-ons", and "smashons."

Carabiners

These are oval-shaped rings with a snap gate used as connecting links between a piece of climbing hardware and the rope; they are usually forged from high strength aluminum alloy. Some carabiners have a lock sleeve for the gate so that it can't open accidentally. Other special purpose carabiners are made from alloy steel.

There are some carabiners which can be converted into rope brakes by means of a cross bar. These carabiners can easily overheat and burn or damage the rope if stopped when they are moving quickly; the necessarily tight bend can also damage the rope. Inspect your carabiners occasionally to make sure the gate closes properly. If it does not it is a sign that the carabiner has been overloaded or distorted.

Each carabiner weighs about two or three ounces and generally tests out at about 3000 lbs. A combination of a carabiner and another piece of climbing hardware such as a climbing nut, can be expected to support a 2000-pound load.

Climbing Nuts

The idea of using pieces of metal which are of an appropriate size and shape to lodge in cracks originated in Great Britain. There are many varieties of these "artificial chockstones" on the market today, some of which are only ⅛ inch by ¼ inch in cross section, while others are 6 inches or more along the major axis. Each chock is affixed to a wire or nylon loop to which a carabiner may be clipped. These devices are quicker and easier to place than pitons, although in some placements they may be dislodged by a sideways pull of the rope. Climbers carry an assortment of "nuts" and "stoppers" for use in the varied circumstances encountered. The widespread adoption of climbing nuts is responsible for the reduced use of pitons.

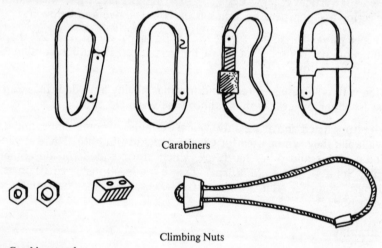

Carabiners

Climbing Nuts

25. Carabiners and Climbing Nuts

"Friends"

Climbers also use camming devices which can be inserted into parallel-sided or flaring cracks and which can resist an outward pull by exerting pressure on the sides of the crack. Although several brands are currently (1982) on the market, the "friend" is by far the most popular. This device has several advantages—for example, placing it is very straightforward, it is easier to remove than nuts or pitons, and it will sometimes work when nothing else will. It is definitely a useful supplement to other climbing tools.

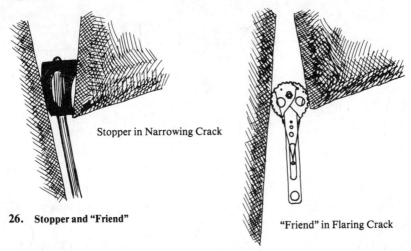

Stopper in Narrowing Crack

26. Stopper and "Friend"

"Friend" in Flaring Crack

Ascenders

As with many other skills nowadays, prussiking has been mechanized. The type of ascender now usually used is the "jumar." Such devices are used in pairs, and with the chest sling keep the climber upright. As a precaution though, a prussik knot should be placed above the top ascender.

Slings and Cords

Loops of nylon webbing or rope called "runners" or "slings" are ubiquitous in the climbing world. Typically, a loop is between 18 and 24 inches long, although some climbers carry runners which are double this length and some carry runners which are only about 8 inches long. Runners are used for tying into fixed chockstones, trees, horns of rock, and so on. They are also used to lengthen the sling on a nut or "friend".

Climbing Shoes

For many climbers, the shoe is the single most important piece of equipment. Specialized climbing shoes fit the foot snugly, are usually very flexible, and have soles of special rubber which has a high coefficient of friction. A pair of climbing shoes (a.k.a. "varappe" or "kletterschue") is a logical first purchase for a beginning climber. Hiking boots are a poor substitute for climbing shoes. Some tennis shoes or all-purpose athletic shoes will suffice for easier climbs.

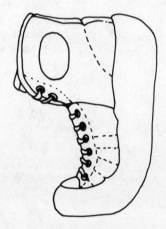

Miscellaneous

A **harness** or **swami belt** is a must for rock climbing. Several models are commercially available.

A **belay plate** is a mechanical device which allows the belayer to lock the rope and stop a falling climber.

Some climbers wrap their hands and/or fingers with **athletic tape** to protect them from abrasion when working on rough rock.

Gymnastic chalk is popular in warmer areas where the perspiration on the climbers' hands makes for a slippery grip. For beginning climbers chalk is unnecessary; the dry powder provides an advantage only on very difficult, steep rock. In some locales, chalk is thought unnecessary, and the discoloration of rock offends some climbers.

Because many climbers are injured by rockfall, more and more climbers are wearing **hard hats**.

11.4 Roped Climbing

This chapter on rock climbing is subdivided into a number of independent subjects: equipment, rope knots and roping up, belaying, types of climbing, positions and signals, balance and stress climbing, placing of chocks, etc. Rock climbing is nothing more than recognizing which of these we must select and appropriately utilize to safely master a specific difficult climb.

Groups engaging in roped climbing form into rope teams, which usually consist of two or three climbers. One climber in each team is the rope leader. Each climber on a team climbs for him- or herself: their teammates do not assist them in free climbing, either directly or indirectly (through the rope). On occasion a climber may ask for aid in the form of tension on the rope, but each climber prides her or himself on having climbed the "pitch" on their own. For the sake of the illustrations below, we will assume two rope teams, on which the second person in each rope is an intermediate climber who wants to lead easier pitches, with the third climber being a beginner.

Values of the Rope

The purpose of the climbing rope is not to haul people up but to guard climbers against serious injuries from falls. Without the rope, climbing is limited to relatively easy terrain where a mistake, a yield of hold, a slip, or a misjudgment cannot lead to serious accidents.

The rope enables all the members of a climbing team to take advantage of a secure position held by one member and to benefit from their leader's ability. With the rope, all the team members are united by their mutual dependence. When climbing within the rope's safety margin, your ability, enjoyment, and confidence increase and nervous strain decreases. Less experienced climbers have a chance to develop more advanced skills.

Rope Knots

The most important knot to know is the "figure-eight" knot. It is used for tying the climber to the anchor. The diagram below shows the completed knot. When a harness is not used, the knots used for roping up are the "bowline" (for the end person) and the "butterfly" (for the middle person). Knowledge of these is essential. Climbers must practice them until they can tie in rapidly under the most adverse conditions, such as darkness and/or extreme discomfort. If you are a beginner, practice coiling the rope, then quickly uncoiling it (without snarls), and tying in. Then check your knots.

In addition to the knots mentioned above, all climbers should know the "fisherman's knot" and "sheet bend" (for joining two ropes). Another important knot is the "prussik" knot. All these knots are preferred because they perform the needed functions and do not weaken or damage the rope. With the exception of the butterfly, they are easy to undo, even when wet.

The Rope Team.

In rock climbing a rope team consists of two, three, or more members. A "rope" of only two climbers is preferred because with that number much faster progress is possible. Two or more rope teams may follow each other on the same route.

28. Bowline and Butterfly Knots

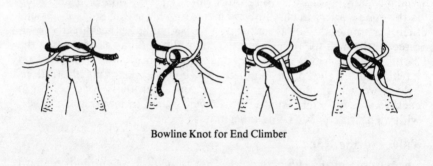

Bowline Knot for End Climber

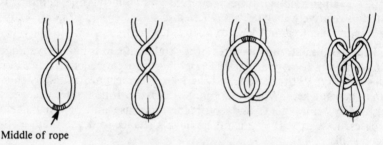

Middle of rope

Butterfly Knot for the Middle Climber

Whenever a team member feels insecure or nervous, he or she must not hesitate to ask for roping up. It is important to rope up *before* reaching exposed places. All climbers should be belayed, including the rope leader (the most experienced person on the team).

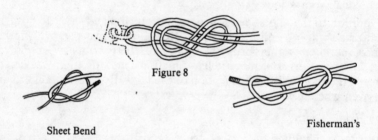

Figure 8

Sheet Bend

Fisherman's

29. Figure 8 Sheet Bend, and Fisherman's Knots

The order of roping up may take various forms, depending on the climbers' abilities and the difficulties expected. One member of the rope team may be better qualified to lead a rock pitch, another better on snow or ice. When the climbers are of equal ability, they may shift leads often during the course of a climb. When there are marked differences in the abilities of the climbers, they rope up for the *ascent* with the best climber going first, the second-best climber next, etc. On a three-person rope, if a difficult traverse is expected, the least experienced climber goes second.

On the *descent* the second-best climber goes first if there is a route-finding problem; otherwise the least experienced climber descends first and the second-best climber descends last. This line-up is the most efficient for the usual team, but a different order in roping may be decided upon because of special reasons such as training, strength, or weight of the individuals in the team.

Both the butterfly and the bowline are economical in the use of rope, but they provide only one coil around the body. If two coils are desired, and this does not shorten the usable length of the rope too much, the use of the double bowline is recommended for both end climbers and the middle climber. The double bowline knot is similar to the single bowline knot except for doubling the rope.

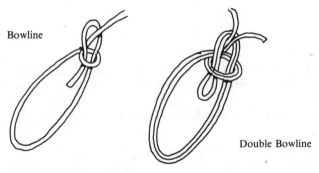

Bowline

Double Bowline

30.   Bowline and Double Bowline Knots

The prussik knot consists of a double wrap of a small rope (usually about ¼-inch in diameter) around a climbing rope. Applying a little force along the larger rope permits the whole knot to slide up or down. However, if the force is applied on the extension of the sling, the tension in the coils generates sufficient friction to lock the coils to the rope and prevent motion. Thus a climber's weight on the sling will enable the climber to be held securely. If the weight is released, the sling and the knot can be pushed with finger force to a higher or lower position.

31. Prussik Knot

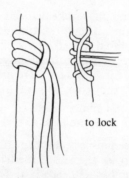

to lock

11.5 Belaying and Signals

Belaying

A rope team is considerably stronger than a single climber because each climber is protected by the other members of the rope team. This situation permits more difficult climbs than a single climber could accomplish. The procedure for providing this protection is called "belaying"; it is made possible by the friction of the rope around the belayer's body.

Importance of Belaying

Belaying is half of rock climbing. This important skill must be learned so well that each belayer is thoroughly trustworthy and aware of his or her responsibility. Unfortunately, even a well-belayed fall may be serious because the climber may sustain rope strains and burns, serious abrasions, and even fractures, from striking rock walls. Fortunately, serious falls are few when belayers are well-trained and constantly alert. *The success of a climb depends on the belayer!*

Location of Belayer

In case of a fall, a strong pull on the rope will occur which must be sustained by the belayer. The belay position must be in a safe and well-chosen location and provide a good stance so that the belayer can absorb a load without being upset, thrown, rolled over, or pulled from the belay position. Even a good stance often requires an anchor to a rock or to a piton which has been placed behind the belayer. The anchor must be situated in line with the direction of the pull from a possible fall.

A belayer keeps the rope from fouling, out of a climber's way, and clear and ready to be paid out—while anticipating the climber's movements. The leader needs just enough rope for climbing and no more, in order to keep the distance of a potential free fall to a minimum. The less rope there is, the less kinetic eneregy will have to be dissipated in a fall.

A climber may, at times, ask a belayer for tension on the rope in order to lean out for route study, to rest, or to overcome momentary insecurity. See "Signals" (this section, below) for the appropriate forms of request and reply.

Standard Belay Positions

In all belays a glove, at least on the braking hand, is necessary. If you are only lightly clothed, a jacket or sweater should be put around your back to guard against rope burns.

Sitting Hip belay: This is considered the strongest and most easily controlled belay position. In this position, facing the direction of expected pull, you can brace your spread legs against the rock, forming a wide base. An anchor will further improve the position's stability. The hip has enough length and curvature to supply a good friction base. Remember to keep the rope on fairly thick clothing, not just on the skin or a thin shirt.

Standing Hip Belay: This position has at best only two points of support and is therefore not as strong a position as the sitting one. In preparing for a down pull, you place one foot close to and in line with the rope. Combined with an anchor to the rock, this belay is quite adequate and often desirable for up pulls or light down pulls.

Standing Shoulder Belay: This belay is not recommended because the load is applied too high above the feet, making it easy for the belayer to lose balance or collapse under sudden pull. Even with an anchor and a foot close to and in line with the rope, it is not a strong enough position for a substantial down pull.

Sitting
Hip Belay

Standing
Hip Belay

Standing
Shoulder Belay

32.   Belay Positions

161

Indirect Belay: The use of a rock or tree as a direct belay was customary in early climbing. However, this practice is recognized today as being completely inadequate and the cause of many accidents. Rocks and trees can be very helpful when used in indirect belays, though. For an indirect belay from any of the above basic positions or stances the rope can be run behind a rock or tree. When doing this, be sure that the rope will not shift and pop out, wedge in a slot, or run over sharp cutting edges.

Sticht Plate Belay: The use of a belay plate is common practice, although many Americans prefer body belays. In the sticht plate belay a loop of rope is pushed through a slot in a metal plate and clipped into a carabiner atttached to the belayer's harness. A firm grip on the braking end of the rope is usually sufficient to lock the plate against the carabiner and prevent movement of the rope in case of a fall. With this belaying method it is easier to stop a severe fall or to lower a climber on the rope than with the body belay.

Belaying Signals

Climber and belayer communicate with oral signals. These must be short and given in a clear voice to offset wind or distance. A standard set of climbing signals is usually agreed upon in most clubs. Use these signals even when the actions of the climbers or belayers appear obvious. Here are some examples of the most commonly used sets of signals.

Climber: "Belay on?"
Belayer: (when ready) "Belay on!" or "Belay *NOT* ready!" (so that climber knows signal was heard).

Climber: "Testing."
Belayer: (when ready) "Test." Climber applies jerk to indicate direction in which pull would occur.

Climber: "Ready to climb."
Belayer: "Climb."

Climber: (as needed) "Up rope" or "Slack."
Belayer: (as needed) "25 feet," "10 feet," etc.

Climber: (when arrived and secure) "Off belay."
Belayer: (confirming) "Belay off."

Both: (when needed) "Rock!"

Climber: (in precarious position, if needed) "Tension." (if in doubt) "Prepare for fall." (or if it happens) "Falling!"

Belayer: (if position needs to be altered or becomes insecure — at the opportune moment) "Belay off." (wait for answer)

162

Climber: (confirming) "Off belay."
Belayer: (when ready) "Belay on." etc., as above.

When rappelling signals must also be given: "Rappel on," and after descent, "Rappel off." The latter is important to keep action going

Note: Both belayer and climber should always wait for confirmation before discontinuing a belay or starting to climb.

11.6 Route Finding

Examining (from a distance) the rock you are going to climb is an important aid in selecting the best route; experienced climbers take every opportunity to view the rock from as many angles as possible before approaching it. As you see more details you may alter your first tentative route and select alternate routes in case your original route proves impractical. Of course the route you take will also depend on the climbers' abilities, the type of rock, the time of year, and the weather conditions.

11.7 Balance Climbing

Rhythm in climbing is necessary. Continuous, smooth, even if slow, progress is preferable to fast, "stop and go" movements. The climber should appear to "flow" over the rock. Balance climbing is no different from the normal type of walking you do every day except that it is adapted to precipitous and irregular terrain. In this type of climbing the rope can be of physical assistance as well as moral support.

Upright Walk

On some kinds of rock—for example, on a steep succession of steps—you can "walk" in a body-upright position. This is the least tiring way to move, because your weight is carried primarily by your feet, thus freeing your hands for use in balancing.

With rubber or other kinds of soft soles you can walk up very steep slopes, relying on friction alone. Balance your body over your feet and *don't lean in*, as this lessens the weight on your soles and reduces the friction by generating an outward force.

33. Upright Walk with Friction Hold

Three-Point Support

When steps or holds become very small and it becomes impossible to remain in a body-upright position, or the position becomes very delicate, you can move upward with the help of foot and hand holds. Progress is still made by shifting your balance, but now three-point support should be used. The three points can be either your two feet and one hand or one foot and two hands. The remaining hand or foot is left free for reaching for the next hold or step. As a rule only one limb moves at a time, because this gives two points of support even if the third gives way.

Foot Holds

Small, conveniently located protrusions or ledges are used for foot holds. In placing your foot, use the edge of it rather than the toes. Your boots will help determine which edges provide you a safe hold. Stiff rubber with a narrow welt will provide the best stance on narrow, inclined foot holds.

Do not use your knee in a hold. It is not only uncomfortable to put weight on a knee, but it is difficult to place a foot on a hold occupied by a knee.

Hand Holds

Hand holds, sometimes only finger holds, are often used for balance while one foot reaches higher; they are also sometimes used for actually lifting the weight of the body. Such holds are usually small and can be cling or pressure type.

Cling holds provide the most secure support. They are easiest to use at shoulder level or just above, when the pressure of the hands is downward. However, they tend to be very tiring.

Pressure holds utilize the palm of the hand for pressing downward. The best pressure holds are those not over the height of your shoulders.

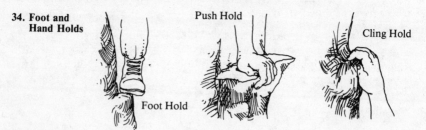

34. Foot and Hand Holds

Push Hold

Cling Hold

Foot Hold

Hold Testing

Before using a step, test it in the direction of expected load and then don't load it differently. Some loose holds can be used when the load is put on in the right direction.

11.8 Stress Climbing

When there are no suitable holds or steps, the climber must create his or her own forces in order to stay in balance or to move upward. In "stress" climbing the rope is often of physical assistance rather than just moral support.

Chimney Stemming

"Chimney" climbing is a typical example of stress climbing. A chimney consists of two vertical or nearly vertical walls, facing each other, one to three feet apart, and generally devoid of holds. The width of the chimney determines the method of stemming used. One method is to place your back against one wall and your feet against the opposite side, somewhat lower than the back. Your hands are used to provide alternating cross pressure. One foot is moved up, then the back, then the other foot. The holding force is the friction created by back and feet being pressed against opposite walls. The body exerting these forces is under a "stress."

If one wall of a chimney is smoother than the other, one foot may be kept under the body against the smoother side and the other foot on the opposite side, thus supplying a continuous counterforce.

Chimney Stemming

Lie-back

35.   Chimney Stemming and the Lie-Back

The Lie-Back

When a crack narrows down so that you can't get inside it (and, hopefully, is not exactly vertical), you can use a method called "the lie-back." In this maneuver you use both hands to grip one edge of the crack and pull against your feet, which are pressing at right angles on the opposite edge of the crack. This is usually easier if your hands and feet are not close together. The lie-back is most useful on inclined cracks or at the edge of large slabs, but because it is tiring, climbers will often stop to rest on longer cracks.

Jam Hold

A hand, arm, foot, or leg can be jammed into a narrow crack for a short period of time. This should be done very carefully, though, because the hold may really jam, perhaps stranding you. The jam hold is most useful in balance climbing.

Cross Pressure

In narrow, vertical cracks you can insert fingers of both hands and pull in opposite directions—i.e., exert cross pressure— to stay in balance or move upward.

Under-Cling Hold

When making use of an inverted hold, you use your hands to pull up and your feet to push down—as in the lie-back.

Hand Jam Hold

Foot Jam Hold

Cling Under Hold

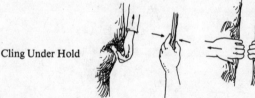

Opposite Pressure Holds

36. More Hand and Foot Holds

Combination Holds

Ordinarily, climbers use a combination of balance and stress climbing holds. For example, you may stand on a good foot hold and pull yourself up by means of a hand jam hold. A great many combinations can be worked out, some of which are much less tiring than others. Practice will allow you to quickly select the most useful of these combinations.

11.9 Downward Climbing

Climbing down can be one of the most pleasurable aspects of climbing. Too few climbers are as experienced in climbing down as in climbing up and thereby miss half of the fun of a climb. Surprising as it may seem, climbing down is often more difficult than climbing up. Fatigue, lack of visibility, and inability to test holds are difficulties that sometimes make climbing down difficult or inadvisable.

Friction Slope

On friction slopes you can walk down with the soles flat and knees slightly bent for maximum friction. Use of the third point (seat of pants), though often convenient, has obvious disadvantages. Crouching and using your hands can provide more friction if needed.

Pressure Hold

Sitting down and facing outward places your center of gravity closest to the rock and gives the best view downward. You will find that you can ease yourself down by using a succession of pressure holds — without resorting to the seat of your pants. A good hold can be used first by one foot and then by a hand. Proceeding while facing sideways is next best and facing in is least desirable, as the view downward is almost nil.

Looping down

Climbing down with
pressure holds

37. Down Climbing

However, very steep faces with good holds can only be climbed down while facing in.

Rope Loops

On very short pitches or on very loose rock, you can use a rope or long sling to throw a loop around a prominent, solid rock and then ease yourself down.

Rappelling

Often climbers may rappel down to avoid the difficulties of climbing down steep faces or just to enjoy sliding down a rope using friction for full and instantaneous control of speed. The procedure is rather simple but requires considerable practice to gain the confidence and agility necessity to rappel correctly and safely.

In rappelling, the rope is usually doubled so that it can be passed through a loop at the highest point and then be recovered after the last climber has descended. If the rappel anchor has been properly placed, friction will not prevent the rope from being pulled freely through the loop after descent is completed. To indicate which of the two ends of the rope is to be pulled for retrieval, tie a knot at that end. During rappelling, sudden jerky stops must be avoided. Such quick stops may impose a momentary load on the rope far in excess of the climber's weight.

There must be no doubt about whether the anchor is strong enough to serve its purpose. The preferred anchor is a tree or a protruding sound

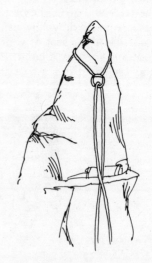

38. Rappel Anchoring

rock, with a stance below it from which the rappel can start. If slings are used, there must be two of them. Because it is difficult to arrange for each sling to carry an equal load, they should each be capable of comfortably carrying the whole load—two ¼ " rope slings should do the job. Fisherman's knots are safe to use for joining ropes, etc. The lower side of the slings should not be tight across, but should sag to where the rappel rope is doubled over (a rappel ring is desirable here). Any sharp point on the anchor should be padded with flat rocks, moss, or other material. If friends or chocks are used there should be at least two, preferably three, of them; they should not be in the same crack.

Several mechanical descenders are available for rappelling. It is also possible to assemble a carabiner brake for use in rappelling. Using a mechanical device is safer and far more comfortable than the "Dulfersitz" method described below. Most climbers never use the "Dulfersitz" or only use it on low-angle rock or for short rappels; its only advantage is that it requires no equipment beyond the rope and is very simple to use.

In beginning the Dulfersitz rappel, the climber faces the slope and straddles the rope. She or he then reaches with one hand for the double rope behind them and lifts the loop over their head to the other shoulder. Thus, after going around the hip, the rope reaches across the climber's body, over the shoulder, and around the back to the controlling hand (as shown in the sketch). The uphill hand is on the rope only to maintain balance and must at no time grip the rope. The controlling hand regulates the speed with which the rope is allowed to slide around the body and in that way controls the speed of descent. Although either hand can be the controlling hand, many climbers cultivate a preference (not necessarily the stronger hand). The function of this operation is analogous to that of a snubbing post—i.e., the rope is fixed and the climber acts as the post.

Control hand

39. Dulfersitz Rappel

169

Depending on the anchor layout, starting any rappel may be awkward and a belay may be in order. (It is customary for the person who plans the rappel to descend first.) While descending, lean well back, attempting to suit the slope of the rock and provide sufficient friction between boots and rock. Keep the feet apart for lateral stability; hold one foot lower for ease in keeping the rope in the crotch (see Illustration 39). During the descent, also hold a finger of the upper hand between the two ropes to prevent their twisting. Beginners should always be given a belay during their first rappelling trials.

Note: The setting up of a rappel should be done by an experienced climber, because of the importance of anchor safety, of choosing the rappelling route, and of deciding on length, joining, and retrieval of ropes. However, this is the time for an up-coming climber to help and learn.

11.10 Prussiking

By using the jumar (See Section 11.3) and/or prussik knot and attaching three slings to a rope, it is possible to climb directly up the rope. One of these slings should be much shorter than the other two; its purpose is to go from the rope to and around the body in order to keep the climber upright. The other two slings (one 6 inches longer than the other) are for the feet. They should be long enough to reach the climber's shoulders. Both slings must closely follow the legs, a feat usually accomplished by passing each one through a strong belt loop, then twisting each around a leg from the inside, behind the knee, and finally to the outside of each foot. By alternately moving each sling up, you can make progress up-rope.

The boot sling must be made of material having minimum elastic stretch, or much of progress up-rope will be lost. Nylon is not recommended

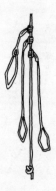

40.   Prussik Slings in Place on Rope

unless it is braided. Manila rope was used for many years because of its low stretch, but it deteriorates quickly and requires repeated replacement. It is easy to test a boot sling by measuring its length before and during application of body weight. A three-inch stretch results in about 20% loss in progress up-rope; this amount of stretch is regarded as an acceptable upper limit.

11.11   Climbing Procedures

When climbing with a two-climber team, the leader anchors in a safe location and prepares to belay their teammate up to their position.

The second climber, using proper signals, starts to climb the same route. During the climb he or she will remove the hardware left in the rock. When the climber reaches the leader's stance they return the recovered hardware to the leader and prepare for belaying the leader on the second pitch.

However, if the second climber is sufficiently experienced and willing to lead, they may take over the lead upon reaching the leader's stance—in which case the leader will belay them.

The leader has the climbing rope above the anchor rope while acting as belayer in bringing the second climber up. If the second climber now takes over the lead, the original leader—who is now belayer—will have to readjust the belay for an up-pull by moving the climbing rope to below the anchor rope. Under favorable conditions some climbers place a carabiner on each side where the climbing rope is close to the anchor rope and omit adjusting the relative position of the climbing rope and anchor rope.

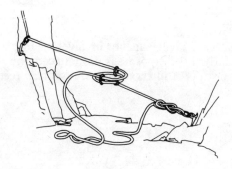

41.   Carabiner Placement

When the "now" leader reaches the end of the second pitch and stops at a likely belay position, the original leader follows them, cleaning the rock face on the way. Upon reaching their teammate, the leader continues to lead the third pitch. Again, it is necessary to shift the relative positions of the climbing and anchor ropes unless the two carabiners mentioned above are in place.

Class 3 Climbing and Roped Walking

If during the approach to the target peak the teams come through an area where the exposure is moderate and which requires intermittent balance climbing, the leaders may want everyone to rope up. Roping up should be done before it is absolutely necessary to do so. If there are intervals during the approach when the rope is not needed, a team usually walks — with each climber carrying a few rope coils in their hand — and avoids fouling, dragging, or jerking on the rope. The leader watches the team's general progress and tries to keep an even pace.

Class 4 Climbing

When the exposure becomes more pronounced and climbing requires a continual balancing, only one climber on the team moves at a time. The moving climber is protected by a belay and the others are protected by an anchor to a rock or tree.

For this class of climbing the second person on each rope sets up a belay stance. Soon after the start of the climb, the leader places a nut or chock well above the level of the belayer and attaches a rope to it with a carabiner. This nut or chock is placed to stabilize the belayer position by providing an up-force in a definite direction.

If the climbing continues to be balance-type climbing, but the leader finds it necessary or prudent due to bad weather or some other reason to place additional nuts or chocks, this does not change the class of the climb. It would just mean that a Class 4 pitch was climbed with Class 5 protection.

Class 5 Climbing

If the climbing after the belay anchor involves balance and stress climbing, and particularly if the exposure is pronounced, the leader places additional chocks or nuts at intervals of ten to fifteen feet, depending on the exposure.

Class 6 (Aid) Climbing

Aid (or Class 6) climbing is done on rock faces where there are no places for a belay stance. The only cracks are often hairline ones. There are no grips or holds. Climbers use standard nuts and friends along with smaller hardware, when the cracks are not large enough. Because the climber's weight is carried at all times by these climbing aids, all moves are slow and deliberate so that too much force will not result. Both climber and belayer are "tied in" with the same rope (this rope should be smooth and very elastic).

At the beginning of a pitch, a climber reaches from the starting point as high as practical in the direction of the climb and places a climbing aid in the rock. A carabiner is then attached to the aid and a stirrup is attached to the carabiner. The climber steps on the stirrup, inspects the aid, and if satisfied climbs up the stirrup as far as he or she can. After getting some slack on the belay rope the climber clips the rope into a third carabiner.

Next, the belayer provides tension on the rope and the climber proceeds to place the second aid — usually two to three feet above the previous aid. Again, the hanger with carabiners is placed on the end, a second stirrup is clipped to one of these carabiners and the climber transfers his or her weight to it. After inspecting the aid, she or he steps higher up on the stirrup and clips the rope into a carabiner anchored to this aid, leaving it clipped to the previous aid. Before doing this the climber retrieves all unused carabiners and the stirrup from the previous bolt, because from a higher position they will not be able to reach them.

Again with tension on the rope, the climber places a third aid, attaches a carabiner and a stirrup to it, and then transfers their weight to it, climbing up on the stirrup and placing the rope through the carabiner without removing it from the carabiner on the previous aid. The climber then retrieves the unused carabiner and stirrup from the last position.

This sequence is repeated many times, but may be altered to suit conditions. The higher the climber proceeds, the closer he or she comes to the end of the belay rope. A suitable spot to set up a new belay position must then be found. (At this point the climber has left behind a rope attached to the rock with various pieces of aid hardware.) As soon as the climber chooses a new belay spot and is secured, the belayer comes up using ascenders and "cleaning up the rock" by removing all hardware. Upon reaching his or her teammate, the climber (the last belayer) may proceed on and take the lead, using the hardware just recovered.

It is possible to rappel down from most climbs if a spare rope is available. If not, return is accomplished by means of stirrups, jumaring or prussiking, or ascenders.

On long climbs hammocks are used for bivouacking. Bivouacking stops are planned for places on the rock where climbers can use hardware that will hold a heavy load or where there is a broad ledge.

11.12 Good Advice

Until recently, climbing—and especially rock climbing—has been characterized as a young man's sport. In recent years, though, many women have begun to climb and some climb very well indeed. There can be no doubt that climbing is more strenuous than golf or bowling, but one need not be a hulking brute to achieve a high level of skill and competence in rock climbing; no body type is clearly superior for climbing rock. Rock climbing technique has improved enormously since a quarter of a century ago. It is not an exaggeration to say that middle-aged women are now climbing routes then considered impossible for the strongest men. The most important requisite for climbing skillfully is the desire to do so.

Climbing guidebooks supply information about some climbing areas you may be interested in. From these books you can learn about approaches to climbs, possible routes, and the climbing history of various areas. There is now a tendency not to write up new climbing routes, the reason being that some feel the challenge is greater if climbers experience some of the same difficulties that occurred on the first ascent.

Checking in and out for all climbs is necessary in places such as Mount Rainier, Mount McKinley, and the Tetons. In these areas the climbing ranger inspects your equipment to see if it is adequate and helps you determine whether your proposed routes are commensurate with your experience. Don't forget to check in after a climb—otherwise the rangers may search for you.

As mentioned before, this chapter is only intended to inform you about some of the basics of rock climbing. The subject is not easily translated into words, certainly not the few words in this book. However, reading this chapter has probably helped you to realize that many skills must be mastered before you can consider yourself a good and responsible climber. For example, you must know the rope knots exceptionally well. Belaying and belaying signals must become second nature. (Some schools or clubs have rigs you can practice holding a falling weight with, and so experience the forces involved in breaking a climber's fall.) You need to be very adept at properly managing the rope in all kinds of situations. You must be familiar with and be able to appropriately choose and use many kinds of climbing hardware. And this is just the beginning. Where you go from here is up (to you!).

Chapter 12

Winter Travel

Snow is white, clean, and beautiful—it is one of nature's most decorative substances. It can smooth out the rough places and make travel easier and faster. It can be a delight to behold and a great source of outdoor fun. But snow is also cold, soft, and wet. It can make travel difficult, hazardous, and even impossible. The snow temperature will always be below freezing; the air temperature can be warmer, but it too is often below freezing. Snow conditions change very rapidly, depending on the weather and temperature, time of day, sun direction, and amount of shade. In open areas there may be a frost crust on the snow; in the shade, the snow may be icy. Wind in open areas will hardpack the snow. No two slopes will have exactly the same snow conditions.

Because snow is cold, warm clothes are necessary for the wilderness traveler. Wool and synthetic fiber batting or down are needed to keep warm. Necessary clothing includes lined boots, warm jacket and sweater, thermal underwear, long wool trousers, windbreaker, windproof overmitts with wool or down inner mitts or gloves, and a warm cap with windbreaker or parka hood for the head. Face protection is also often needed; woolen balaclavas work well.

Because snow is wet, exterior clothing should be water repellent. Boots, mittens, overmitts, and gaiters should be treated with appropriate water-repellent preparations. If snow gets on your clothing, brush it off before it melts. Spraying the rest of your clothes with Scotchguard or something similar is also a great help.

Because snow is white, it is highly reflective. Nearly all sunlight striking snow is reflected, and sunburn can be severe. You can wear light clothing for warm days, but cover arms, neck, and head. Wear snow goggles to protect against snow blindness, a sunburn of the eyes. Use adequate sunburn protection in the form of lotions or salves. At high altitudes, complete blocking with zinc oxide or something similar is recommended for particularly sensitive areas such as nose, lips, and tops of ears. You may even want a mask for the entire face if you sunburn easily or you are going to be exposed for a long time.

Because snow is soft, it generally will not support your weight. Snowshoes or skis are often needed for snow travel. Foot travel is difficult if you sink in more than six inches. Old, compacted snow and wet, frozen snow are firmest and thus most suitable for foot travel. Avoid traveling over soft snow. New snow, wet snow, or snow in areas protected from wind is generally soft. Due to temperature variations, snow may be hard at night and in the early morning, but soft during the day. Learn to judge the hardness of snow in order to avoid breakthroughs.

Snow is also unstable; on steep slopes avalanche hazards are always present. A fall on a snowy or icy slope can be very serious; you can quickly develop great speed on such a slope. Belays should be used to prevent dangerous slides when hiking in snow.

In winter many mountains are at least partly covered with snow. In some areas new snow seldom arrives after May, but the pack on the ground may last until late summer. At high elevations, particularly on north slopes, snowfields can even last until the following winter. On winter wilderness trips—depending, of course, on the area and altitude—you will usually have to be prepared for snow conditions. This means you will have to have proper clothing and equipment and know how to use them. Travel on snow requires considerable practice. Most of the low impact and safety suggestions mentioned in previous chapters apply to snow travel, in addition to the suggestions given below for dealing with winter's special problems.

12.1 Equipment

What has been said about basic clothing in previous chapters needs to be supplemented here because of the demands of winter travel.

Boots

Lined, top-grain leather boots with Vibram soles are usually required for winter wilderness trips. Gaiters will keep snow out of your boots. You should wear at least two pairs of wool socks; wool is warm even when wet. Keep in mind, though, that too many pairs of socks will cut off circulation in your feet, thus predisposing you to cold feet and possible frostbite. Your boots should be treated with a water-repellent preparation before any winter trip. Wet feet can lead to cold feet, and from there to frostbitten toes.

Clothing

Wear wool shirt/s, sweater/s, and pants. If the weather is going to be very cold, windy, and/or snowy, long underwear is in order. Do not wear anything made of 100% cotton — once it gets wet, it takes a long, cold time to dry. Take a down- or synthetic-filled parka with a hood and a windbreaker; don't forget a wool cap that comes down over your ears, wool gloves or mittens, and overmitts.

Polypropylene underwear is new and works well because it does not absorb water. It is also non-allergenic, soft, and very comfortable. Fiber-pile — another synthetic — has insulating qualities similar to wool. However, the pile is lighter and more bulky. It is also non-allergenic.

Ten Essentials

These are listed in Section 3.1. The candle, used for fire starting, can be important for winter camping. Dark glasses, preferably with protection from side glare, or ski goggles with ventilation, are necessary on snow. It doesn't hurt to take a spare pair of sunglasses or goggles along.

Snowshoes and Skis

Using snowshoes or skis off the practice slopes or trails is advisable only if you have had considerable experience with them, and even then they should be used with extreme caution. It is easy to misjudge your endurance in winter; summer is a much more forgiving season.

Rope

If you expect to travel over steep snow slopes, a minimum of one climbing rope for every three in the party should be included in your equipment.

Crampons

If you expect to travel over hard snow surfaces, as in the early morning, crampons may be required. Detailed descriptions of crampons and their uses are found in Sections 12.1 and 13.2.

Ice Axe

The ice axe is a necessary piece of equipment for travel on ice or snow; it can be obtained from most mountaineering equipment stores. If the shaft is wood, it should preferably be of straight-grain hickory, with no knots; ash is a second choice. Aluminum and fiberglass handles are also strong. A 12-inch head is customary for large people; axes for smaller people usually have a 10½-inch head. The following table shows the lengths recommended for different heights.

Height	Length of Axe
5′3″ to 5′6″	31 to 33 inches
5′6″ to 5′9″	33 to 35 inches
5′9″ to 6′	35 to 38 inches

Individual arm length should also be considered when selecting an ice axe. Measure distance from floor to wrist bone with arms loose at the side. Add one or even two inches to the measured length for penetration of point.

To preserve the axe's wooden handle, it is advisable to apply a few coats of linseed oil after lightly sanding the surface. Do this at least once a year, when the shaft is dry. The bottom six to eight inches of the shaft should be wrapped with vinyl, cloth, or electrical tape to lessen the damage from hitting sharp rocks. When storing the axe for longer periods, the metal parts should be lightly oiled.

42. The Ice Axe

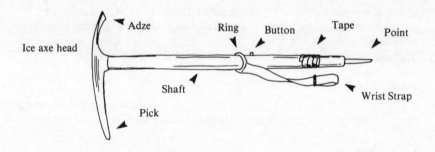

12.2 Ice Axe Use

The ice axe is an invaluable tool when traveling on snow or ice; it can be used in the following ways:

— as a ballast on level ground, snow, or ice. Keep point where user can see it; keep the pick where it cannot be fallen upon.

— to probe for crevasses. Party should be roped.

— as a cane for traverses, held on the uphill side.

— with shaft buried in snow, as a handhold for step-kicking.

— with point into slope for balance on high angle ice. Keep body vertical and sidewise or facing out; keep crampons flat on slope.

— for step-cutting. On steep slopes cut belay positions; anchor belayer to ice axe or piton and use body belay.

— when descending, as a rappel point, but not for the last person unless absolutely necessary. Rope must be low on buried shaft of axe as in the shaft belay.

— for support in steep, direct descents with crampons. Keep crampons flat on slope and clear of snow.

— for self-arrests. Put one hand on head of ice axe, the other on the shaft; pick can be used as brake if turned into the ice gradually.

— as a rudder and support in standing and sitting glissades.

— for balance in crevasse jumps, held ready for self-arrest.

The ice axe is very dangerous if incorrectly used. You must, therefore, practice using it until what you do becomes automatic. If practice is combined with constant preparedness and alertness, the ice axe becomes your best aid on snow and ice. Without the axe, most snow travel would be impossible.

Walking with the Ice Axe

The most common use of the ice axe is as a walking stick. On the level or on gentle slopes—even on easy rocks—it acts as a welcome third leg to help maintain balance. When walking on the trail with the ice axe as a walking stick, it may be carried in either hand with the pick forward. If it is carried horizontally, the adze should be up, with the point forward and on the *uphill* side. On steep slopes the axe is always carried on the uphill side.

When you are rock climbing, the ice axe can be carried on the wrist by means of the strap. It also can be attached to the back of your rucksack or carried with head inside the rucksack and the point up.

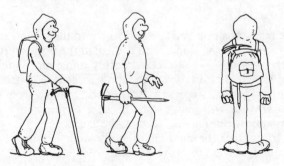

43. **Walking with Ice Axe**

The Ready Grip

The main use of the ice axe is for self-arrest, in case you fall on a snow or ice slope. (On the trail the axe is carried differently, in ways which do not permit immediate self-arrest.) On reaching a snow area, put on your mittens and grasp the head of the axe in the "ready grip." This means reversing the axe so that the pick faces *backward* and placing your thumb under and partly around the adze, with the other four fingers over the pick. You must be able to grip very firmly when necessary. On steep slopes the axe should ordinarily be in the uphill hand, although some people prefer to always carry the axe with their strongest arm and hand.

The Ready Position

If you carry the axe with the "ready grip," you can go into the "ready position" by raising the hand holding the axe to just above the shoulder, as indicated in the illustration. The shaft is then brought diagonally in front of the body, and the other hand grips the shaft near the point of the axe, holding it firmly and close to the hip.

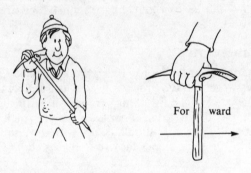

For ward

44. Ready Position and Ready Grip

The Self-Arrest

From the ready position you can easily go into the self-arrest. To do this, you fall facing into the slope, with the axe in the position just described. You apply pressure to the pick smoothly and immediately to prevent gathering speed (the faster you go, the harder it is to stop). You must hold tightly to the axe to prevent it from being pulled from your grasp or forced to arm's length above your head, a position in which its effectiveness is almost eliminated. Keeping the axe close to your chest will permit you to control the amount of body weight you put on the pick. Spread your feet wide to prevent rolling over.

In soft snow, when your weight on the pick is not sufficient to stop a fall, digging in with elbows, feet, and knees helps. If you wear crampons it is important that in a fall you hold your feet off the ground, particularly when you're in a prone position. On very hard snow or ice, you can prevent the pick from glancing off the surface by gradually applying pressure with your body weight.

Regardless of the way you are falling down the slope—whether head first, feet first, or sideways—digging in the pick will turn you so that you are facing up the slope. When turning or rolling to face the slope, avoid rolling toward your low hand—the one holding the point of the axe near your hip. If you hit the point, it might dig in and throw you out of control. Always yell "Falling!" when you go into the self-arrest.

45. Self-Arresting with Ice Axe

Traversing a Slope

The position in which the ice axe is held when traversing a slope is similar to the "ready position" described above. Your controlling hand is on the downhill side and the axe is extended sideways with the point toward the slope and touching it. When using switchbacks, reverse the position of the ice axe as you cut back and forth across the slope. Make sure the point is always toward the slope. When using the wrist strap while crossing steep and exposed slopes, you don't need to shift the wrist loop from hand to hand. The ring slides, and what was the controlling hand shifts to near the point and the other hand becomes the controlling hand. If you lose your balance, fall at once into the self-arrest position and yell "Falling!"

46. Traversing a Snow Slope with Ice Axe

Using the Wrist Strap

Attaching the ice axe to your wrist will prevent loss of the axe if it should fall out of your hand. However, because falling with the axe attached to your wrist is dangerous, the strap should be used in only the few situations where losing your axe would compromise the safe completion of your trip. A few examples of such critical situations are:

— on rock

— on glaciers

— on long, steep, snow or ice slopes

— when crossing deep and swift currents

The strap should be off in other situations, particularly when glissading.

Ice Axe Substitutes

If the grain in the shaft of your axe is not straight and free of knots, a side-load applied at the head can break it. If the shaft breaks near the point, you just have a shorter axe. (You can wrap something around the splintered end.) If the break is in the middle or near the head, the short stub could dig into the snow and twist the head out of your grip. In this case use the point like a vertical stick: one hand as a pivot, the other above and braced against your shoulder. If you lose your axe or forget it, you can substitute something long and *strong* like an ice piton or screw, piton hammer, long angle piton, tent pole, etc. Even a long, slender rock can be used.

12.3 Ascending Snow Slopes

A snow field or snow-covered couloir (gully) often provides a convenient route to a peak when the other possibilities are difficult rock routes. Although a snow route can save much time, you must be prepared to traverse surfaces ranging from hard ice to deep powder snow. On hard snow, you can kick or cut steps; on soft snow you often have to wallow through as best as you can. In both cases, a rhythmic pace is essential, and the lead should be changed often to avoid tiring the leader.

Safety is, of course, one of the primary reasons for choosing a particular route. Avalanche slopes and crossings below avalanche slopes should be avoided except in early morning or evening, when it is colder and slopes may be less unstable. Routes through woods, dense vegetation, or over ridges are safer and should be used whenever possible.

Level Ground or Gentle Slopes

When you are walking on level ground or gentle slopes, the heel generally hits first and the foot is then flattened to provide a horizontal platform. In soft snow, "bucket" steps are formed naturally, and the ice axe provides extra stability. Follow in the footsteps of the leader and improve his or her steps. To change the lead, the leader steps aside and the second person assumes the lead, with the ex-leader going to the end of the line.

Steep Slopes

What has just been said about traversing level ground also applies here. In addition, the leader may have to kick or cut steps in hard snow; these should be improved by the people following. When kicking steps, stand with the body vertical (have a good horizontal platform) and use your ice axe for additional stability.

The route can go straight up, but switchbacks are less tiring and make it easier to maintain a steady pace. When using switchbacks, try to keep out of the fall-line of the person above you. When going straight up and using the steps of the climber above you, be prepared to get out of the path of anyone who falls and to go into self-arrest on either side of the steps you are climbing up. To turn on a switchback, kick your inside foot into the slope at 45°, then kick your outside foot straight into the slope, and finally kick the inside foot again at 45°, in the direction of the new track.

Summit Ridges

Routes along ridges, particularly if wide, are safest from avalanche dangers—even though they are usually windy. The summit, or any ridge, may have a cornice. A cornice is a projecting overhang resulting from a strong, prevailing wind sweeping over a ridge (see illustration). When approaching a cornice from below, you may find a cushion of loose, unstable snow just beneath it. Because the cornice may overhang the lee side of the ridge as much as 50 feet, you may have to cut a trench or path through it to gain the ridge.

Prevailing Wind ►   Cornice

Cushion of Loose Snow

47. Approaching a Cornice

When approaching a corniced ridge or summit from the windward side, do not go out too far on the cornice because it may break away from under you. Corniced ridges can be traversed, but you should stay well down on the windward side while traversing. The ridge with a cornice overhanging both sides is especially dangerous, but fortunately rare. *A belay is necessary when approaching any type of cornice.* The belaying techniques for snow travel are discussed in Sections 12.5 and 12.6.

The Rest Step

This technique for maintaining smooth, upward travel has already been described. However, because of its importance in climbing long, snow-covered slopes, the rest step description is here repeated:

— Lift left leg, place it forward unweighted.

— Pause, rest left leg.

— Shift weight and raise right leg. Repeat sequence.

12.4 Descending Snow Slopes

Descending a snow slope is often more difficult than ascending, particularly when the slope is icy. Therefore, on difficult climbs a group will usually return over the same route they used for the ascent. Walking in single file on the ascent and improving the leader's tracks leaves a convenient and usually safe return route.

Steep Snow Slopes

On a short, steep slope, face into the slope and jam your ice axe into the snow for a solid anchor. Then hold the ice axe with both hands and step down, kicking steps into the slope. Repeat the process until the slope becomes gentler.

The Plunge Step

If the snow is soft enough, use the plunge step by facing out from and down the slope, standing upright, and holding your ice axe in the ready or traverse position. Then, with all your weight, plunge a heel, stiff-kneed, into the slope (see illustration). After a short skid, your boot will pack the snow into a somewhat inclined step and come to a stop. Don't lean backward to prevent a skid or you will sit down and may even break out of the step and start falling. The "plunge step" is the most common step used when going down a snow slope; it can be adapted to a wide range of slope and snow conditions.

48. The Plunge Step

The Skating Step

On gentle slopes you can progress faster by holding your ice axe in the ready position and using a skating motion. Be on the lookout for holes or any irregularity in the slope. Avoid icy spots.

The Standing Glissade

When you are on medium-steep slopes with suitable snow, glissading is an enjoyable way of descending quickly. Glissading is something like skiing in that it has its dangers and requires quite a bit of practice to do well. The basic glissade position is with hand on your ice axe in the ready position and body facing out from the slope and squatting, as if sitting in a chair. You then lower the axe from the ready position to form a "third leg," with the point facing backward and digging into the slope, taking part of your weight. Keep one foot slightly in front of the other and your knees slightly bent. To increase speed, flatten your feet and bring your body into an almost upright position. To slow down, dig your heels in and lean more on the axe. To stop, turn your feet sideways and lean hard on the axe and your feet. Control your direction by shifting your weight and using the axe as a rudder.

If you lose control while glissading, immediately go into the self-arrest. One danger of a standing glissade is that it is very easy to lose control on icy slopes or hard snow. Also, unseen holes or ridges may cause headfirst falls. Wear mittens. *Do not use the wrist strap while glissading.*

Sitting Glissade

For this glissade, the basic position is sitting on the snow with body facing out from the slope and your axe in the ready position. To control the glissade, dig in the axe, as in the standing glissade, or use your heels for braking. Shift your body and apply pressure on the ice axe to control direction. For more speed, lean back and raise your legs.

185

Facing-In Glissade

This type of glissading is used only on steep slopes. In the self-arrest position, lie on the slope, facing in. Release the pick slowly and slide. Dig the ice axe into the slope to control your speed. This technique can also be used to determine the type of glissading that can safely be done on an untested slope. In testing a slope one person is belayed from above so they can safely try the glissade.

Precautions for All Glissades

Because chances to glissade are eagerly welcomed by snow travelers, a few notes of caution are in order:

— Never glissade unless you can see the whole length of the slope below.

— Beware of rocks (especially those barely covered by snow), particularly when executing a sitting glissade.

— Wear mittens to avoid bruising your hands on hard snow or ice.

— Do not use the ice axe wrist strap.

12.5 Roped Snow Travel

As previously outlined in detail in Section 11.4, the rope is a means of collective security for your group. Your party should rope up *before* reaching exposed territory. The safest team on snow and ice has three members. If there is a marked difference in ability and experience in snow and ice climbing, the most skilled person should go first on the rope, then the next best, and finally the person with least experience.

Continuous Roped Travel

This is analogous to third-class climbing and is used on moderate slopes where there is some danger. It is difficult for the team to move smoothly during roped travel on snow or ice because of the incovenience of rope handling. This is especially true at switchbacks, where keeping up an even pace is almost impossible. When traveling as part of a roped team, keep an even distance between climbers. Hold one or two coils of rope in one hand and, as much as possible, avoid dragging the rope on the snow. Observe your teammates and try to keep the team moving at a steady, even pace by slowing down when necessary. All climbers on the team should be ready to go into self-arrest if anyone falls. If you sense you are losing your balance, immediately go into self-arrest and shout "Falling!"

One-at-a-Time Roped Travel

This is analogous to fourth-class climbing and is used on severe slopes where a fall would require a long distance to stop by a self-arrest. In this kind of travel, the leader goes first and is belayed by the second climber, who is anchored by the third. After the pitch is completed, the leader and third climber belay the second up to the leader's stance; then the second, anchored by the third, belays the leader on, and brings up the third climber while anchored to the leader. Sometimes the second and third climbers may follow together on the leader's belay, because steps kicked or cut by the leader lessen the difficulties of following.

12.6 Belays on Snow

A belay given from a snow slope is seldom perfect, but a fall on a snow slope is usually a sliding fall and may not be as difficult to stop as a "free fall" in rock climbing. If rock belays are possible, they are preferred to any of the snow belays.

Sitting Hip Belay

Sometimes you can find or dig a hole or flat place in the snow in which the belayer can sit. The belay, rope handling, signals, etc., are then the same as for a belay on rock (see Section 11.5).

50. Sitting Hip Belay on Snow

Ice Axe Belay

A very simple belay can be rigged with just an ice axe. For this belay, the shaft is plunged into the snow above the belayer, with the pick uphill. The head is held by the uphill hand and the rope is coiled around the shaft. You may also run the rope over your thigh or around your hip. Although this method is adequate for belaying from above, the boot-axe belay should be used for belaying the leader.

51. Ice Axe Belay on Snow

Boot-Axe Belay

The most common ice axe belay is the boot-axe belay. For this belay, jam your axe into the snow as far as possible. The pick *must face the slope,* and your boot should be placed close against the shaft and below it. Place your *uphill hand* on the head of the axe to hold it firmly in the snow; be ready to self-arrest if necessary. As lbelayer, you face across the slope in the direction of the climber and assume a comfortable, braced stance. The rope runs from the climber across the toe of the belayer's boot and around the shaft and boot heel to the lower side of the boot. The rope is then held in your downhill hand. To apply friction, bring the rope further around the boot and apply hand pressure. The rope should be free to run just enough to eliminate the impact of a fall, no more. To brake, bring the rope further around the friction surface (side of the boot heel) and apply hand pressure. The tension on the rope has a tendency to push boot and axe shaft together.

Be sure to handle the rope so that it does not snarl. In case of a fall or on a descent, a snarl can endanger the belayer's position. If the belay appears to be pulling out, ease up on the friction slightly. If the belay does pull out, go immediately into the self-arrest and call "Falling!"

It is very important that the uphill hand hold the head of the axe so that the pick faces uphill. Only this position assures the "ready grip" and "ready position" in case you must fall into a self-arrest.

The Seattle Mountaineers have tested the various ice axe belays on snow slopes and glaciers under a variety of conditions. The results of these tests indicate that the simplest, strongest, and fastest use of the ice axe for belaying in snow is the boot-axe belay.

52.   Boot-Ice Axe Belay on Snow

Alternate Boot Belay

In this belay, the rope, after running around the shaft, passes in front of the boot, forming an "S" instead of a "C." This alternate method is awkward, but does furnish more friction.

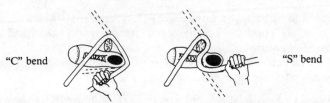

"C" bend   "S" bend

53.   Alternate Boot-Ice Axe Belays on Snow

Thigh Belay

This belay is used on steep slopes, but is not nearly as effective as the boot belay. To set up the belay, you put your thigh or leg against the axe's shaft and run the rope around shaft and thigh.

12.7   Avalanches

When snow ceases to adhere to the slope or to the previous layers of snow or melting causes snow slopes to become unstable, large masses of

189

snow may suddenly start sliding down to the valleys below in an "avalanche." Any climber on the slope or below it when an avalanche occurs is in serious danger.

In choosing a snow route, always try to pick a route which will not be in the way of potential avalanches or likely to trigger one. In rugged mountains during winter and spring, an avalanche is always possible. If you have any suspicion at all about a given slope, avoid it.

The number and complexity of conditions affecting avalanches make it very difficult to know whether or not any particular slope will or will not avalanche. With proper knowledge and experience, however, it is possible to predict whether a slope *may* avalanche. The following brief discussion will acquaint you with some conditions under which avalanches are likely to occur.

Conditions Contributing to Avalanches

Steepness of Slope: The steeper the slope, the more likely the avalanche. However, if conditions are conducive, avalanches can occur on slopes as gentle as 15°, while snow on very steep slopes may not move.

Shape of Slope: Avalanches are more likely to occur on convex slopes than on concave slopes. Most avalanches occur in chutes or couloirs.

Anchorage of Snow to Ground Surface: Terrain type has an influence on snow anchorage. Rocks, brush, and dense woods hold the snow well; grass, wet soil, and sparse woods do not.

Anchorage of Snow to Lower Snow Layers: It may take more than a day for a stable bond to form between new snow and the hard or smooth crust of old snow. Before that bond has been established, a "dry" snow avalanche can occur. During a thaw, the bond between snow layers may be weakened by water flowing along the bonds.

Internal Cohesion of Snow Layers: The more branches snowflake crystals have, the more firmly interlocked the branches are and the more internally stable the layers are. For this reason, "corn" snow may avalanche more readily than snow with complicated snow crystals.

When branches of snow crystals melt, this weakens the stability of snow layers and may cause them to "flow" in a "wet" avalanche. This melting may be accelerated by a dry wind or by the weight of accumulated snow. Although the surface layer of snow may be internally stable, the buried layers may have lost the branches between crystals and be unstable. The branches tend to melt as snow consolidates.

Weather Effects: Temperatures—especially during a snowfall—affect the anchorage or bonding between snow layers. For example, if during a snowfall the temperature is high enough for wet snow or for rain, the snow may become saturated with water. The extra weight that results may destroy the original cohesion of the snow layers.

Destruction of bonds between snow layers may also be accelerated by wind packing the snow. On lee slopes exposed to wind, the simultaneous deposition of drifting snow and packing may result in a wind slab. A slab is very unstable; soft snow may underlie it and it may slide away in blocks when disturbed.

Depth of Snow: The greater the snow's depth, the more weight must be supported by internal cohesion or by bonding to lower layers. Thus, avalanches are more likely in deep snow. However, even the upper few inches may slide if disturbed.

Other Causes: Seracs, rocks, or cornices may fall or collapse and trigger avalanches on the slope below them.

A skier can trigger an avalanche by skiing across the slope and cutting the surface layer.

Sound is known to have been the cause of avalanches (a good reason for *not* trying to make an echo!).

Common Types of Avalanches

Dry Snow Avalanche: This type is generally expected after a cold snowfall. Cold powder snow is very unstable, especially on steep or frozen slopes. This is the most common avalanche of the early winter season. Avalanche danger is highest immediately after a snowfall and may persist if the temperature remains low. On slopes which do not get much sun (north-facing slopes) the danger may last longer than on sunny slopes. Wind packing tends to reduce the danger. A dry snow avalanche is light, moves very fast, and contains much air.

Wet Snow Avalanche: This type of avalanche can result from water saturating snow layers and consequently destroying bonds between layers of snow crystals. The wet snow avalanche is the most frequent type after mid-winter and is the most dangerous. The snow mass is heavy, contains little air, and rapidly freezes solid after it has avalanched. The danger of this type of avalanche increases as the temperature rises during the day and decreases in the late afternoon as the temperature falls.

Slab Avalanche: Slab avalanches occur when a wind-packed or frozen surface layer of snow collapses or caves into a loose layer below it. Slabs fall in large blocks.

Dangers of Typical Avalanches

Although climbers may be completely buried in a dry snow avalanche they may still survive because the dry snow contains air.

In a wet snow avalanche, buried climbers may die because the wet snow usually freezes quickly and contains little air.

Wind-slab avalanches often crush climbers with blocks of compacted snow.

When and Where to Expect Avalanches

From what has been said so far about avalanches, it is evident that certain conditions increase the probability of their occurrence. Here is a brief summary of some of those conditions:

— Wet snow avalanches occur more frequently around noon, because the sun has warmed the top surface of the snow and destroyed bonds between snow layers.

— Avalanches may occur on any slope after prolonged warm weather or wind, or after deep, new snow has fallen on hard snow.

— Old avalanche trails, chutes, slopes below cornices, unstable rock, and grassy slopes covered with snow are good candidates for avalanches.

— Less obvious places of danger are wind-slabs, particularly if they are buried or mistaken for wind-packed crust.

— A slope which settles with a crunching noise when you step on it or one with loose snow pockets under a crust should be suspected of being a wind-slab. Sometimes it is possible to detect a buried crust or wind-slab by probing with your ice axe or a pole.

— A powdery slope's instability may become apparent if you throw a snowball into it.

— Slopes that are unsafe at mid-day may be safe in the cool, early morning.

Please use these facts to help you avoid the dangers of avalanches. Keep in mind that danger is not limited to the slope itself, but also includes the area where the avalanche comes to a standstill. Here, huge masses of unstable snow collect very quickly.

Avalanche Precautions

A climbing party should make every effort to avoid being caught in an avalanche. Any slope which looks doubtful should be avoided by taking another, even if longer, route. If you must proceed through a possibly unsafe area, prepare well and use extreme care; your team probably has very few tools suitable for rescue work.

A good leader will make sure all members of a party know how to avoid starting an avalanche, what to do if caught in one, and what rescue efforts to make if necessary.

What to Do in an Avalanche

If you are caught in an avalanche, make every effort to stay on top of it and avoid being buried. Remove your pack and other encumbering gear and stay on top with swimming motions — feet downhill and held high. Cover your mouth and nose to avoid suffocation by the snow cloud accompanying a dry snow avalanche. If buried, create an air space in front of your face and chest.

Avalanche Rescue

After an avalanche, rescuers should remove all rope, loosen packs, skis, and other encumbering gear, and tie on an avalanche cord. This latter is 30 yards of colored cord which you may be able to use as a marker to aid other rescuers in locating a buried climber. (It could also be used to locate you, in case of another avalanche.) Before any rescue operations are commenced, someone should be appointed to watch for any other avalanches which may occur in the area.

A rescue procedure commonly used after an avalanche is to have rescuers probe the snow systematically (using ice axes, skis, poles), following the directions and pattern given by a rescue leader. Usually, rescuers are asked to space themselves far apart (100-300 feet) and to move one at a time, if feasible. Whenever possible, they are asked to go straight up or down the fall line on slopes where people may be buried in the snow. When rescuers locate a person buried in the snow the place is marked with an avalanche cord or pole and digging is begun immediately.

Note: In this book no attempt is made to present an extensive treatment of avalanches. People who intend to travel in rugged mountains in the winter or spring should take it upon themselves to become well informed on the subject of avalanches. In any case, words are no substitute for observation and experience in the (snow) field in the company of knowledgeable mountaineers.

12.8 Good Advice

In Section 9.4 the dangers of hypothermia are described. Read the section again. In winter, loss of heat from skin and lungs can take place very quickly; if you lose more heat than you can generate, hypothermia can result. Thus, one of the winter skills you need to cultivate is that of keeping a layer of warm air next to your skin. This can be accomplished with the "layering system" described in Section 3.2.

Cold, however, is not the only or necessarily even the main winter culprit responsible for carrying away warm air from your skin: wind can be even more of a problem. In fact, a warm wind can remove that warm air just as fast as cool, still air can. If your skin or clothes are damp, evaporation will cause a drastic loss of heat — with or without wind. In other words, it's not just the air temperature that makes you cold; when there is wind, it seems cooler — and it *is* cooler, cooler than your thermometer may indicate.

This phenomenon, which takes place when moving air removes your body heat faster than still air would, is called "wind-chill." Though a nice breeze in summer is often very welcome, in winter it can be the end of comfort and the beginning of hypothermia — if you are not properly prepared for cold weather. A wind of just 20 mph can turn a balmy winter day of 45° into a below-freezing one. So be prepared. Below is a wind-chill chart that will help you understand the difference just a little wind can make.

Estimated Wind Speed MPH	Actual Thermometer Reading °F										
	50	40	30	20	10	0	-10	-20	-30	-40	-50
	Equivalent Temperature °F										
Calm	50	40	30	20	10	0	-10	-20	-30	-40	-50
5	48	37	27	16	6	-5	-15	-26	-36	-47	-57
10	40	28	16	4	-9	-21	-33	-46	-58	-70	-83
15	36	22	9	-5	-18	-36	-45	-58	-72	-85	-99
20	32	18	4	-10	-25	-39	-53	-67	-82	-96	-110
25	30	16	0	-15	-29	-44	-59	-74	-88	-104	-118
30	28	13	-2	-18	-33	-48	-63	-79	-94	-109	-125
35	27	11	-4	-20	-35	-49	-67	-83	-98	-113	-129
40	26	10	-6	-21	-37	-53	-69	-85	-100	-116	-132

Wind speeds greater than 40 MPH have little additional effect

Little danger for properly clothed person

Increasing danger

Great danger

Danger from freezing of exposed flesh

54. Wind-Chill Chart

Chapter 13
Snow and Ice Climbing

In winter, when the mountains are dressed in their finest and the air is crisp, travel on snow can be a memorable experience. A snow route often provides an easier approach to the summit of a peak than a rock route. Snow techniques are just as interesting as rock techniques, and some feel that the most perfect type of mountaineering is that which combines both snow and rock climbing. However, glaciers and icefalls should never be underestimated, as incompetence or carelessness in crevassed areas can prove fatal. Before venturing onto a glacier or icefall, you must be experienced in crevasse rescue, proper use of crampons, route selection on snow and ice, and other techniques of glacier and ice climbing. Travel over glaciers and ice climbing involve all of the problems of snow climbing plus a great many more. For this kind of climbing you will need special equipment and should have mastered some basic techniques. To enjoy this kind of mountaineering, adequate knowledge and the ability to apply what you know are required; the safety of a party on snow depends on these preparations.

The following discussion is intended to provide information on the basic techniques you need to master for safe snow and ice climbing. For advanced ice and glacier travel, what is presented in this chapter must be supplemented by experience, mastery of advanced techniques, and knowledge of the technical literature on the subject. Careful study and practice of these can result in supremely rewarding mountaineering experiences.

13.1 Glaciers

Origin

Glaciers are a characteristic and beautiful feature of high mountains. All glaciers do not look alike, but all are caused by excess of the winter snowfall beyond the summer melting. The force produced by this increasing snow depth, solidified into ice, causes outward or downward flow from the source. The flow is outward for an icecap and downward in most other glacier types. Valley glaciers are essentially streams of ice in the same sense that rivers are streams of water. Ice flow is, of course, much slower than water flow—ranging from 8 to 12 inches a day for glaciers on Mt. Rainier to 30 to 40 feet per day for some Alaskan glaciers.

Crevasses

The movement of ice in a glacier is like the flow of an extremely heavy liquid; however, the stresses and strains created on the glacier by irregularities in the terrain produce rifts or cracks called "crevasses." Crevasses may be completely or partially exposed. A partially exposed crevasse may have a bridge over it that can be used for crossing. Such a bridge should be approached with extreme caution and examined carefully before it is used.

The crevasse depth can range from a few feet to a few hundred feet, depending on the depth of the glacier. Crevasses taper in width either horizontally (if caused by a bend in the direction of flow) or vertically (if caused by changing slope of the terrain). Thus, a crevasse that looks innocently small could actually be very dangerous; it may widen further down and be very deep. Due to continuous motion of the whole ice field, crevasses change in size, disappear, and are recreated. Each time you travel over the same glacier, you will find it changed.

55. Cross-Section of a Moving Glacier

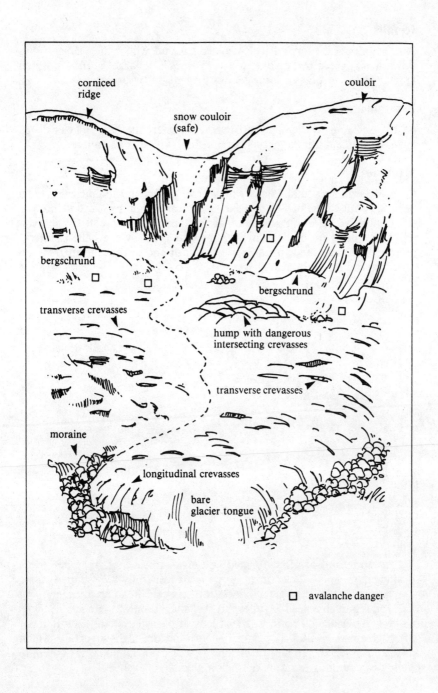

56. Anatomy of a Glacier (Good Line of Traverse Indicated with Dashed Line)

197

Icefalls

An "icefall" is a jumbled ice formation found where the glacier flows down a very steep bed or over cliffs. "Seracs" are large ice blocks which appear at the icefalls or large blocks pushed up by pressure.

Bergschrund

A "bergschrund" is the uppermost crevasse where the "live" glacier drops away from the stationary rocks or ice field which is its source.

Moraines

Piles of large and small rocks which have fallen on the glacier or have been torn out of the bed of the glacier and carried on by it are eventually left behind when the glacier changes its course or retreats. When the rocks are piled up at the sides of the glacier, they are called "lateral moraines." When they appear at the snout or end of the glacier, they are called "terminal moraines."

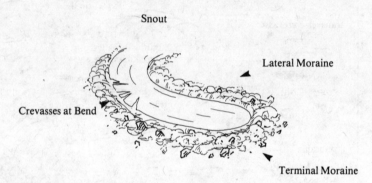

57. **Glacial Moraines**

Valleys

When mountains are first formed and eroded by water, they develop a drainage system. Valleys in this system are generally "V"-shaped; these are "pluvial" valleys. If glacial periods then occur in an area, the moving ice erodes and changes the valleys to "U"-shaped ones; these are "glacial" valleys. After glacial periods, the creeks of pluvial systems are often cut off high on the valley slopes — thus forming the high waterfalls which now add much to the natural beauty of these glacial valleys. (Yosemite Valley is a famous example of such a glacial valley.)

13.2 Equipment

In addition to the equipment necessary for serious snow travel (mentioned in the preceding chapter), glacier travel requires the items below.

Slings

In glacier travel a set of Prussik slings is always attached to the climbing rope. These slings are used, when necessary, for getting out of crevasses using the Bilgeri method. Prussiking techniques allow you to progress up a rope without having to use sheer muscle power alone (see Section 11.10 for details).

Crampons

Crampons are of two principal types, the standard "10-pointer" and the "12-pointer." The latter's two additional prongs in front enable you to kick straight in and thereby climb directly up very steep slopes. Army surplus frame crampons are not recommended because of their tendency to break or bend. When purchasing crampons, be sure they are fitted to your boots. If you borrow them for a trip, the fitting should be done before you leave home.

58. Crampons

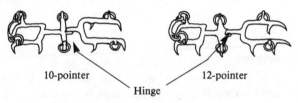

10-pointer   12-pointer

Hinge

Crampons are made from tempered steel and cannot be bent except when heated. Heating and bending should be avoided because this weakens the metal and could make the crampons dangerous to use. Once crampons have been damaged in this way, only retempering by a blacksmith will restore their strength.

Crampons are very helpful on both glacier ice and hard-frozen snow. If you are going to travel on snow at high altitudes in the early morning or at lower altitudes on exceptionally cold mornings, crampons are essential. In order to get maximum bite when walking on crampons you must be sure to place all points of the crampons on the slope.

There are certain dangers involved in using crampons. To avoid spiking your leg or tripping and falling, you must walk carefully. If you have loose pant legs, tie them snugly with a cord between your knee and ankle. Where there is soft snow over ice, your crampons will jam up with snow, making footing insecure. You then need to tap the crampons with your

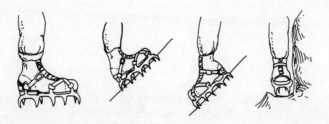

ice axe to free them from snow.

When carrying crampons in your pack, be sure to protect the points so that they will not tear up other equipment in your pack or injure you in a fall. Carrying bare crampons on the outside of your pack is not a safe practice.

Ice Axe

The ice axe and its use have been mentioned in connection with snow climbing (see Section 12.2). An important point to remember here is that whenever crossing a glacier or chopping steps, the strap should be on your wrist.

Other Equipment

Use of ice pitons, hammers, and other equipment is not discussed here. Advanced work using this equipment closely resembles 5th class rock climbing and falls outside the realm of "basic" mountaineering techniques.

13.3 Travel Over Glaciers

The Party

Before stepping onto a glacier, *rope up first*. Three make the safest rope team. The most experienced person should be first on the rope, the second best the second person, and the least experienced person should be the last on the rope. There should be a minimum of two rope teams to a party. Keep the rope strung out between climbers in order to limit the length of fall. Prussik slings should be in place on the rope.

Crevasses

The greatest danger inherent in glacier travel is crevasses — they should be carefully avoided. Crevasses frequently lie in parallel lines and tend to occur along the sides of glaciers, at bends in valleys, on steep slopes, and near obstructions; however, they can occur anywhere on a glacier.

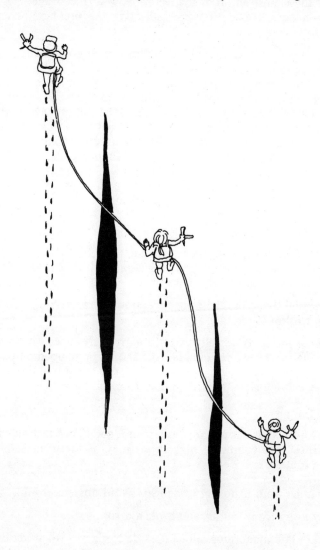

60. Traveling in Territory with Suspected Crevasses

Winter snow covers and hides crevasses, but as spring and summer progress these crevasses reappear. The ones which are wide open and clearly visible are of little danger. It is the ones hidden by snow which constitute the greatest danger and necessitate extreme caution. Because visible crevasses frequently have hidden continuations, you should be on the alert for these. Inspection of the ice or snow surface sometimes reveals dips or changes in snow texture indicating the presence of crevasses and/or their continuations.

When walking on a glacier, use your ice axe to continually probe the strength of the ice ahead of you. Each person should probe. Not only do people often miss dangerous areas, but what is safe for, say, a lightweight person, may not be safe for a heavy person. Avoid obvious breakups when possible and go well around the end of crevasses in order to avoid possible hidden continuations. When it is necessary to travel through obvious or suspected crevasse systems, cross them at right angles to lessen the chance of more than one climber going into the same crevasse. If it is necessary to travel parallel to crevasses, walk in echelon formation with each person kicking their own steps. When a crevasse bridge must be crossed, follow this procedure:

— Set up a belay.

— Examine the snow or ice bridge carefully from the side. Probing with your ice axe may give an indication of its thickness and strength if you cannot get a side view.

— Walk lightly across the bridge, cautiously transferring weight from step to step.

— Step or jump across fully exposed narrow crevasses. (A crevasse requiring much of a running takeoff should be jumped only as a last resort. Belayer should be prepared for a possible fall and should leave enough slack for the jumper to reach the opposite side.

Route Finding

In addition to what has already been mentioned in connection with safe glacier travel, the following suggestions may be useful in helping you find safe routes:

— Minimize your exposure to danger; avoid obvious trouble.

— Stay away from icefalls and broken areas.

— Follow lateral moraines along the side of glaciers whenever possible. Avoid ice.

— Stay away from cliffs at sides of glaciers, especially on volcanoes where debris is continually falling.

— Stay away from tottering seracs in icefalls. Although an ice tower may last for years, it could fall when you are under it.

— Mark your route when on any long or complicated snow or glacier trip. (Deep tracks in snow can be obliterated by bright, warm sun or snow flurries. If fog or a storm rolls in, it is often very difficult to return by your carefully selected ascent route—even if you have good visibility. Marking the route with wands flagged with colored material will help you find the return route.)

13.4 Crevasse Rescue

A Successful Rescue

If someone falls into a crevasse, it is necessary to *get them out very quickly* because the ice inside a crevasse will quickly chill them, increasing the danger of hypothermia and severe shock. The importance of speed in the rescue makes it imperative that every member of the party on a glacier climb be trained in the details of crevasse rescue. Smooth, competent action can, in a few minutes, save a life that might otherwise be lost.

The following incident illustrates a successful rescue:

A five-person party, with one rope of three and one of two, is returning from the summit of a mountain. They are crossing a glacier known to have some crevasses, which they avoided on the ascent. Although following their exact route on the descent, the lead person of the rope of three falls through the snow cover of a hidden crevasse. This occurs on a fairly level part of the glacier, and the other two on the rope immediately go into self-arrest in order to stop the leader's fall. This leaves the leader hanging by a waist loop against the side of the crevasse, about 25 feet below the top.

The climbers on the two-person rope then immediately drive an ice axe into the snow between the middle person and the crevasse and anchor the three-person rope to it with a Prussik sling. This reinforces the hold on the person dangling below and allows the other two on that rope to join the rescue operations. Carefully belayed, one person from the two-climber rope approaches the crevasse opening, crawling to lessen the pressure on the edge. The climber finds that the victim is apparently uninjured and thus can help. The rescuers decide to use a modified Bilgeri rescue.

The Bilgeri method requires two rope ends in the crevasse, so one climber of the two-person rope unties. A bowline loop is then tied in the end of the rope, which is then lowered to the person in the crevasse—who then

61. The Accident

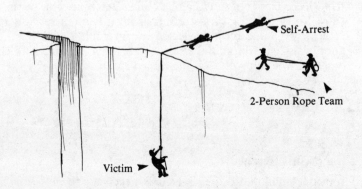

passes the loop down through a waist loop, around the back of their left leg, and over their left foot. The person then steps onto this loop, which is being held with a couple of turns around an ice axe driven solidly into the snow. The weight is now off the victim's waist loop, leaving that rope slack.

Before lowering the second rope, a rolled-up parka was placed on the lip of the crevasse to prevent the first rope from sinking into the lip. Now that the weight is off the other rope, it is also shifted onto the parka, and an axe is driven in the snow so this rope can be anchored with turns around the shaft.

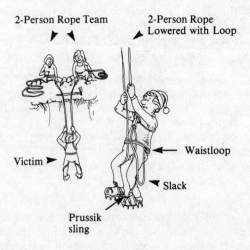

62. Bilgeri Rescue

The victim then pulls down a couple of feet of slack from their team's rope and pushes the Prussik knot of their sling up the rope. Now they are able to pass the bowline loop of this sling down through their waist loop, around the back of their right leg, and over their right foot. Then the hanging climber puts weight on each foot alternately, while those above take up rope around the axes as each rope in turn is made slack by the shifts in weight. Within just a few minutes, the dangling leader is helped out over the lip of the crevasse and a highly efficient and successful rescue is ended.

Possible Complications in Crevasse Rescues

There were no complications in the above illustration of an efficient and fast crevasse rescue, but here are some of the things that can occur, along with action that should be taken:

— A victim can be unconscious or too injured to give assistance. If the victim is light enough and there are enough people in the party, the person can simply be hauled out. If this is impossible, another climber can be lowered into the crevasse to remove the victim's pack (which can then be pulled up separately), to give first aid, or to put warm clothing on the victim. With a small party it may be necessary to set up a "Spanish windlass" type of rescue, which takes much more time and requires more equipment and experience.

If another climbing party is in the vicinity, its help should usually be summoned in case of a crevasse fall. The added strength and additional equipment will increase the chances of a successful rescue.

— Sometimes a victim may be able to climb out of a narrow crevasse if they are wearing crampons. Even though the walls are vertical, the climber can stem out, as in a rock chimney. Rope assistance can be given by other team members.

13.5 Good Advice

Glaciated mountains are beautiful, and climbing them can be highly enjoyable. However, before venturing onto a glacier, you should be familiar with crevasse rescue, proper use of crampons, route selection, and other techniques of glacier and ice climbing which have only been mentioned here. Careful study and practice of these techniques and methods can reward you with extraordinary mountaineering experiences.

Chapter 14
Desert Travel

During summer and fall, the desert is very hot and dry and usually unsuitable for mountaineering activities. During the winter and spring, however, most desert regions are pleasantly cool and beautiful. During this time, you can enjoy the desert's magnificent views and clear, star-studded nights in relative safety and comfort.

There are many stories about the rigors and dangers of the desert. Most of these are overstated. You needn't fear the desert, but you should respect it. In other words, desert trips take a lot of advance planning. Be sure to check into local weather patterns and get up-to-date trail information before embarking on a trip. (For example, do you know which trails have been washed out since last year?) Give special consideration to water supply, temperature, and type of terrain. At least one member of your group should be familiar with the route you plan to take.

When you go to the desert, as with all mountaineering trips, let someone—preferably a park ranger—know where you are going, when you will be back, and what routes you expect to travel. Don't change your plans. Follow your course carefully so that you always know where you are at all times. Upon returning, be sure to let the ranger know.

14.1 Equipment and Supplies

Most of the equipment used for mountaineering is adequate for desert wilderness travel. However, there are a few additional considerations, some of which are listed below.

Boots

Be sure your footwear is in good condition when hiking in the desert. Heat and perspiration can cause some very serious problems, as can sand. Sturdy, well-ventilated shoes or boots are a necessity. If you wear shoes with thin soles and the weather is hot, you are liable to raise a painful crop of blisters. Many people who hike in the desert prefer sturdy, flat-soled shoes or boots for walking on sand or gravel, rather than heavy mountaineering boots. For canyons with streams, tennis shoes stand up better than leather under repeated wadings, so it's a good idea to bring a pair along on a desert trip.

Clothing

In the desert it is possible to wear lighter weight clothing than in the mountains, but you must keep in mind that although the desert may be very warm in the daytime, it can be as cold as higher mountain areas in the evening. Although heavy clothing is not always essential, you should carry a wool sweater or shirt and windbreaker. Light-colored, loose clothing is most comfortable because it reflects the heat and gives better air circulation during the heat of the day. Cotton or a cotton-polyester blend is best because it absorbs perspiration and then cools you by evaporation. If you wear shorts during the day, either use a sunscreen or make sure you are already sufficiently tanned not to burn. The greater the area of skin you expose, the greater your water loss through perspiration will be. If water is a consideration, as it often is in the desert, you should keep your body lightly covered by wearing long sleeves and trousers.

Keep your head covered in the heat of the day; sunstroke or heat exhaustion is not fun. Carry and use plenty of sunscreen lotion. Protect your eyes from glare and dust by good dark glasses; well-ventilated, goggle-type glasses are best. Optically coated lenses are recommended; plastic scratches easily.

Ten Essentials

When you travel in the desert, always carry your Ten Essentials. You may want to add tweezers (for cactus spines), sunscreen lotion, chapstick, and spare sunglasses. Make sure your first aid kit contains a snake bite kit.

Sleeping Bag

A sleeping bag for the desert can usually be lighter than one for mountain travel, but here again what you need depends on the time of the year and the temperature expected. It is not unusual for night temperatures in the desert to fall below freezing in winter, early spring, and late fall. A ground cloth is necessary, but an air mattress is usually not because sand can be easily shaped to your body contours; many people carry an Ensolite pad because it insulates well from both heat and cold.

Food and Water

The food suggestions included in Section 9.2 can also be used for desert travel. The only exception is dehydrated foods — these require quite a bit of water for preparation. On extended desert trips the weight of additional water may prohibit their exclusive use. You should also avoid greasy foods and those which create thirst or spoil easily.

Water supply is almost always the major problem in the desert. Experience has taught travelers that in very dry climates and warm temperatures (80-90°F) anything less than four quarts total intake per day will affect the body's efficiency and cause considerable discomfort. With higher humidity and lower temperatures (60-70°F), the minimum requirement may be reduced to two quarts total intake per day. The above suggestions are for average physical effort. With great activity or higher temperatures, the requirement increases very rapidly. Always take more water than you think you will need.

You need all the water you drink. As long as you want it, your body uses it better than your canteen does. The most practical ways to economize on water use are to remain in the shade, to shift all activities to the cooler hours, and to avoid activity that will cause you to produce more sweat. Remember that in the desert sun sweat is saved by wearing clothes, not discarding them. If you must walk during hot weather, travel early or late in the day or night if moonlight allows enough visibility and the terrain is not hazardous.

Non-drinkable water can be used on clothing or skin to help your body keep cool. Eat foods that are high in water; most fruits and vegetables contain large amounts of moisture. Foods high in protein and salt should be kept to a minimum, as they require large amounts of water for digestion and excretion.

Springs which do not attract the wildlife of an area may not be safe to drink even when purified, due to dissolved minerals which may be poisonous or irritating to the human digestive system. Be very suspicious of a water source if there are no signs of animal prints and droppings or even of dead insects. If good water locations are known, campsites and stops for water replenishment should be planned around them. Do not camp too close to a waterhole, as wildlife will visit it during the night. You are a visitor in the desert and should not unnecessarily disrupt the lives and habits of its inhabitants. When reaching a suitable campsite, proceed as in mountain camping by setting up camp before dark.

Cooking in the desert differs little from mountain cooking except that the scarcity of water makes cleaning pots and plates more difficult. A more positive difference is that foods take less time to cook than in the mountains.

One of the main concerns of the trip planner is to provide for replenishing the water supply without making water carrying a heavy burden (a gallon of water weighs eight pounds). It is well to remember that although desert water often does not have a refreshing taste (because of being sometimes stagnant and/or alkaline), it does satisfy the demand for liquid if proper precautions are used to insure its safety. (See Section 7.2 for water purification suggestions.)

14.2   Desert Hiking and Camping

Car Approach

In flat areas, many miles of desert travel can be by car if some sort of road is available. Because you will have to walk many miles if anything goes wrong, your car must be in good operating condition, especially the radiator and cooling system. For rough road driving a spare tire (or even two) should be taken, along with a tire pump and tools for tire changing and minor mechanical repairs. You will need not only a jack, but a board to support it. For possible trouble in sand it is advisable to have a couple of boards, strips of lath wire, or carpet (2 x 6 feet), a cupped shovel (not a flat one), and a piece of plastic to lie on. Carry some cork or a bar of soap for a possible hole in the pan.

Distances between gas stations are often great and on some desert trips it is wise to carry extra gas and oil. Check your mileage before starting and refill the tank at every opportunity. Take extra water for the radiator as well as for your own needs. Do not use glass jugs or any breakable containers, as a bumpy road may break them and cause loss of water or gas.

Keep your car on the road tracks — they are most likely to be hard-packed through use. Don't drive closely behind other cars; you may need additional momentum to clear deep sand traps or other road irregularities. Anticipate when you will need to shift to another gear and do it before the need arises. Do not attempt to turn around or get off the tracks without first checking the road. Know the clearance of your car, being sure to take into account the loss of clearance due to a heavy load or to reduction of the pressure in your tires in order to obtain better traction.

When you begin to sink into sand or gravel, do what you can to provide traction for the wheels before trying to drive again. Do not spin the wheels — this will only make the situation worse. Letting the air our of your tires down to minimum of 20 pounds will make it possible to get better traction (a flatter tire gives you more surface area). The tires should be pumped up again before traveling on pavement. (If this is not possible, drive slowly.) In case you forgot the carpet, brush or rocks can also help you to get some traction. If you have a breakdown, stay with your car until help arrives. Stay even if it takes a couple of days for you to be found. (See Section 10.6 on "Your Car Can Save Your Life.")

On back country trips cars should travel together whenever possible, so that the travelers can assist each other in case of emergency. On narrow roads, ascending cars have the right of way. When you see a car coming, stop at the first wide spot; there might not be another. When driving in the desert, remember that desert back roads demand slow speeds — not in excess of 15 to 20 miles per hour for many stretches. Use low gears and low driving ranges; many desert roads are steeper than they appear.

When climbing slopes in late afternoon, up-canyon tail winds often increase the chances of your radiator boiling. To hasten cooling, head the car into the wind and keep the motor idling. During warm weather, cars sometimes vapor lock and refuse to start again after brief stops. The only way to remedy this condition is to wait for the motor to cool. Leaving the hood open and wrapping a wet cloth around the fuel pump will help speed the process. At the trailhead, turn your car around so that it will be easier to get back on the road when you return. Don't park at the bottom of a wash.

Hiking in the Desert

Like other trips by a group, progress in desert travel should be at an even pace that the whole party can maintain and enjoy. Rest stops should be made at regular intervals. The group should remain together unless the leader says otherwise; all should be aware that separation in the desert can contribute to loss of time and more serious situations. Visibility in flat, brushy territory is very poor, and in the middle of the day there is often distortion due to haze and heat waves. Few natural leads, such as creeks and valleys, are available. When resting, utilize any available shade, even of low vegetation, to minimize dehydration. Drink water at regular intervals.

In some desert areas, summer temperatures as high as 125°F are not uncommon. Trips should not be taken during such heat. A person can survive only one to one-and-a-half days without water at this temperature if exertion is necessary. With 20% loss of body fluids, death can occur. If you expect daytime temperatures to be high, plan to use the comparatively cooler evening and early morning hours for travel. Walking at night should be done in sufficient moonlight or with flashlight.

The desert flora include many distinctive and wonderful plants found in no other biotic area. Among them are a number which are thorny — for example, many types of cacti and trees such as the ocotillo and cats-claw acacia. Rattlesnakes and scorpions are also common in the desert, particularly in brushy areas where the ground is not visible. In warm weather snakes may be out at night. The experienced desert traveler has a trained eye on the watch for these reptiles and for thorns and at the same time is able to enjoy the surrounding view. Walking in single file minimizes dangers from thorns, snakes, separation, etc. and also damages the desert less.

Hiking Navigation in the Desert

One of the difficulties of desert travel is orienting yourself with regard to your location, the direction you are heading, and the safest way back to your point of origin (unless you have arranged a car shuttle for a one-way trip).

When you are planning a desert trip, study the maps and decide the course or compass bearing to follow. It may appear from the map that you can take a bearing directly to your destination; at other times major obstacles, such as hills, may necessitate plotting a multi-bearing course. The almost complete lack of distinctive landmarks or leading ground configurations such as valleys or washes makes hiking navigation in the desert difficult. Despite what the map may indicate, desert trails often are partially obliterated or divide and become barely recognizable. Unless someone has previously scouted the trail your group is planning to use, you should assume that you will probably have to navigate by compass at least part of the time. If you are not proficient in this skill, be sure to choose a well-known trail.

If the trail is poor or nonexistent, you can hold your direction by transferring the compass bearing of a landmark to an equivalent objective that you can follow, perhaps for many hours. This will also permit you to temporarily follow washes or ravines or avoid bad sandy or rocky areas. Whenever such a deviation is necessary, estimate the distance you go off the original course and then return an equal distance. To follow a course consisting of more than one bearing, first follow one direction to a specific point, then change direction, using the same procedure until you reach the next predetermined point. This may be repeated until you reach your destination.

Many desert trips involve hiking down or up water courses. Some of these canyons, ravines, and arroyos have year around spring-fed streams and borders of lush greenery; others have only intermittent streams, with the springs drying up in hot weather when the water table drops; yet others only have water during and directly after rains or snows in higher mountain areas. Even if the weather is clear when you are hiking in a canyon, rains elsewhere can cause flash floods — so keep informed of the weather in surrounding areas and never camp in a water course. It is a good idea to carry a rope and know how to use it if you plan on traveling in desert canyons.

Your return trip may be by the same route taken when entering the area. In this case it is helpful to keep a written record or sketches of the compass bearings and distant objectives followed on the way in. Another precaution is to sight an objective not only in one direction but also in the reverse direction—as it will be when you follow it on the return trip. It is a good idea to form the habit of looking back toward your starting point after traveling some distance and recording the appearance of the horizon and landmarks in detail. This will aid you in finding your car when you return. One member of the group should keep these records.

Do not rely on memory, especially on an extended trip into unfamiliar territory. It is not at all difficult to become confused in the desert. Because your survival margin is slim, you need all the help you can get to set you back on your proper course if you inadvertently wander off. It is at times like this that such records can become lifesavers. If, despite reasonable precautions, you do become lost or a member of your party becomes separated from the rest of the group, follow the suggestions in Section 10.1.

Camping in the Desert

Except in the dead of winter, desert trip gear need not be as heavy duty as for mountain travel. If you are not taking a tent, you can take along the fly or a tarp and a tent pole or two so that you can set up a lean-to or canopy during the hottest part of the day. Don't use sandy washes as campsites, as they are often cold and damp at night—and if it rains you may find yourself in the middle of a river!

14.3 Surviving in the Desert

If, due to accident or carelessness, you have not begun your hike out when you still have plenty of food and water, you must immediately begin to economize your resources—including physical strength as well as food and water—and think seriously about what you will do if you run out of water.

Max. Daily Temp. in Shade °F	Expected Days of Survival for Amount of Water					
	none	1 qt.	2 qt.	4 qt.	10 qt.	20 qt.
120	2	2	2	2.5	3	4.5
110	3	3	3.5	4	5	7
100	5	5.5	6	7	9.5	13.5
90	7	8	9	10.5	15	23
80	9	10	11	13	19	29
70	10	11	12	14	20.5	32
65	10	11	12	14	21	32
50	10	11	12	14.5	21	32

(Taken from "Thirst," *Natural History,* Dec. 1956.)

63. How Long Can You Survive in the Shade?

In order to conserve body moisture, do not walk in the hottest part of the day or exert yourself unnecessarily; rest in the shade during the day. Keep covered; exposure to the sun will use up more water. If you have a choice, avoid eating fats or use them very sparingly; fat digestion takes more water than carbohydrate digestion and will shorten survival time. You may have to dispose of useless weight and return and recover it later.

Food

There is plenty of life in the desert — but for the perhaps desperate visitor to discover and use this life requires time and knowledge. Catching animals is not easy, except for lizards (whose tails can furnish at least some nourishment) and snakes, which are also edible. Toads are not edible. Catching birds, rabbits, or field rats is nearly impossible for the inexperienced. Do not eat plants unless you know they are not poisonous. If you find moist and grassy areas, investigate for wild onion; their leaves look much like those of small green onions. If you pull one up and smell it you'll have no difficulty telling it is an onion. Cactus apples can also furnish some nourishment.

Water

If you are looking for water, head for the top of canyons which have green vegetation in them, as the higher levels sometimes have springs. There is usually water where you see palm trees. If water is not available, there are two sources of moisture you can use in emergencies: plants (usually cacti) and air.

Cacti: The meatier the cactus, the juicier it will be. The barrel cactus is considered the best candidate for moisture extraction. To obtain liquid, break up a cactus and squeeze the juice out of the pulp. Juicy succulents will also supply a fair amount of liquid. A fairly efficient way of getting the moisture out of a cactus is to set the outside on fire (it should burn easily), then cut off the top and with a knife or any suitable tool hollow out the top to a cup shape, chipping the meat to a watery pulp. The liquid is drinkable and the pulp will at least stop hunger pains. Another recommendation is to knock over a barrel or fish-hook cactus, cut off the top, hollow it, set it up again with the lid in place, and build a fire around it. The heat drives the water to the hollow-ed out part of the cactus.

Dew Method: Scoop out a large hole in the ground, line it with plastic, parka, poncho, or what have you and fill it with cool pebbles. Dew will form on the cool pebbles overnight, then trickle down and collect on the canvas or plastic. The quantity can be very small or as much as a cup, depending on the amount of moisture in the air.

214

14.4 Low Impact Pointers

Our deserts have enough problems without hikers adding to them. Mining, overgrazing by both domestic and feral animals, and off-road vehicles are major problems. However, when too many hikers use an area the result can be similar. Although the desert may look as if it were hard to damage (after all, what can you do to harm sand and rocks?), the opposite is actually true. Desert ecosystems are fragile and easily disrupted — perhaps because they exist on the edge, the farther reaches of adaptation, where there is little room for sudden change or disruption without fatal consequences. In the desert, the brush, cacti, and rocks are important habitats for desert creatures. When brush or cacti are trampled, their already slow growth rate is slowed even further and wind and water erosion can set in. In this way, a whole area can eventually become devoid of plants and animals. At the very least, careless hikers visibly mark the desert for decades, perhaps centuries, to come.

Again, remember to leave desert waterholes for the native inhabitants; do not camp near springs or streams. Animals such as the dwindling bighorn sheep will not remain in areas where they have to compete with people for water.

Appendix A
Spring/Summer/Fall Trip Checklist

This list includes what you will be wearing at the trailhead. Extra clothing, food, and water are just that — items you wouldn't use except to cope with the unexpected.

Backpack

Permits
(Wilderness, Fire, Fishing)

Ten Essentials

Map of the area
Compass
Flashlight (with extra batteries and bulbs)
Sunglasses
Extra food and water

Extra clothing
Waterproofed matches
Candle or firestarter
Pocket knife
First aid kit (See Section 9.2 for checklist)

Emergency

Optional: signal whistle, metal signal mirror, extra prescription glasses

Repair & Maintenance Kit

Needle and thread
Buttons
Wire (#24, brass or copper)
Nylon string
Ripstop nylon patches

Rubber bands
Safety pins
Clevis pins and rings for pack
Shoelace/s

Clothing

Hiking boots (broken in, water-proofed)
Wool outer socks
Light inner socks
Long-sleeved, lightweight, "sun" shirt
Long pants (wool for cold weather

Shorts
Synthetic or down parka with hood
Bandana
Underclothes
Windbreaker with hood
Short-sleeved shirt
Wool watchcap or balaclava

Wool sweater or shirt

Sun hat (something with brim)

Rain poncho, cagoule, or jacket
  with hood

Optional: camp shoes (sandals, old tennies), wind pants, rain pants, swimsuit, fishnet shirt, gaiters (ankle-high), gloves, belt, raincover for pack, long underwear

Cooking

Cookset or pots

Stove with accessories (fuel
    funnel, etc.)

Fuel

Aluminum foil

Dishrag or sponge

Potgripper

Matches

Can opener (if not on knife)

Measuring spoon (tablespoon)

Candle or firestarter

Frying "pan" (metal plate)

Plastic scouring pad

Cup/s (marked for measuring)

Spoon

Nylon bags for hanging food

⅛" nylon cord for same
    (80' for bears)

Extra plastic bags and ties

Optional: pancake turner, large plastic trash bags, grill, collapsible water carrier, windscreen for stove, long-handled stirring spoon, biodegradable soap, paper towels, small wire whip

Food

Breakfasts, lunches, dinners, snacks, condiments (see Appendix E and Chapter 8 for suggestions)

Shelter

Tent with fly, tube tent, tarpaulin, or mini-tent (with poles, lines, stakes, etc.)

Ground cloth, plastic (3'x7-½' minimum)

Sleeping

Sleeping bag, 3-season, synthetic
    or down

Sleeping bag straps

Stuff sack for sleeping bag

Sleeping pad, closed-cell foam
    or air mattress
    (with patch kit)

General (frequent use)

Water bottle/s, wide-mouth,
    1-qt size

Moleskin

Lip balm

Sunscreen

Toothbrush

Toothpaste

Dental floss

Nail clippers

Comb

Insect repellent	Small, thin towel and washcloth
Pencil and small notebook	Biodegradable soap
Toilet paper	Trip information sheet

Optional: security strap for glasses, hand lotion, clothespins, water purification tablets.

General (infrequent use)

Identification	Important phone numbers
Keys to car	Dimes for phone calls

Special Equipment (for rock climbing, etc.)

Luxuries

Watch	Games
Camera and accessories	Musical instrument and music
Field books	✗ Fishing gear
Area guidebooks	Candle lantern with extra
✗ Binoculars	candles
Insoles for hiking boots	✗ Day pack or fanny pack
(closed-cell foam)	

Water

Stuff Bags (marked)

To Be Left in Car

Extra car keys	Dirty clothes bag
Water	Spare tire
Pencil and paper	Small piece of plywood
Car repair tools	or carpet
Change of clothes	Checkbook and/or credit cards
Food	(well-concealed)
Gas can	Money (well-concealed)
Tow rope	Shovel
Antifreeze in radiator	Jumper cables
Trip information sheet ✗	

Winter Mountaineering Trip Checklist

Backpack

(probably soft pack or one with interior frame)

Permits

(Wilderness, Fire, Fishing)

Ten Essentials

(same as for Spring/Summer/Fall)

Emergency

(same)

Optional: avalanche cord, signal flares, bivouac sack

Repair and Maintenance kit

(add any items necessary to repair skis, snowshoes, or other winter mountaineering equipment)

Clothing

(same, except for following changes and additionsl)

Heavy wool socks	Gaiters (calf-high)
Wool shirt *and* wool sweater	Wool long pants
Wind pants (nylon, not waterproof)	Heavy down or synthetic parka with hood
Wool mittens	Long underwear (wool, thermal knit, fishnet)
Overmitts	
Wool balaclava	

Optional: wool knickers, synthetic or down booties, glove liners

Delete: shorts, short-sleeved shirt

Cooking

(same)

Food

(same)

Shelter

Tent with fly and accessories (must have proper ventilation if you plan to cook in tent)

Ground cover for inside tent
Ground cloth

Optional: tent vestibule (for cooking, storage), frostliner

Sleeping

Sleeping bag adequate for winter, down or synthetic
Stuff bag and straps for sleeping bag

Sleeping pad, closed-cell foam, full-length

General (frequent use)

(same, except for following changes and additions)

Snow goggles
Waterproof cover for pack (can use large plastic garbage bags)

Glacier cream for lips, ears, nose
Waterproofing for boots (e.g., "Snow Seal")

Delete: insect repellent

General (infrequent use)

(same)

Special Equipment

Optional: skis, snowshoes, bindings, waxes, poles; rock or ice climbing equipment; and so on

Luxuries (same)

Water

Stuff Bags

To Be Left in Car

(same)

Appendix B

Mountaineering Mail Order Houses*

Adventure 16, 4620 Alvarado Canyon Rd., San Diego, California 92120, 283-2374

Alpenlite, P.O. Box 851 (108 S. Spring), Claremont, California 91711, (714) 626-6400

Altra, Inc., 5541 Central Ave., Boulder, Colorado 80301

Eddie Bauer, Third & Virginia, Seattle, Washington 98124

L. L. Bean, Inc., 3871 Main St., Freeport, Maine 04033

Black Ice, 120 Woodland Ave., Reno, Nevada 89523

Camp 7, 802 So. Sherman St., Longmont, Colorado 80501, (800) 525-3707

Camp Trails Co., P.O. Box 23155, Phoenix, Arizona 85063

Caribou Mountaineering, P.O. Box 3696, Chico, California 95927, (916) 345-1671

Class 5, 1480 - 66th St., Emeryville, California 94608, (415) 653-6366

The Coleman Company, Inc., 250 North St. Frances, Wichita, Kansas, 67201

Co-Op Wilderness Supply, 1607 Shattuck Ave., Berkeley, California, 94709 (414) 843-9300

Damart, 1811 Woodbury Ave., Portsmouth, New Hampshire 03801

Early Winters, Ltd., 110 Prefontaine Pl., South, Seattle, Washington 98104

Eastern Mountain Sports, Inc., 1041 Commonwealth Ave., Boston, Massachusetts 02215

Eureka Tent, Inc., Box 966, Binghamton, New York 13902

Frostline Kits, Frostline Circle, Denver, Colorado 80241

Gerry, 5450 North Valley Highway, Denver, Colorado 80246

Great Pacific Iron Works, P.O. Box 150, Ventura, California 93001, (805) 643-8616

Gregory Mountain Products, 4620 Alvarado Canyon Rd., #13, San Diego, California 92120, (714) 284-4050

Holubar Mountaineering, Ltd., 3650 So. Bristol St., Santa Ana, California (714) 549-8541 Box 7, Boulder, Colorado 80306

Jansport, Paine Field Industrial Park, Everett, Washington 98204

Kelty Pack Inc., 9281 Borden Ave., Sun Valley, Idaho 91352, (213) 768-1922

Lowe Alpine Systems, P.O. Box 189, La Fayette, Colorado 80026

Mountain Safety Research, 631 So. 96th St., Seattle, Washington 98108

The North Face, 1234 Fifth St., Berkeley, California 94710, (415) 524-8532

Pacific Mountain Works, 2670 Via de la Valle, Del Mar, California 92014, 481-SKIS

R.E.I. Co-op, 405 E. Torrance Blvd., Carson, California 90745
  P.O. Box C-88125, Seattle, Washington 98188

Robbins Mountain Paraphernalia, Box 45-36, Modesto, California 95352

Sherpa Designs, Inc., 3109 Brookdale Rd. East, Tacoma, Washington 98446

The Ski Hut, P.O. Box 309, Berkeley, California 94701, (415) 843-6505

Trailwise, 2407 Fourth St., Berkeley, California 94710, (415) 548-0568

Wilderness Experience, 20120 Plummer, Chatsworth, California 91311,
  (213) 248-9438

Yak Works Corp., 10706 Twelfth Ave., N.W., Seattle, Washington, 98177

* Most, if not all, of these companies will send you a free catalog!

Appendix C

How To Make Gaiters

Procedure:

1. Make pattern. See drawing below.
2. Hot cut material. Cut 2 pieces
3. Sew drawhem at top. See drawing below
4. Sew hem at bottom.
5. Install hook or set grommet. Center at front. Install hook upside down.
6. Install grommets or loops on sides.
7. Sew up rear seam.
8. Install drawstring at top.
9. Install tie-down string. (Ties under boot, to hold gaiter down.)
10. Install front tie-down string.

Height of gaiters varies slightly for longer or shorter legs.

How to Form Drawhem at Top

Step 1   Step 2   Step 3

fold   fold   stitch

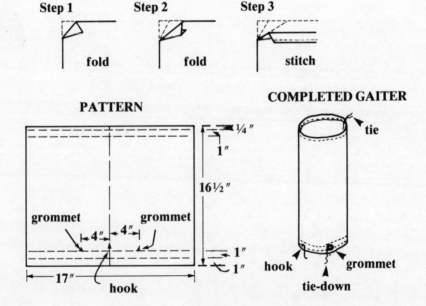

PATTERN

COMPLETED GAITER

How To Make Mittens

Procedure:

1. Draw outline around hand on piece of paper. Allow enough room for liners.

2. Cut pattern out of paper. Allow ¼ inch for seams.

3. Trace pattern on material. Side of pattern opposite thumb should be along fold so that when it's opened out, it will look like the middle drawing.

4. Cut material. Hot cutting is best so material won't ravel.

5. Sew seams together, wrong side out. Double stitch. Elastic may be used at the wrist if desired.

6. Wool liners may be made the same way. Use old sweaters for material. Use cuff and sweater bottom ribbing as selvage.

Size should just fit hand. Remember to allow enough room for liners.

fold

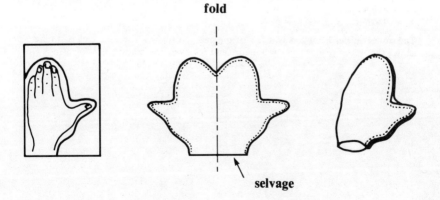

selvage

Appendix D

Stove Comparison

Stove name	Type of Fuel	Weight of Stove (oz)	Fuel Capacity (oz)	Burn Time Full On Hrs:Min	Approximate Boil Times (Minutes)		
					Sea Level	5000'	10,000'
Bluet S200	B	14.3	6.8	2:45	7.5	7.0	9.5
Instaflam	B	20.5	6.8	3:25	8.0	11.0	12.5
MSR X-GK	Various	15.0	32.0	4:00	3.5		5.0
Optimus OO	K	22.5	13.3	5:10	6.0	7.5	5.5
Optimus 8R	WG	22.5	3.3	1:10	10.0	7.0	9.0
Optimus 80	WG	18.0	4.5	1:10	6.5	6.5	8.5
Peak I	WG	28.0	10.0	1:50	4.5	4.5	5.5
Primus Grasshopper	P	11.5	14.0	6:15	7.0	9.0	9.5
Primus Mini-Ranger	B	15.3	7.3	4:05	7.0	8.5	11.0
Svea 123	WG	17.0	4.0	1:05	6.5	8.5	9.0

Key to Types of Fuel: B, butane; P, propane; WG, white gas; K, kerosene.

Stove weights are for empty stove (without fuel bottle). Stoves using fuel bottles can be used with pint quart bottles.

The stoves on this list are only a few of the many available. These were chosen because experience h shown that they are efficient, well-made, and relatively inexpensive.

Appendix E
Trail Food Suggestions

Carbohydrates

Breads, whole grain*
    English muffins
    tortillas
    chapatis
    loaves, uncut (they keep better)
    crackers
    pita (pocket) bread
    quick sweet breads (e.g., banana)

Cereals, whole grain*
    oatmeal (quick-cooking)
    cream of whole rice
    cream of whole rye
    whole wheat
        flakes (bran or other)
        bulgur
        cream of whole wheat
    mixed grains
        "Grapenuts"
        "Familia"
        "Bear Mush"
        granola

Trail Mix (with whole grains, dried fruits, nuts, seeds, carob and/or chocolate chips, etc.)

Noodles/Macaroni/Spaghetti, whole grain*

Brown rice, long grain (cooks faster)

Vegetables (fresh, freeze-dried, dehydrated)
—be sure to include potatoes (whole, instant), they are particularly
quick and easy to prepare

Fruits (fresh, freeze-dried, dehydrated)
—please carry out your citrus peels!
—many hikers become addicted to home-made fruit leather

Cookies and dessert bars, whole grain

Candy
sesame seed bars made with honey
various high-energy bars made with fruits, nuts, honey, etc.
halvah (made from ground sesame seeds and honey—doesn't melt)
various nut and fruit "clusters" coated with carob or chocolate

Flours, whole grain (for pancakes, biscuits, bread, gravies, sauces, etc.)*
—you can put together the pancake, bread, and biscuit mixes
at home

Honey, dried honey, date sugar, malt sugar, cane sugar**

Proteins

Meats, etc.
fish, chicken, or beef (freeze-dried, dehydrated, or fresh)
salmon or albacore packed in water (too much oil is hard to digest)
sardines packed in water or mustard/tomato sauce

Dairy products
cheese, natural, pasteurized (raw goes bad too fast without
refrigeration, except in cool weather)
eggs (fresh or freeze-dried)
cottage cheese (freeze-dried)
milk, non-instant, spray dried, whole or skim (reconstitute using
wire whip or add to various recipes for enrichment)

Beans, etc. (freeze-dried or dehydrated)
red, kidney, pinto, white, navy, lima, black, etc.
lentils (cook quickly)
split peas (cook quickly)
soy grits (cook quickly, use as enrichment)
soy "nuts", toasted (for snacks)

Nuts and seeds (all kinds)
nut and seed "butters" (good on almost anything)
almonds, peanuts, cashews, pecans, walnuts, sunflower, sesame,
pumpkin, etc. (toasted or raw)

Fats and Oils

Butter (granules are now available—they don't spoil)
Polyunsaturated oils (safflower, soy, corn, etc.)
Nuts, seeds, cheeses, and eggs also have quite a bit of fat and oil
    in them

Seasonings

salt, pepper
garlic powder
onion powder or flakes
green pepper flakes
parsley, dried
cloves, cinnamon, nutmeg
chili powder, cayenne, curry
basil, oregano, rosemary, thyme (or whatever)
bouillion cubes
gravies, dressings, sauces (dehydrated)
parmesan or romano cheese, grated
soy sauce, miso
sesame seeds

Hot and Cold Drinks

Orange, lemon, grapefruit, tomato crystals (freeze-dried)
Chocolate or toasted carob drink mixes (hot or cold)
Instant coffee or coffee "bags" (with ground coffee!)
Tea, regular or herb (instant or no)
Non-caffeinated cereal beverages, instant (e.g., Pero, Cafix, etc.)
Bouillion cubes (they come in several flavors)
Electrolyte replacement drink mixes (avoid those with FD&C coal tar
    dyes; remember to dilute with 2-3 times more water than called for,
    so your stomach will tolerate them better

Ready-Made ("Instant") Whole Foods

Soups and puddings (try whole food stores for brands without sugar and
    unnecessary additives)
Hummous (a dip made from garbanzo beans, high-protein—just add
    water)
Ramen, whole grain (just add hot water)
"Burger" mixes (can be used with or without meat—just add water)
    felafel
    sesame burger
    sunflower burger
    soy burger

* Whole grains are recommended because they supply complex carbohydrates. Complex carbohydrates are higher in protein, fiber, vitamins, and minerals than the simple carbohydrates found in white flour products. Ounce for ounce, you'll get more energy from whole grains than from highly processed ones.

** Sugar is sugar, but cane sugar (including brown sugar) can give you more of an unpleasant "blood sugar bounce" than the sugars found in less refined honey, date sugar, and so on. These latter tend to be used more slowly by the body.

Appendix F

California Wilderness Areas

A Wilderness Permit is required before entering any of the 24 special Wilderness or Primitive Areas in the National Forests of California. Getting the permits is the responsibility of the trip leader.

Wilderness permits are free to anyone who will agree to follow simple rules intended to protect the visitor as well as the wilderness resource. The permit also authorizes the building of campfires in some areas. A permit is issued for a single trip during a specified period of time. Only one permit is required for a group traveling together, but a separate permit is necessary for each trip.

To obtain a permit, contact the appropriate ranger station or other forest service office listed below. You may apply in person or by mail. If your trip extends through more than one wilderness, or through more than one national forest, you should obtain your permit from the office covering your starting point. If your trip starts in a national park, obtain a permit from the national park office. This permit is valid in National Forest Wilderness and Primitive Areas.

If you expect your trip to last more than 10 days, please include your approximate route of travel in general terms.

Northern California

CARIBOU
Lassen National Forest
707 Nevada Street
Susanville, CA 96130

MARBLE MOUNTAIN
Klamath National Forest
1215 S. Main Street
Yreka, CA 96967

SALMON-TRINITY ALPS
(for south side entry)
Shasta-Trinity National Forest
P.O. Box T
Weaverville, CA 96063

(for north side entry)
Klamath National Forest
1215 S. Main St.
Yreka, CA 96067

SOUTH WARNER
Modoc National Forest
P.O. Box 220
Cedarville, CA 96104

THOUSAND LAKES
Lassen National Forest
707 Nevada Street
Susanville, CA 96130

YOLLA-BOLLY-MIDDLE EEL
(for south side entry)
Mendocino National Forest
420 E. Laurel Street
Willows, CA 95988

(for north side entry)
Shasta-Trinity National Forest
Platina, CA 96076

Central California

DESOLATION
Lake Tahoe Basin Mgt. Unit
Box 8465
1062 Tata Lane
South Lake Tahoe, CA 95705

EMIGRANT/EMIGRANT BASIN
Stanislaus National Forest
19777 Greenley Rd.
Sonora, CA 95370

HIGH SIERRA
Sequoia National Forest
Miramonte, CA 93641

HOOVER
(for east side entry)
Toiyabe National Forest
Bridgeport, CA 93517

(for south side entry)
Inyo National Forest
P.O. Box 10
Lee Vining, CA 93541

JOHN MUIR
(for west side entry)
Sierra National Forest
P.O. Box 300
Shaver Lake, CA 93664

(for east side entry—central portion)
Inyo National Forest
798 N. Main Street
Bishop, CA 93514

(for east side entry—south portion)
Inyo National Forest
P.O. Box 8
Lone Pine, CA 93545

(for east side entry—north portion)
Inyo National Forest
P.O. Box 148
Mammoth Lakes, CA 93546

KAISER
Sierra National Forest
P.O. Box 306
Shaver Lake, CA 93664

MINARETS
(for west side entry)
Sierra National Forest
North Fork, CA 93643

(for east side entryk)
Inyo National Forest
P.O. Box 148
Mammoth Lakes, CA 93546

MOKELUMNE
Eldorado National Forest
P.O. Box 1327
Jackson, CA 95642

(for south side entry)
Stanislaus National Forest
P.O. Box 48
Arnold, CA 95223

VENTANA
Los Padres National Forest
406 S. Mildred
King City, CA 93930

Southern California

AGUA TIBIA
Cleveland National Forest
332 S. Juniper, Suite 100
Escondido, CA 92025

CUCAMONGA
San Bernardino National Forest
Box 100, Lytle Creek Star Route
Fontana, CA 92335

DOME LAND
Sequoia National Forest
P.O. Box 6
Kernville, CA 93238

GOLDEN TROUT
Inyo National Forest
P.O. Box 8
Lone Pine, CA 93545

(for west side entry)
Sequois National Forest
32588 Highway 190
Porterville, CA 93257

(for south side entry)
Sequois National Forest
P.O. Box 6
Kernville, CA 93238

SAN GABRIEL
Angeles National Forest
150 S. Los Robles Ave., Suite 300
Pasadena, CA 91101

SAN GORGONIO
San Bernardino National Forest
Box 264, Route 1
Mentone, CA 92359

SAN JACINTO
San Bernardino National Forest
P.O. Box 518
Idyllwild, CA 92349

SANTA LUCIA
Los Padres National Forest
1616 N. Carlotti Dr.
Santa Maria, CA 93454

SAN RAFAEL
Los Padres National Forest
1616 N. Carlotti Dr.
Santa Maria, CA 93454

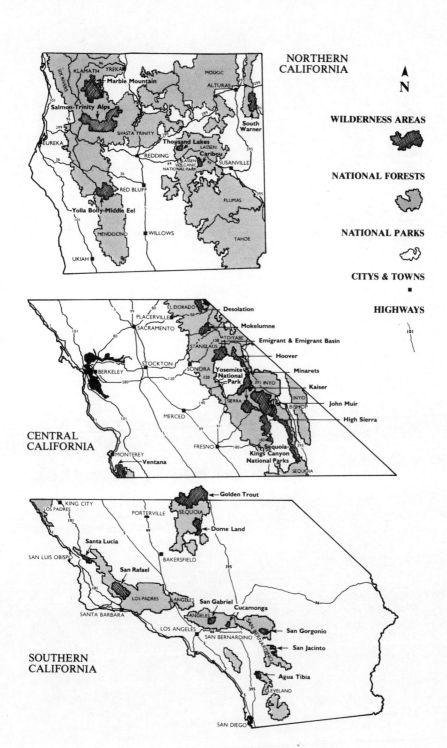

NORTHERN
CALIFORNIA

N

WILDERNESS AREAS

NATIONAL FORESTS

NATIONAL PARKS

CITYS & TOWNS

HIGHWAYS

CENTRAL
CALIFORNIA

SOUTHERN
CALIFORNIA

INDEX

knots, 158-160
  bowline, 158, 159
  butterfly, 158
  double bowline, 159
  figure 8, 158
  fisherman's, 158
  sheet bend, 158
  prussik, 160

lacerations (see First Aid)
leading mountaineering trips, 11
lie-back (see Rock Climbing)
lightning (see also Weather)
  first aid for lightning
    strike, 61-116
  ground current paths, 63
  strike attractors, 62
looping down (see Rock Climbing)
lost (see Search and Rescue)
low impact wilderness use (see
  Wilderness)
lunch, 92

mail order mountaineering catalogs,
  addresses for obtaining, 222
maps (see also Hiking Navigation)
  addresses to order from
    (USGS), 40
  how to read, 40-42
meal planning (see Planning)
minerals (see Nutritional Needs)
missing or lost people (see Search
  and Rescue)
mittens, how to make, 225
moraines (see Glaciers)
mosquitoes, 83, 127
mountaineering mail order catalogs
  (see Mail Order)
muscle cramps, 125

nausea, 125
North Star, 53
nutritional needs (see also

Food), 85-88
  calories, 85
  carbohydrates, 86, 227
  fats, 86, 229
  fiber, 88
  minerals, 87
  protein, 86, 228
  vitamins, 86

orienteering (see Hiking
  Navigation)

pace
  measuring for hiking
    navigation, 42
  on trail, 71
packing, 67-70
  pack, 68-70
  food, 99
packs, types of, 31
permits (see Wilderness)
physical conditioning, 7-10
  aerobic training, 9
  elevation gain training, 8
  heart rate, target, 9
  jogging, 8
plague, 130
planning
  fuel, 97
  meals and snacks, 88-94
  travel with children, 11-13
plotting bearings (see Hiking
  Navigation)
plunge step, 184
pneumonia (see First Aid)
poison oak, 127
Polaris (see North Star)
pressure points (see First Aid)
protein (see Nutritional Needs)
prussik (see also Rock Climbing)
  knot, 160
  slings, use of, 170